YES You Can!

Reaching Your Potential While Achieving Greatness

The interviews found in this book are conducted by David Wright, President of International Speakers Network and Insight Publishing

If you need that extra boost to get where you're going, I can tell you with confidence that this book will provide the advice you need to know that "yes, you can" get there! We are proud to present authors whose chapters will give you some tools to help you along your journey to wherever you want to go.

I have to admit that there have been times in my life when I definitely thought, "No, I can't!" All successful people get discouraged sometimes. But they don't let discouragement stop them. When you've hit a wall, you have to push through, knowing that eventually yes, you can make it.

The authors I interviewed for this book gave me fascinating and innovative ideas about how to push through to achieve that "Yes You Can" mindset. "Yes you can" is a mantra that you can use every day for encouragement. Like the "Little Engine that could" in the children's book, you can say, "Yes I can, yes I can," all the way up the hills in your life until you grasp what you are reaching for.

The preparation for this book was done by way of the authors' education and their impressive experiences in business. But the primary source of their preparation was life itself. Each author's life experiences provided unique insights into what "yes you can" truly means. Their suggestions will help you succeed in every area of life—business and personal.

I highly recommend that you not only read this book but also use it for encouragement and for new ideas about how you can push through every obstacle with confidence, knowing that *Yes You Can!*

- DAVID E. WRIGHT, PRESIDENT
INTERNATIONAL SPEAKERS NETWORK
& INSIGHT PUBLISHING

TABLE OF CONTENTS

CHAPTER ONE

Career Contentment Trumps Job Satisfaction

by Jeff Garton

David Wright (Wright)

Jeff Garton is an organizational consultant, career coach, speaker, and ASTD best-selling author. His background is specialized in HR for twenty-three years with the Philip Morris Companies. He is noted for pioneering the field of *career contentment,* a topic that shows employers how to improve employee resilience, productivity, and retention, despite work conditions that can't always be satisfying. His groundbreaking works on this new topic have been featured on Fox Business, ABC *Sunday Morning,* NPR Radio, *The Wall Street Journal,* and *Chief Executive* magazine. His consulting has been instrumental in helping employees and organizations to cope with the challenges posed by the failed economy, global competition, cost-cutting, and sustainability issues.

Jeff, welcome to *Yes You Can!*

Wright

What is career contentment?

Jeff Garton (Garton)

First of all, contentment is a *human emotion*. Like any emotion, it is the direct result of how you think. You think first, feel second (emotion), and then you take action based on how you feel. You act on your emotions because of what you think or as the result of how you are caused to think. This is a fact that leaders, teachers, coaches, and salespeople rely on to motivate human behavior.

You can motivate yourself (self-motivation) in this same manner—by simply improving how you think in a non-negative manner. This is what positive psychologists refer to as thinking realistically and optimistically.

You want to do something, for example, because you thought about it first. What gets you up and moving is how you feel. You can improve how you feel and the effectiveness of how well you perform by simply improving how you think.

- If you *think you can* do something, you inspire performance *enhancing* emotions to act upon: joy, optimism, excitement, enthusiasm, gratitude, and contentment. This creates an *ease response,* thus improving your chances of accomplishing what you want. At the same time, you create favorable impressions: you're perceived as joyful, optimistic, excited, enthused, grateful, and content.

- If you *think you can't* do something (or you waste your time complaining), you inspire performance *inhibiting* emotions to act upon: fear, worry, envy, doubt and anger. This creates a *strain response*, thus decreasing your performance potential. You procrastinate, do the wrong thing, or you deliver half-hearted efforts. At the same time, you create unfavorable impressions: you're perceived to be a poor performer, afraid, worried, envious, uncertain and upset.

Because your life circumstances and work conditions are never consistently satisfying, the idea is to learn how to *think non-negatively* (realistically and optimistically) so as to maintain your own good performance despite your circumstances. You think or reason to recognize the agreeable middle ground between the extremes of satisfaction or dissatisfaction. By taking the approach of intentionally recognizing your contentment, you create an ease response to act upon that improves your own performance and perceptions about you.

Is this possible? It's a scientific fact! Your circumstances are random and meaningless until you assign them a meaning and react. You assign the meanings, which makes you responsible for how you feel, what you do, and how others react toward you. Your circumstances, therefore, are secondary or subject to your thoughts about them. In other words, *you don't live in response to your circumstances, but in response to your emotions caused by what you think about your circumstances.* This means that you have the power to create your own heaven or hell on Earth by how you choose to think.

Not only do you have the freedom to think whatever you choose, you also have the freedom to create any emotion you prefer to act upon, regardless of whatever your external circumstances or conditions might be.

- You can think to feel confident, and therefore act confidently, even though your external conditions may be frightening. For example, when you have to give a presentation or perform a challenging task.
- You can think to feel enthusiasm, and therefore act enthusiastically, even though your external conditions are boring or dreadful. For example, when you have to interact with someone you don't particularly like or when you have to do something you don't really enjoy.
- And you can think to feel contentment, and therefore act contentedly, even though your work conditions are made dissatisfying. For example, when you enjoy your work, but you have to endure long hours, low pay, or a bad boss. You can be content even though not entirely satisfied.

By controlling your thoughts to produce the emotion of contentment to act upon, you have the self-sufficient ability to improve your own self-motivation to perform and resilience to persevere despite circumstances that can't always be satisfying. This also gives you the ability to create favorable impressions to enhance your relationships with others. Otherwise, you can allow your circumstances to have control over how you think and feel, and jeopardize getting what you want out of your life and career.

Career contentment is both a process and an end result:

- As a process, career contentment is the self-sufficient control of your thoughts and emotions to manage your career to achieve your purposes independently of conditions that can't always be made satisfying.
- As an end result, it is the peace and pleasure you derive from work that you decide is meaningful to the fulfillment of your most valued purposes for working.

Contentment Is An <u>EMOTION</u>
(experienced regardless of conditions)

If Feeling	Thinking	Result
Pessimistic	Optimistic	You can think to *muster* either of these emotions to enhance your self-motivation to perform and resilience to persevere regardless of your conditions
Afraid	Confident	
Impatient	Patient	
Apathetic	Enthused	
Dissatisfied	Content	

Workers can't simply muster job satisfaction because it's not a human emotion they control

Wright

How does career contentment compare to traditional job satisfaction?

Garton

Job satisfaction is based on the assumption that other people (employers) are responsible for your wellbeing and career fulfillment. Career contentment, on the other hand, is based on the premise that individuals are responsible for their own wellbeing and career, with or without job satisfaction.

Contrary to popular thinking, job satisfaction is not a human emotion, but a condition. For example, you can't have intrinsic or extrinsic job satisfaction without the job and rewards that are budgeted for and controlled by employers. And why employers invest in providing job satisfaction is to attract, motivate, and retain workers to fulfill the employer's purposes. If a return on this investment is not realized, the worker and/or job is repaired, replaced, or eliminated.

Career contentment is a human emotion that is controlled exclusively by individuals in order to fulfill their own life and career purposes. By reasoning alone, workers can choose to be content and stay in their job even if not made entirely satisfied (resilience)

4

or they can choose to be discontent and leave their job even after being made satisfied (resolve). People's independent ability to flex their emotions in this manner enhances their resilience to persevere or their resolve in order to make changes to their life and career as their purposes for working continue to evolve. This insures their ability to achieve authentic vocation despite the allures or challenges posed by their work or employer.

Ultimately, a person's life and career are not indentured to any one job, career, or employer. Their career choices are also not guided exclusively by external motivators or transient rewards supplied by employers. Careers are guided from within by an individual's pursuit of contentment derived from work that he or she decides is meaningful to his or her deep interests and evolving and most valued purposes for working.

Job Satisfaction Is A <u>CONDITION</u>
(not an emotion that you control)

If Feeling	Thinking	Result
Cold	Hot	Won't change the temperature
Hungry	Full	Won't put food in your stomach
Sick	Well	Won't improve your health
Poor	Wealthy	Won't put money in your bank
Dissatisfied	Satisfied	Won't give you a better job, boss, wages, benefits, etc

Complete satisfaction may never be possible because you lack total control over conditions

Wright

Why do people assume that being made satisfied is good, and that contentment means laid back or settling for less?

Garton

Don't assume that contentment means laid back or settling for less. For example, that you love someone deeply enough to overlook their flaws doesn't mean you are settling for less. If you truly love someone and wish to maintain the relationship, your decision to be content despite their flaws enables your resilience to persevere. You are content even though not entirely satisfied, and this ability enhances your potential for greater fulfillment despite circumstances. Contentment has been overlooked as a source of resilience in situations where satisfaction isn't always possible.

Due to our lazy misuse of terminology over the years, the original meanings for the words *satisfy* and *content* have been lost:

- The word, *satisfy* originates from the French and Latin words for *sad* and *factitious*. It's sad because being made satisfied is dependent on someone doing something and is conditional on whether your expectations were fulfilled. You can't simply choose to be satisfied. It's factitious or artificial because it doesn't originate from within but is dependent on people and things outside of you. And because you lack total control over these matters, the probability exists that you may never be completely satisfied. This sad realization was made over a thousand years ago and explains why the word *contentment* was created.

- The word, *content* originates from the French and Latin words for *contain* and *enclosed*, meaning from within. In situations where satisfaction isn't possible, the contented person endures with a calmness protected by their own self-sufficiency. By reasoning alone, you can choose to be content even if not made entirely satisfied. The emotion of contentment is overlooked as a source of self-motivation and enduring resilience in situations where satisfaction isn't always possible.

Unlike job satisfaction, which involves expecting more—something new or different—career contentment involves wanting what you already have. It is the result of an inner choice without regard to outer conditions that are never completely satisfying. More than doing what you love, it involves learning how to love what you do.

"He who is not contented with what he has, would not be contented with what he would like to have"—Socrates.

"Riches are not from an abundance of worldly goods, but from a contented mind"—Muhammad.

"Contentment furnishes constant joy. Much covetousness, constant grief. To the contented even poverty is joy. To the discontented, even wealth is a vexation"—Ming Lum Paou Keen.

"Our content is our best having"—William Shakespeare.

Wright

Why would someone choose to be content in a dissatisfying job?

Garton

Career contentment makes a distinction between work preferences and work conditions. That work conditions are satisfying or dissatisfying is something an employee can't control except by quitting or through some form of bargaining. But in regard to their work preferences, employees do have control over which jobs they choose and how long they prefer to stay before deciding to change jobs.

When an employee chooses work that they believe is worth fighting for or that is highly meaningful to their calling and most important purposes for working, they are more likely to want to keep that job, despite instances of job dissatisfaction. It's a matter of how important their purposes are. Those purposes can be on the job (vocational) or even off the job and unrelated to their employer (e.g., family, financial).

Meaningful work is an ingredient to employees' willingness to recognize their career contentment and to leverage their resilience to rise above their dissatisfactions. If an employee believes his or her work is not sufficiently meaningful or worth fighting for, it's unlikely the employee will choose to recognize his or her career contentment or leverage his or her resilience in order to stay.

Job Satisfaction Highest Goal

vs.

Career Contentment Highest Goal

EMPLOYERS INVEST IN JOB SATISACTION TO FULFILL THEIR BUSINESS PURPOSES	INVESTMENT	EMPLOYEES WORK TO FUFILL THEIR EXTRINSIC AND INTRINSIC PURPOSES
(Highest Goal) Profits, increase efficiency, improve productivity	JOBS	Paybills, put food on table, improve lifestyle
Attract, motivate, retain employees to reduce turn-over and other costs	CAREERS	Make contributions, achieve recognition, and enhance development
(Not Relevant to business)	CALLINGor MEANINGFUL WORK	(Highest Goal) Fulfill deep interest, vocation, purpose

Wright

Does career contentment replace job satisfaction?

Garton

No! Career contentment supplements job satisfaction but does not replace it. Employers will always need to provide employees with the traditional elements of job satisfaction, including: jobs, wages, benefits, supervision, training, working conditions, career path, promotions, and so forth.

However, if employees are going to work and expect employers to make them satisfied, it's guaranteed that they will be become disappointed and dissatisfied. Employers offer no guarantees on job satisfaction. Also, employees should not limit themselves or their career only to what their employer is willing to provide that might later have to be reduced or taken away due to circumstances beyond even the employer's ability to control.

Between Conditions
Exists An Agreeable Middle Ground

Either You Have Job Satisfaction		Or You Don't

Career Contentment Is Recognized As The Agreeable Middle Ground <u>When Purposes Are Worth Fighting For</u>

Wright

Why should organizations emphasize career contentment in addition to job satisfaction?

Garton

After years of uncertainty caused by cost-cutting, job eliminations, and layoffs, workers realize that job satisfaction is transient and unreliable due to circumstances beyond their control or the control of their employers. In some regions affected by the down economy, just the mention of job satisfaction provokes feelings of contention and entitlement among workers. More than remuneration, people are searching for career contentment, which is deeper and more meaningful than mere job satisfaction.

Organizations espousing the belief that people are their greatest asset cannot minimize this asset by neglecting the control workers have over their emotion of career contentment. People's lives and careers are guided by the control of their emotions, not by transient rewards. In comparison, external motivators are never more powerful than what people can do for themselves, from within. In either case, people are not called to job satisfaction, but to work that is meaningful to their most valued purposes for working.

Consider this analogy: disease and dissatisfaction are both conditions that create discomfort. In the same manner that patients should play an active role in mobilizing the innate energies of their body to combat disease, workers should play an active role in leveraging their contentment to rise above their inevitable dissatisfactions. Workers should not rely exclusively on employers to make them satisfied just as patients should not rely exclusively on physicians to make them well.

Wright

How was the idea for career contentment developed?

Garton

Career contentment was developed based on research from across multiple fields of study, including: positive psychology, self-efficacy, self-motivation, emotional intelligence, self-transcendence, and resilience. The first book and learning resources on this new topic were published in 2008 by the American Society for Training and Development. I authored these original works and my career specialty is in human resources and career coaching.

Positive psychology teaches us that people don't live in response to their circumstances, but in response to their emotions caused by what they think about their circumstances. Whatever occurs during your life and career is random and meaningless until you assign it a meaning and react. Because you assign the meanings, this makes you responsible for feeling satisfied or dissatisfied. Consequently, work conditions are secondary or subject to your thoughts about them. You can improve how you feel and the effectiveness of how you perform by improving how you think to achieve contentment rather than expect satisfaction.

This is not the power of positive thinking, but what positive psychology refers to as "the power of thinking non-negatively." This involves reasoning that intentionally combines thoughts that are both realistic and optimistic. By reasoning in this manner, you are able to recognize and leverage your contentment as the agreeable middle ground between the two extremes of satisfaction and dissatisfaction.

CAREER CONTENTMENT	JOB SATISFACTION
Wants to be there	Paid to be there
Content to be there	Made satisfied
Self-motivated	Made motivated
Naturally engaged	Made engaged
Self-reliant	Dependent on others
Low maintenance	High maintenance
Learns to love what is	Finds reasons to complain
Resilient to endure	Low tolerance
Attitude of gratitude	Entitlement mentality
Makes things happen	Mixed results
Responsive to career callings	Always shopping

Wright

Is career contentment the same thing as employee engagement?

Garton

No! Employee engagement is comparable to job satisfaction. It's dependent on employers providing jobs or modifying job content, and it's also conditional on whether an employee's expectations were fulfilled as a result. If employees are not satisfied, employers must make them satisfied, and if employees are not engaged, employers must make them engaged.

However, employers cannot make employees have career contentment. Employees have exclusive control over their own emotions or career contentment, and this is feasible independently of employer efforts to make them satisfied, dissatisfied, engaged, or disengaged. You could say that career contentment is engagement that occurs naturally or without the employer's involvement.

Wright

How will career contentment affect how employees manage their career?

Garton

Because career contentment is an emotion controlled only by employees to manage their career and fulfill their purposes, and this occurs independently of employer efforts to make employees satisfied, it's up to employees to achieve their own career contentment. In this regard, employees are responsible to clarify their career intentions and purposes and to take the steps that they believe are necessary to keep themselves in the right jobs that will fulfill their most important purposes for working.

It's also the responsibility of employees to avoid complaining about job dissatisfactions that are inevitable to every job, career, and employer. When employees have the option to leverage their contentment to endure, or otherwise leave to fulfill their purposes elsewhere, complaining is pointless and also detrimental to the individual and to the business.

Wright

Can employees find contentment in an interim job that is outside of their normal career path?

Garton

Yes! One of the most valuable features of career contentment is an employee's ability to recognize their contentment in work situations where traditional job satisfaction isn't feasible. Career contentment is not associated with having a corner office, company car, expense account, or promotions. It is associated with work that an employee decides is meaningful to the fulfillment of his or her most important purposes for working.

In situations where employees feel obligated to take or stay in a job they need but don't want, or an interim job that is outside of their preferred career path, it is typically for purposes that are off the job and linked with caring for themselves and their family. In these situations, the employee's highest purpose is just a job for income and/or benefits. As such, the employee should not be expecting job satisfaction or to advance up the company ladder. If an interim job fulfills employees' highest purposes for working, they can reason to recognize their career contentment with what they have and leverage their resilience to endure until they can turn their situation around.

Where employees often need help is in realizing that there is virtue or goodness in working with a clear conscience—that they are doing their best with what they have to fulfill their highest purposes. In every situation, employees have the option to look for ways to love what they do until they can turn their situation around or they can look for reasons to complain, thus prolonging their own agony.

Wright

How can the introduction of career contentment make organizations stronger?

Garton

The objective of career contentment is to enhance the resilience, fulfillment, and performance of workers while simultaneously reducing costs and improving productivity and retention for organizations. This is contingent on workers learning how to recognize their emotion of contentment and leverage it to transcend their inevitable dissatisfactions and occupational rigors.

Currently, organizations seek to attract, motivate, and retain workers with the prospect of being made satisfied. But as we know, complete satisfaction is never possible and can't be sustained. Organizations that maintain an emphasis on job satisfaction without supplementing it with training on the topic of career contentment, are establishing expectations they can't fulfill due to circumstances they can't control (e.g., the economy, global competition, acquisitions). Organizations are unintentionally contributing to the very problems they are investing to prevent.

Career contentment acknowledges that conditions inside any organization are never perfect or consistently satisfying—and workers should never be encouraged to expect that they will be. Career contentment training shows workers how to empower their self-motivation to perform and resilience to persevere despite their inevitable dissatisfactions. The net result is fewer complaints and reduced costs associated with fixing problems resulting from those complaints.

In the meantime, organizations must always do their part in addressing unfavorable work conditions. But if workers continue to complain after they have the option to leverage their career contentment, it's an indication that: a) their expectations are unrealistic; b) they lack control over their thoughts and emotions, which raises issues regarding their ability to perform; c) their career purposes are unclear or not sufficiently meaningful; or d) they're in the wrong job.

Organization Impact
Make Employees Better

REDUCE COSTS
Contented Workers are
less likely to complain

IMPROVE PRODUCTIVITY
Contented Workers are
purpose focused

IMPROVE RETENTION
Contented Workers are
less likely to leave

Focused on the virtues of working for the sake of working – not just for rewards

Wright

Why is training or coaching on the topic of career contentment a better investment than other programs currently being used?

Garton

Career contentment was not created with the intention of replacing any programs that organizations believe are necessary to the development of their workers. More so, training and coaching on the topic of career contentment intends to enhance the effectiveness of those programs. Therefore, it's not a question of which program is best, but which should be implemented first.

Because career contentment is not a program, per se, but an emotion, it already exists in the minds and hearts of workers. It's already guiding their career choices and self-motivation despite whatever programs employers may offer. This helps us to finally understand why workers continue to complain and quit after programs are implemented to make them satisfied and engaged. Any programs offered by employers are: a) powerless compared to an individual's control of their decision to be content or discontent; and, b) pointless unless workers decide first that they are content to be there and stay there. To insure the effectiveness of your programs, focus first on the career contentment of workers.

Training on the topic of career contentment teaches workers how to take command of their innate faculties to enhance their productivity and resilience despite circumstances that can't always be made satisfying. Once this is accomplished, employers can invest as much as they like in any program they prefer—but by this point, some programs may no longer be necessary because contented workers are naturally engaged, self-motivated, and resilient to persevere.

Wright

What is the process for implementing career contentment inside an organization?

Garton

Although the idea of career contentment challenges existing paradigms, it's overlooked by most people how they unconsciously rely on their contentment already. The fact is that contentment is *natural* whereas job satisfaction is *artificial* or man-made. Once this is understood, the paradigm shift is completed. However, the learning must be reinforced because our conditioning is strongly oriented to expecting satisfaction.

The process of shifting paradigms begins with awareness-building and resolving expectations, starting with the leadership team developing a vision and objectives for career contentment inside the organization. This is achieved through presentations, group discussion, the review of learning resources, and individual coaching where necessary. Thereafter, it's a matter of staff becoming involved in action-planning and execution.

To facilitate this process, it is recommended that in-house trainers or your outsourced training team become certified to offer and reinforce learning and coaching on the topic of career contentment. In addition, human resource departments must participate in updating processes that are necessary to support a career contentment culture. For example:

- **Recruitment:** Incorporate career contentment into employer branding statements, integrate the discernment of purposes into recruitment and selection processes, and incorporate career contentment competency-based interview questions into the selection process.

- **Development:** Expand on-boarding programs to provide introductory training on career contentment and the resources that are available to achieve it. Integrate career contentment competencies into existing competency models and expand repertoire of training to include career contentment principles and advantages.

- **Performance:** Integrate career contentment competencies into existing performance management systems, 360 instruments, and provide for individual coaching to achieve and maintain career contentment as a fundamental benefit to workers.

- **Retention:** Expand survey instruments used to examine job satisfaction trends to include an examination of career contentment trends. Enable workers to self-assess whether leaving is contradictory to their authentic vocation or whether they need to reinvigorate their resilience through reinforcement training.

- Explore cost reduction opportunities resulting from not continually chasing after workers with new and improved job satisfactions or reinvesting to fix their dissatisfactions.

Wright

How is the effectiveness of career contentment measured?

Garton

Employee surveys generally measure how effective the organization has been in making work conditions satisfying to workers. Where these surveys fall short is not measuring if workers are content with their choice of work, independently of whether their work conditions are satisfying or not. If workers are content with their work, they are naturally more tolerant of dissatisfying work conditions. But if they are discontent with their work, it's unlikely that improving their work conditions will make a difference in their performance or retention. Few people are willing to waste their time and talents for very long in the wrong job just because their work conditions are made satisfying.

Following are the metrics associated with career contentment:
- Increased employee resilience as measured by decreased complaints and their associated high costs linked with resolving: job stress, illness, absences, apathy, poor performance, low productivity, and turnover.
- Higher employee productivity as measured by an improved ratio between total employee costs and total company revenues, but also reduced downtime and costs associated with job related stress and illnesses.
- Improved employee engagement as measured by employees reporting a higher degree of control over their work and career, and improved

perceptions regarding their contributions to fulfill their purposes for working.

- Improved recruiting efficiencies as measured by shorter time periods required to fill positions, increased number of employee referrals, reduced turnover among new hires within their first and second years on the job, higher average scores for new hires on performance evaluations compared to previous year, and improved perceptions of managers regarding the quality of hires.
- Improved employee retention as measured by reduced turnover among high performers in key positions where turnover should be prevented, and where it's essential for the business to maintain diversity balance.
- Reduced percentage of low-performing employees as measured by reduced instances of employees being recommended for performance management programs.
- Increased percentage of employees who believe they are on track to achieve their purposes as measured by improved perceptions regarding on-the-job learning and growth opportunities, job rotations, job expansions, and the availability and relevance of training to support employee purposes.
- Increasing percentage of new hires and existing workers who report their reasons for taking their job, and choosing to stay there, are for reasons of career contentment. Referring to the pleasure and fulfillment linked with the virtues of working, not just for traditional elements of job satisfaction: income, benefits, training, supervision, working conditions, etc.

Wright

Today we have been speaking with Jeff Garton. Jeff I've enjoyed this conversation and hope our readers will learn more by visiting your website, www.careercontentment-thebook.com

Garton

Thank you, David, for allowing me the opportunity to contribute to this book. I love the inspirational title, and I hope that everyone who reads this book develops a *Yes You Can* attitude in regard to their life and career.

JEFF GARTON is an organizational consultant, career coach, speaker, and ASTD best-selling author. His background is specialized in HR for twenty-three years with the Philip Morris Companies. He is noted for pioneering the field of *career contentment*, a topic that shows employers how to improve employee resilience, productivity, and retention, despite work conditions that can't always be satisfying. His groundbreaking works on this new topic have been featured on Fox Business, ABC *Sunday Morning,* NPR Radio, *The Wall Street Journal,* and *Chief Executive* magazine. His consulting has been instrumental in helping employees and organizations to cope with the challenges posed by the failed economy, global competition, cost-cutting, and sustainability issues.

Jeff Garton

Career Contentment, Inc.
8 Queens Way
Lincolnshire, IL 60069
847-607-8854
www.careercontentment-thebook.com

CHAPTER TWO

A Special Interview

by Warren Bennis

David E. Wright (Wright)

Today we are talking with Warren Bennis, PhD. He is a university professor and a distinguished professor of business at the University of Southern California and chairman of USC's leadership institute. He has written eighteen books, including *On Becoming a Leader, Why Leaders Can't Lead,* and *The Unreality Industry,* coauthored with Ivan Mentoff. Dr. Bennis was successor to Douglas McGregor as chairman of the organizational studies department at MIT. He also taught at Harvard and Boston universities. Later he was provost and executive vice president of the State University of New York—Buffalo and president of the University of Cincinnati. He published over nine hundred articles. Two of his books have earned the coveted McKenzie Award for the "Best Book on Management." He has served in an advisory capacity for the past four U.S. presidents, and consultant to many corporations and agencies and to the United Nations. Awarded eleven honorary degrees, Dr. Bennis has also received numerous awards including the Distinguished Service Award from the American Board of Professional Psychologists and the Perry L. Ruther Practice Award from the American Psychological Association.

Dr. Bennis, welcome to *Yes You Can!*

Warren Bennis (Bennis)

I'm glad to be here again with you, David.

Wright

In a conversation with *Behavior Online*, you stated that most organizations devaluate potential or emerging leaders by seven criteria: business literacy, people skills, conceptual abilities, track record, taste, judgment, and character. Because these terms were somewhat vague, you left them to be defined by the reader. Can we give our readers an unadorned definition of these criteria, as you define them?

Bennis

There's no precise dictionary definition that would satisfy me or maybe anyone. I'll just review them very quickly because there's a lot more we want to discuss.

Business literacy really means: do you know the territory, do you know the ecology of the business, do you know how it works, do you know where the plugs are, do you know who the main stakeholders are, and are you familiar with a thing called business culture.

People skills: This is your capacity to connect and engage, because business leadership is about establishing, managing, creating, and engaging in relationships. Conceptual abilities is more important these days because it has to do with the paradoxes and complexities—the cartography—of stakeholders that make life at the top (more than ever) interesting and difficult, which is why we've had such a turnover in CEOs and leaders over the last few years.

Track record: Now, if I want to know about a person—if I were a therapist—one of the first questions I would ask is, "Tell me about your job history." That tells me a lot. On the whole, as my Dad used to say, "People who get A's are smart." People who have a successful track record tend to be effective. We don't always go on that, because sometimes these people don't grow. But, if I had only one measuring stick, it would be that one: Tell me your job history. Let's talk about whether it looks successful or whether you view it as successful or not. It's hard to define, but it's about whether or not you have the capacity a good curator has, a good selector has, to know people. It's always a tough one; God knows we all make mistakes. Your taste means your capacity to judge other people in relation to the other six characteristics.

I think taste and judgment are combined. I dealt with them separately because I thought taste was specifically the selection of people in an intuitive and objective way, but also in a subjective way. It has to do with the range of such things as being bold versus being reckless. It has to do with the strategic implications and consequences of any decision and what you take into account in making any decision, especially the tough ones. The easy ones are different; everyone looks good in a bull market. It's when things get tough, vulnerable, difficult, and in a crisis mode that judgment really counts the most. Taste and judgment are the hardest things to learn, let alone teach.

Character: Here I have in mind a variety of things such as size of ego, the capacity to listen, emotional intelligence, integrity, and authenticity—basically, is this a person I can trust? That's what character is all about.

Wright

You said that businesses get rid of their top leaders because of lapses in judgment, and lapses in character, not because of business literacy or conceptual skills. Why do you think this is true?

Bennis

It's true simply because it's true. Look at the record. I wasn't just stating a hypothesis there that looks to be proved. I was stating experiences with leaders and I'll give you three quick examples.

Let's take a recent one. Howell Raines had the top job in journalism in the world. He had great ideas, great business literacy, and all the things in the top five. He did not have taste, judgment, or character. This is a guy who had an ego the size of Texas. He played favorites, had the best ideas, was a terrific newspaperman and no one would argue with that. But, his way of treating people—of not harnessing the human harvest that was there, and his bullying, brutalizing, arrogant behavior and his inability to listen; that's what I mean by character.

Eckhart Pfeiffer was fired after seven or eight very good years at Compaq. He had terrific ideas, but he did not listen to the people. He was only listening to those on his "A" list who were saying, "Aye, aye, sir." People on his "B" list were saying, "You'd better look at what Gateway and Dell are doing; they're eating our lunch on our best china." He didn't listen; he didn't want to listen. That's what I mean by character. Let me just stay with those two examples, I don't think it's ever about conceptual abilities—ever. There may be some examples I just don't know about. But, with over fifty years of leadership research, I don't know of any leader who has lost his or her job or has been ousted because of a lack of brainpower.

Wright

You said that teaching leadership is impossible, but you also said leadership can be learned. How can that be?

Bennis

Let me qualify that. I teach the stuff, so no, it isn't impossible to teach you. As is the case with everything, teaching and learning are two different things. One has to do with input into people; the other has to do with whether or not they get it. You know very well, and your listeners and readers know very well, that there's a difference between listening to a lecture and it having any influence on you. You can listen to a brilliant lecture and nothing may happen. So, there's a disconnect to teaching and learning.

Actually, how people learn about leadership varies a lot. Most people don't learn about leadership by getting a Ph.D., or by reading a book, or by listening to a tape, although that may be helpful. They learn it through work and experience. You can be helped by terrific teaching from a recording, a tape, a book, or a weekend retreat.

Basically, the way people learn about leadership is by keeping their eyes open, being a first-class "noticer," having good role models, and being able to see how they deal with life's adversities. You don't learn leadership by reading books. They are helpful, don't get me wrong. I write books; I want them to be read. The message you are trying to get out to your people—to listen and to read—is also important. I think it's terrific. That's my life's work. That's what I do for a living, and I love it. I'll tell you, it has to be augmented by the experiences you face in work and in life.

Wright

Trust me, I have learned, after reading many of your books, that they are teaching materials.

Bennis

Thank you. I hope you also learn from them, David.

Wright

As I was reading those books, I wondered why I did the things you said to do, and they worked when I did it. It's simply because I learned by doing.

Bennis

Thank you. I'm really glad to hear that.

Wright

Since leadership is where the big money, prestige, and power is, why would seasoned business executives, who are monitored more closely than the average employee, let character issues bring them down? One would think it would be like a person who constantly uses profanity, just deciding not to curse in church.

Bennis

I wish it were that easy. It's a really good question. I wish I knew the answer, but I don't. I will give you a real quick example. Howell Raines, as I said before, executive editor of the *New York Times* (people would die to get that position) was an experienced newspaperman, and there was a seventeen thousand-word article about him in *New Yorker*, June 6, 2002 (he had been on the job since September 2001, so it was written not a year later). The article exposed him; it was a very frank and interesting article. It called him arrogant, a bully, playing favorites, all the things I said earlier, and called him a hell of a good man and a terrific editor. He'd been around the track; he had business literacy up the wah-zoo. He was as good as they get.

He read that article and everybody at the *New York Times* read it. Do you think it might have made him want to change a little bit? Did Julius Caesar not hear the warnings, "Beware the Ides of March?" Did he not hear, "Don't go to the forum?" There were so many signals and he wasn't listening. Why wasn't he listening? Didn't he go down to the newsroom and talk to those people? No. The most common and fatal error is that because of arrogance; they stopped listening. It could happen internally, as in the case of Howell Raines, or like Eckhart Pfeiffer, who wasn't listening to his "B" list tell him about Gateway and Dell.

I don't have the answer to your question, but I will tell you, someone ought to be around to remind these people of the voices, stakeholders, and audiences they aren't listening to. That's a way of dealing with it—making sure you have a trusted staff that isn't just giving you the good news.

Wright

I've often heard that if I had been Nixon, I would have burned the tapes, apologized, and moved on.

Bennis

Absolutely.

Wright

I think it's the arrogance factor; you really "hit the nail on the head" when you said that, to put it in my simple terms.

How does one experience leadership when they haven't yet become a leader?

Bennis

How do you become a parent for the first time? There's no book that you are going to read on becoming a parent any more than there is a book you are going to read on becoming a leader that will prepare you for that experience. You're going to fall on your face, get up, dust yourself off, and go on. The only thing you're going to learn from is your experiences and having someone around you can depend on for straight, reflective back-talk. A lot of it is breaks, and chance. Some of it isn't that, but if there's one thing I want to underscore, nobody is prepared the first time they are going to be in the leadership position. You're going to fall on your face, you're going to learn from it, and you're going to continue that for the rest of your life.

Wright

At one time, I had a company with about 175 people working for me; we had business in the millions. I just kept making so many mistakes that afterward, I did wish I had read some of the things you had written about before I made those mistakes. It sure would have been helpful.

In your studies, you found that failure, not success, had a greater impact on future leaders—leaders learn the most by facing adversity. Do you think teachers at the college level make this clear?

Bennis

I can't speak for all teachers at the college level. Do you mean people teaching leadership and business management at the college level?

Wright

Yes.

Bennis

I don't know if they do. But, I would imagine things are much more difficult and complicated today because of the kinds of things that business leaders are facing. This includes problems such as globalization, fierce Darwinian competitiveness, complexity of the problems, regulatory pressures, changes in demography, difficulty of retaining your best talent, the price of terrific human capital and then keeping them, the ability to help create a climate that encourages collaboration, and then there's the world danger since 9/11.

Wright

In my case, I just remember the equations and things in the courses I took, such as controlling and directing and those kinds of things. I don't remember anybody ever telling me about exit strategics or what's going to happen if my secretary gets pregnant and my greatest salesperson is the one responsible for it. Who do I fire? As the owner of a small company that's growing at a rapid pace, what can I do to facilitate the competencies of the people I have chosen to lead this into the future?

Bennis

Your company is how big, again?

Wright

I was talking before about a real estate conglomerate. Presently I have a speakers' bureau/servicing agency and publishing business. I employ about twenty-five people, and we also use about fifty vendors, which I look at as employees.

Bennis

Yes, they are, aren't they? That's a good way of thinking about it. There are several things you can do in any size company, but with a small company, you can get your arms around it—conceptually, anyway. The leader/owner has to model the very

25

behaviors he wants others to model. If you are espousing something that is antithetical to your behavior, then that's going to be a double bind. That's number one.

The second thing is to make leadership development an organic part of the activities at the firm. In addition to encouraging people to read, bringing in people to talk to them, and having retreats, every once in a while, look at leadership competencies and what people can do to sharpen and enhance those capacities that are needed to create a culture where people can openly talk about these issues. All of those things can be used to create a climate where leadership development is a part of the everyday dialogue.

Wright

If you were helping me choose people to assume leadership roles as my company grows, what characteristics would you suggest I look for?

Bennis

I've implied some of them early on as we discussed those seven characteristics. I've become a little leery of the whole selection process; there is some evidence that even interviews don't give you really valid insight. I think what I would tend to do is look at the track record. Talk about that with the person, where they think they have failed, where they think they have succeeded. Try to get a sense of their capacity to reflect on issues and see to what extent they have been able to learn from their previous experiences.

See what you can make of how realistically they assess a situation. Most people rarely attribute any blame to themselves; they always think, "The dog ate my homework." It's always some other agent outside of themselves who is to blame. Those are the things that I think are going to be characteristics of emerging leaders among men and women. That's what I would look for—the capacity to reflect and learn.

Wright

When you made that comment about interviews, I don't feel as inept as I did before this conversation. I'm sixty-four years old and the longer I live, I just feel that when people come in and interview, I want to give them an Academy Award as they walk out. People can say almost anything convincingly in this culture. It's very, very difficult for me to get through, so that's one thing I really had not thought of. It seems so simple though—just follow the track record.

Bennis

I have had the same experience you've had. When I was president of the university and making lots of choices all the time, my best was hitting 700, which means I was off three out of ten times. I think my average here was 60/40; it's rough. It's even harder these days because of legal restrictions, how much you can say about their references, how much they can reveal. We have to pay attention to selection level, no kidding. We can overcome mistakes in the selection level by the culture and how it will screen out behaviors that are not acceptable. That's our best default—the culture itself will so educate people that even the mistakes we make will be resurrected by the culture being our best friend and ally.

Wright

As a leader, generating trust is essential. You have written extensively on this subject. Can you give our readers some factors that tend to generate trust?

Bennis

People want a leader who exudes that they know what he/she is doing. They want a doctor who is competent and they want a boss who really knows his or her way around. Secondly, you want someone who is really on your side—a caring leader. Thirdly, you want a leader who has directness, integrity, congruity, who returns calls, and is trustworthy, who will be there when needed and cares about you and about your growth. Those are the main things. It's not just individuals involved.

A boss must create a climate within the group that provides psychological safety—a holding pattern where people feel comfortable in speaking openly. I think that's another key factor in generating and establishing trust.

Wright

It is said that young people these days have less hope than their parents. What can leaders do to instill hope in their employees?

Bennis

All (and you can emphasize *all*) the leaders I have known have a high degree of optimism and a low degree of pessimism. They are, as Confucius said, "purveyors of hope." Look at Reagan; in a way, look at Clinton and Martin Luther King, Jr. These are people who have held out an idea of what we could become and made us proud of ourselves, created noble aspirations—sometimes audacious, but noble. Leaders have to express in an authentic way that there is a future for our nation and that you have a part in developing that future with me.

Wright

Dr. Bennis, thank you for being with us today, and for taking so much time to answer these questions.

Bennis

Thank you for having me.

Warren Bennis has written or edited twenty-seven books, including the best-selling *Leaders* and *On Becoming a Leader*; both of which have been translated into twenty-one languages. He has served on four U.S. presidential advisory boards and has consulted for many Fortune 500 companies, including General Electric, Ford, and Starbucks. The *Wall Street Journal* named him one of the top ten speakers on management in 1993 and 1996, and *Forbes* magazine referred to him as "the dean of leadership gurus."

Warren Bennis

m.christian@marshall.usc.edu

CHAPTER THREE

The Path to Leadership Fitness

by David Chinsky

THE INTERVIEW

David Wright (Wright)

Today we're talking with David Chinsky. David brings twenty-five years of executive leadership and management experience to his role as a sought-after business advisor and executive coach. Drawing upon his own successful career as an accomplished and effective leader in the healthcare, automotive, and information technology industries, David shares his unique insights into leadership, change management, and teamwork with hundreds of leaders. He is founder of the Institute for Leadership Fitness™, a twelve-month leadership development experience designed for leaders seeking the clarity, confidence, effectiveness, and vitality necessary for achieving their highest levels of professional effectiveness and leadership fitness.

David, welcome to *Yes You Can!*

David Chinsky (Chinsky)

Thank you, David. It's a pleasure to be here.

Wright

So what exactly is leadership fitness?

Chinsky

Leadership fitness is an integrated model of leadership development derived from over twenty years of personal leadership experience and eight years spent professionally coaching and training high-potential leaders. Leveraging these experiences, I identified four crucial components of leadership success that create long-term impact for leaders and their organizations. These components are clarity, confidence, effectiveness and vitality. When leaders can consistently demonstrate all four of these leadership qualities, they become "fit leaders."

Wright

So how did you come to develop this model of leadership development?

Chinsky

After working for many years with high-potential leaders, someone suggested to me that I take the time to document my philosophy and approach to working with and developing our clients. This was an excellent suggestion because it caused me to really think about what we were doing in our practice to create sustainable success for the individuals and the organizations we were privileged to be working with.

Soon after embarking on this process of defining our unique approach to developing leadership talent, four very specific foundations for professional effectiveness and success surfaced.

The first component to emerge in our model of leadership fitness was clarity. We knew from our work with leaders and their teams that to be successful, leaders must first be capable of setting a clear direction. They need to be able to articulate a vision that is compelling and that develops followership on the part of their people. More than anything else, employees seek clarity from their leaders. Leaders lacking clarity and leaders who do not take the time to provide clear direction to their teams create an environment where staff are forced to choose among multiple priorities. This often results in employees concluding "we don't know where we are going" or "I'm not sure what I am supposed to be working on."

The second component to emerge was confidence. While clarity creates a necessary and strong foundation for action, we discovered that the most successful leaders combine their sense of direction with a powerful self-confidence that amplifies their message. Employees have a keen sense, a sort of radar, when it comes to interpreting what they hear from their leaders. While the words may be logical and understandable, if there is a lack of authenticity, or if there is a feeling that the leader does not really believe in what he or she is espousing, the leader's message easily becomes compromised.

Many words exist to capture the power these self-doubts represent. To some, they are known as gremlins. To others, they are known as saboteurs. Regardless of how we label them, these doubts often get in the way of our overall impact by causing us to second guess our beliefs and intentions. Fit leaders learn how to overcome the dampening effect of these inner voices, and develop strategies to effectively push ahead with conviction and self-assurance. They build the resiliency necessary to win others over.

The third component to emerge was effectiveness. Effectiveness comprises the host of execution and implementation skills necessary for leaders to act on their bold visions. Fit leaders know:

- how to leverage and adapt their unique leadership styles to the needs of their organization,
- how to manage conflict,
- how to retain their best people,
- how to plan for their own succession and that of their high performers,
- how to provide feedback at the teachable moment, and
- how to utilize delegation to increase the overall capabilities of their teams.

We have coached and trained many executives with large doses of clarity and confidence who lacked the effectiveness skills to get anything done. Our focus on effectiveness is all about creating accountability around commitments and driving sustainability for the organizations being led.

Once we identified clarity, confidence, and effectiveness as crucial contributors to leadership fitness, I thought our model was complete. I thought to myself, "What else would an organization ask for if we could help them develop clear, confident, and effective leaders?"

Then I realized that we had been asked to coach and train many leaders who were clear, confident, and effective and yet some of these same leaders were failing to go the distance. Even though these leaders were clear on where they needed to take their teams, had the ability to tame their inner voices or gremlins, and they had a complete set of effectiveness tools, they were nonetheless becoming frustrated, overwhelmed, and even ill because they weren't attending to their own health and vibrancy. The result was that these leaders were unable to sustain their influence in the long run because they ran out of steam. Recognizing this limitation, I decided to add vitality to our model, thus creating an integrated model of leadership fitness comprising clarity, confidence, effectiveness, and vitality.

Wright

So what's unique about your model?

Chinsky

Our model is a unique process that integrates training, coaching, and assessment. While other programs tend to focus on only one or two of these important elements of learning, our Institute for Leadership Fitness is a twelve-month leadership development experience comprising four full-day workshops (one every ninety days), eight months of coaching, and three leadership assessments. Participants attend four skill-building workshops during the year-long program.

In addition to these four facilitated learning sessions, one every ninety days, each participant is assigned an executive coach with whom he or she works throughout the year to create and execute a customized development plan incorporating each of the four dynamic qualities of leadership fitness: clarity, confidence, effectiveness, and vitality. Participants also receive an individualized 360 degree Leadership Assessment, along with profiles of their conflict management styles and communication preferences.

When I started in this business, I often would do a talk for an hour or two, or perhaps conduct a one- or two-day training program and then move on to my next assignment. What I didn't realize at the time was that when I left, many of my clients had a difficult time truly implementing what they had learned in our programs. Learning from this experience, I knew that I needed to build more support for my clients over a longer period of time to ensure greater sustainability around the tools and concepts we were teaching.

When we designed our Institute for Leadership Fitness, we decided to adopt a coaching model whereby clients who enrolled in our twelve-month program would come to class four times a year, once every ninety days, and be coached in each of the months that they're not in class. This design element allows us to keep our own skin in the game and to be fully supportive of our clients as they work to implement changes back in their organization. The coaching component of our program enables our clients to work through whatever barriers or resistance they encounter on their way to implementing changes they commit to during our workshops.

Another key differentiation point associated with our program is the inclusion of vitality in our model of leadership fitness. We have had leaders in our program tell us that while they have participated in numerous leadership development programs, ours is the first that treats them as a whole person.

The holistic approach we take to developing fit leaders is rooted in our experience that leaders who do not take care of themselves often fail to succeed in the long run. At first, we wondered how organizations would view a respected leadership development program that spent time on issues of balance, rejuvenation, nutrition, exercise, and time mastery. We were encouraged to find that organizations truly understand how important vitality is for their leaders. There is increasing appreciation that vitality matters, and that leaders who don't take the time to exercise, rejuvenate, and learn the tools of time mastery are at greater risk for failing to lead.

Wright

So why is vitality such a critical component of leadership fitness?

Chinsky

Our work with successful leaders has confirmed the contribution that vibrancy and vitality make to the overall leadership fitness of individuals and organizations. Vital leaders have increased flexibility and a greater range of motion. Without vitality, it is more difficult to achieve clarity. Mental acuity and physical vitality are linked more than we know. Without vitality, it is less likely that leaders will remain confident. Finally, without vitality, the energy it takes to lead and manage effectively becomes depleted.

Wright

So how do leaders benefit from integrating clarity, confidence, effectiveness, and vitality?

Chinsky

Most leaders attending leadership development programs today encounter a relatively fragmented approach to skill development and practice. Participants in these other programs tend to learn tools of leadership in a very isolated fashion.

One of the reasons we believe our model is so effective is that it compels leaders to look at the interrelationships among all four components of leadership fitness: clarity, confidence, effectiveness, *and* vitality. We reinforce this integration by teaching new tools and approaches in each of the four components of the model at each of the four workshops our clients attend during their twelve-month relationship with us.

For example, we do not just focus on clarity during the first workshop, then focus on confidence during the second workshop, and so on. Instead, we introduce new materials in each of the four components of leadership fitness in each of our workshops. Central to the success of our model is the fact that proficiency in all four components is necessary to create the level of leadership fitness our clients are seeking.

Wright

What are some of the important synergies that you've discovered among the four components of your model?

Chinsky

Let me give you an example from our curriculum. One of the effectiveness tools we teach relates to becoming more masterful at managing conflict. In this module, leaders learn their "go-to" style for resolving disagreements. They also explore how they can increase their versatility with colleagues, bosses, and other team members by adapting their conflict management style to the specific situations they face. At the same time, we stress the important contribution of increased confidence when preparing our clients to effectively influence others and successfully win them over to competing points of view. In this example, our clients are shown how increasing their capability in one component of our model (i.e., confidence) can affect their ability in another component of our model (i.e., effectiveness).

Other synergies exist between our clarity modules and our vitality modules. In our module called "The Power of Feeling Your Best," we emphasize the role of certain foods in maximizing energy throughout the day and their effect on our ability to set a clear direction for our teams. In this example, we demonstrate how increasing vitality leads to an increase in clarity. In our module on time mastery, we demonstrate how "calendarizing" contributes to leaders becoming more effective.

Regardless of the specific tools being taught in our Institute, participants can't help but experience a synergistic or multiplier effect with one or more of the other tools they are learning in the program. Because vitality focuses on the whole person and the whole leader, the increased vibrancy, energy, and well-being achieved in the program has substantial affect on the leader's ability to be clear, to be confident, and to be effective.

Wright

So what do you think prevents leaders from becoming fit?

Chinsky

I will point to two barriers we see most often getting in the way of leadership fitness. The first relates to how other programs tend to focus on only one or two dimensions of leadership development without recognizing the important and dynamic relationships that exist between what we see as the four crucial components of sustainable leadership impact. For leaders to truly become fit, it is necessary for them to embrace a more holistic and integrative approach to developing and practicing the skills and behaviors that will optimize their leadership fitness. From our experience, this means developing proficiency in each of the following four areas: clarity, confidence, effectiveness and vitality.

The second barrier to successfully developing fit leaders is the conspicuous absence of solid structures of accountability in many existing leadership development programs. We know from our experience working with hundreds of high-potential leaders that classroom instruction by itself rarely provides what is necessary for lasting change in the skills and behaviors our clients are working on. That is why we have integrated professional coaching into our work with leaders.

Invariably, as leaders attempt to implement and apply their newly acquired skills and processes, they encounter resistance in their own organizations. Without access to a trained coach with whom our clients can work through these barriers and resistance points, and determine adjustments to their approach, it is not uncommon for individuals to simply conclude that "it won't work" or it is simply too hard. Giving up, they neutralize the value of the investment in the learning process altogether, and never go on to realize the profound impact of the changes they were convinced were beneficial in the first place.

Wright

What specific outcomes do you produce for participants in your Institute for Leadership Fitness?

Chinsky

One important outcome is the ability to sort through and prioritize opportunities that compete for the leader's attention. By completing what we call The MVV Equation™, participants get clear on their mission, vision, and values and learn how to identify opportunities that are aligned with the strategic goals of their organizations. This focuses their attention on high payback opportunities and minimizes the ambiguity that sometimes surrounds what priorities others in the organization should be working on.

Leaders completing our program also learn how to utilize delegation as a means to accelerate the development of others on their team. While we often think of delegation simply as a way to get work done through others, we enable participants to begin using delegation as a means to create succession possibilities and to expand the capacity of the people on their teams.

Among the many other outcomes participants in our Institute can expect to receive, the following examples provide an illustration of the results we seek to deliver.

- We prepare leaders to more effectively sell their ideas to colleagues and customers.
- We teach leaders how to create work environments in which high performers thrive and star performers are retained.
- We call attention to the self-sabotaging inner voices that can get in the way of our clients taking action and we provide strategies for managing these gremlins.
- We encourage leaders to develop a repertoire of positive habits that go on to feed their vitality and effectiveness.
- We show clients how to build more oscillation and balance into their lives by dedicating more time in their life to relaxation and rejuvenation.
- We provide leaders with well-researched information on choosing foods, exercises, and other healthy habits that maintain peak performance.
- We coach leaders on how to transform their leadership behaviors to best support the present and future needs of their organizations.

Wright

Would you tell our readers about some of the specific tools and processes you teach in the Institute for Leadership Fitness?

Chinsky

We introduce sixteen separate tools and processes during our twelve-month program. One of our tools is called The Fit Leader's Companion™. The Companion focuses our clients on the specific actions they plan to take during the ninety-day periods between each of the four full-day workshops they attend. Participants complete a different Companion each quarter that creates a personalized road map to guide their implementation of the tools and processes they learn in each workshop.

In The Confidence Net™, participants build a portfolio of positive habits as a buffer to mitigate the effect and lower the volume of their gremlins or self-sabotaging inner voices. This "net" provides leaders with the ability to remain focused on the future, despite the self-doubts and other distractions they may be experiencing.

In The Star Retainer™, participants focus on their people decisions: whom to hire, whom to fire and whom to promote. In this module, we introduce our performance matrix that classifies organizational talent into one of six categories based on level of performance and the degree to which someone is organization centric versus egocentric.

In The Risk Quadrant™, we assess the leader's appetite for risk and explore organizational barriers to risk-taking. Participants are introduced to four risk quadrants determined by the extent to which a leader brings high or low amounts of both clarity and confidence to his or her decision-making process. Leaders also learn how to embrace failure as an essential step in the learning process.

In The Vanishing To-Do List™, we provide leaders with a productivity-boosting tool that allows them to confidently process all items on their to-do lists on a daily basis. After implementing this tool, our clients successfully convert their to-do lists into a temporary accumulator of important commitments and tasks, and then watch their to-do lists vanish at the end of each day as they either implement or schedule the follow-up actions necessary to fulfill each task on the list.

In The Power of Feeling Your Best, leaders learn how to create time in their lives for rest and rejuvenation, and how to create nutrition and exercise regimens that work for them.

We have a great mix of tools, each of which has its own workbook and interactive exercises designed to create the ability for leaders to immediately go back and implement these new processes in their organizations. Each quarter, our clients are introduced to at least four new tools designed to increase their clarity, confidence, effectiveness, and vitality.

Wright

Well, what a great conversation and what a great model. I wish I had met you forty-two years ago when I first started leading companies. This would have been really helpful. I'm so glad that you included vitality and the other elements of sustainability in your model. You have really done a great job, and I'm sure our readers are really going to enjoy learning more about some of the tools and processes you've introduced in this chapter. David, I appreciate your taking all this time to answer all these questions.

Chinsky

David, it's been my pleasure.

Wright

Today we've been talking with David Chinsky, business advisor and executive coach. David has shared his unique insights into leadership, change management, and teamwork with hundreds of leaders. He has developed a twelve-month leadership development experience, called The Institute for Leadership Fitness, which is designed for leaders seeking the clarity, confidence, effectiveness, and vitality necessary for achieving their highest levels of professional effectiveness and leadership fitness.

David, thank you so much for being with us today on *Yes You Can!*

Chinsky

You're welcome.

DAVID CHINSKY brings over twenty-five years of executive leadership and management experience to his role as a sought-after business advisor and executive coach. Drawing upon his own successful career as an accomplished and effective leader in the healthcare, automotive, and information technology industries, David has shared his unique insights into leadership, change management, and teamwork with hundreds of leaders. David is founder of The Institute for Leadership Fitness™, a twelve-month leadership development experience designed for leaders seeking the clarity, confidence, effectiveness, and vitality necessary for achieving their highest level of professional effectiveness and leadership fitness. For more information on The Institute for Leadership Fitness, please visit www.theleadershipfit.com/institute.

David Chinsky

David Chinsky & Associates
7252 E. Aurora
Scottsdale, AZ 85266
866-960-LEAD
dchinsky@theleadershipfit.com
www.theleadershipfit.com

CHAPTER FOUR

Let Us be the Water

by Jane Perdue

David Wright (Wright)

Today we're talking with Jane Perdue. Jane is a consultant, coach, speaker, and author whose career includes twenty years of executive level leadership, with fifteen of those years spent as a Vice President for Fortune 100 companies. As she so humorously states, she earned her business chops by managing twenty-five-million-dollar budgets and thousands of employees, developing and executing strategy as well as creating and implementing numerous leadership development programs.

In 2007, Jane followed her heart and founded The Braithwaite Group, a small female-owned professional development and consulting firm that's poised at the intersection of the art of leadership and the science of business. Her company works with leaders to help them achieve the exquisite balance between head and heart business practices. Jane works to inspire others to embrace possibilities beyond what they think, dream, or believe is achievable.

She believes that leadership isn't a role; but rather, a mindset and a heart direction open to all where purpose, passion, power, and performance connect. She brings a spirit of fun and adventure, along with a sense of limitless possibility to leading people, achieving common visions, and delivering results.

Jane, welcome to *Yes You Can!*

Jane Perdue (Perdue)

David, thank you so much. I'm delighted to be speaking with you today.

Wright

I understand you left a successful career as a Vice President in a Fortune 100 company to work for a small professional development and consulting firm. That's a big career change. Why did you make the move?

Perdue

David, making the move *was* an enormous amount of change. It felt like jumping off a cliff—scary, but energizing at the same time. Sometimes you just have to follow your heart and that's what I did to breathe life into a long-held dream.

Today, in what I call my second act of life, I consult, coach, write, speak, and inspire others to embrace possibilities at the intersection of the art of leadership and the science of business. That intersection is rich with opportunity for that exquisite but rare business balance between head and heart that I am so passionate about.

I believe that leadership is *both* a mindset and a heart direction in which purpose, passion, power, and performance connect. Anyone with a genuine head and heart connection can be a leader, regardless of job title, if he or she is willing to make the commitment to do so.

Wright

Will you give our readers a few examples of head and heart leadership practices so we can understand what they are and how they're different?

Perdue

Of course, I'd be happy to provide some definitions.

Head practices are what I call the fundamentals that exist in every workplace. They are items or activities like process and procedure, finance, policy creation, rules, making money, tasks and systems to get the work done, supervision, meetings, record-keeping and reporting, business development, research, operational efficiency, and compliance. The list goes on and on and represents the nitty-gritty requirements of running a business.

Heart practices touch people emotionally—even spiritually—and encompass workplace essentials like respect, compassion, recognition, and two-way communications that include empathetic listening, a sense of belonging, collaboration and partnership, trust, having fun, growing talent, engagement, vision, and employees feeling connected to the values of the organization. Heart practices create real alignment within the business between the stated mission and employees' actual on-the-job behaviors.

Wright

That makes sense, so what, then, is head and heart leadership?

Perdue

Head and heart leadership is focusing on, believing in, and executing both tasks *and* relationships. Head-and-heart-connected leaders get the work done, and get it done well. However, they also inspire employees so they feel valued and connected to their organization. Both head and heart practices are absolutely vital to business success, both from the Wall Street *and* Main Street perspectives.

Things typically go wrong when leaders concentrate too much on one of these two elements, and it's usually the head-oriented practices that get priority treatment. Having an appropriate balance of attention on tasks *and* relationships is best for both the business and employees.

For success in life and business, one must be able to manage (i.e., to direct and control) things like finances, inventory, work schedules, logistics, sales, compliance, etc. People are not managed per se, they are led—shown the way, inspired, guided.

In my head and heart view, head items are typically managed. Heart items are led. An effective leader touches hearts and balances that with head practices to get the work accomplished. There must be a sincere connection between head and heart to truly motivate people to follow a leader.

Wright

The Braithewaite Group has a fascinating tagline: "inspiring you to embrace possibilities at the intersection of the art of leadership and the science of business." Would you say more about what that means?

Perdue

In short, David, it means that there *must* be room for both head practices (making money, tasks, operational efficiency, and so on) *and* heart practices (compassion, vision, collaboration, trust, fun, and so on) in business today. Employees bring their brains—and their feelings—with them to work each day, so it's only natural that the workplace should represent getting the task done while also building relationships and fostering inspiration and innovation.

During the Renaissance, art and science were intermingled; both were highly valued. However, with the advent of scientific management in the United States in the early twentieth century, work focus shifted to time-and-motion studies, standardization, and concentration on task. A quote from Frederick Taylor, an American mechanical engineer, sums up this scientific management orientation: "It is only through *enforced* standardization of methods, *enforced* adoption of the best implements and working conditions, and *enforced* cooperation that this faster work can be assured. And the duty of enforcing the adoption of standards and enforcing this cooperation rests with *management* alone." Yuck! Who wants to work in an environment focused on force!

While few companies today are as rigid as Taylor's position, many are highly focused on earnings, *whatever the cost*, as the recent recession so powerfully illustrates. Strong elements of that concentration on task alone still exist in today's workplaces, with bottom line results and shareholder value being the foremost measures of business success. Employees, those invaluable assets who perform the work, are considered expense items, not assets, on the company's balance sheet.

It's my hope that a sufficient number of leaders will initiate a movement for a better workplace—a place in practice *and* belief where people matter and aren't simply viewed as just a budget line item. I'm reminded by the quote from Lao Tzu, "Water is fluid, soft, and yielding. But water will wear away rock, which is rigid and cannot yield. As a rule, whatever is fluid, soft, and yielding will overcome whatever is rigid and hard. This is another paradox: what is soft is strong." I help leaders be the water, bringing the power of heart into business.

As David Whyte so movingly states in his book, *The Heart Aroused, Poetry and the Preservation of the Soul in Corporate America,* ". . . finding the soul in American corporate life is blessedly fraught with difficulties . . . any man or woman working in the pressure of a modern corporation is making their way *through* the world, but it may be a world that seems, as the years roll by, to have less and less room for soul." A head and heart connected leader works to assure that this loss of soul at work doesn't happen. Treating employees with respect and compassion doesn't add a penny of expense to the bottom line, yet it produces impressive productivity, engagement, and profit results.

It's my dream that there's sufficient yearning, sufficient passion, sufficient drive, and sufficient purpose among character-based leaders for a better working environment. We can take this yearning, passion, and drive to reclaim the workplace, and then reshape it to a place where there's room for profits *and* principles *and* people, all equally valued.

Wright

So how do we recognize authentic head and heart connected leaders?

Perdue

Their energy, their affect, and influence are so powerful and contagious that it's easy to recognize them! An authentic head and heart leader thinks "we" first, "me" second. Watch for the person who understands the business, who has solid management acumen, and who then brings enthusiasm, laughter, adventure, unbounded possibility and inventive thinking to leading people, attaining goals, and delivering results.

If this individual is a formal leader—someone holding a job title involving overseeing the work of others, his or her department will be the one that hums with positive productivity and high employee engagement. If the individual is an informal leader—someone who does not manage a department, function, or people—he or she will be the person whose involvement and counsel is sought out, *because people want to know what they think or feel about an issue.*

A head-and-heart connected leader inspires everyone he or she touches to be the best they can be.

Wright

You've worked for and with companies of all sizes in both the for-profit and non-profit sectors. Are there any organizations that do manage to combine intellect and emotion, or head and heart as you call it, in running their business?

Perdue

Yes, David, there are organizations, large and small, for-profit and nonprofit, that do balance head and heart practices. A few with highly recognizable names that come to mind are Google, Whole Foods, Starbucks, Zappos, Chick-fil-A and Southwest Airlines. Smaller head-and-heart oriented organizations include the Mayo Clinic and Open Books. As a result of their leadership's consideration to both task and relationship, you can typically find these organizations included in the best-place-to-work survey results that are conducted either locally or nationally.

Proctor & Gamble, Sonoco Products, and Westfield Group have been recognized as top companies for leaders. These organizations have demonstrated a track record of financial success while investing in developing leaders and fostering a leadership culture. Leaders in these firms understand that an investment in their employees improves the bottom line results.

Wright

Why do you think leadership development is so important?

Perdue

Organizations' owners invest in technology or research to further their competitive positioning. Investing in their companies' leaders should be no different. I'm fond of saying that all work gets done by and through people, so why not invest in that valuable resource?

I've always been passionate about leadership development, creating numerous programs throughout my career, and coaching hundreds of leaders. I've seen bad bosses from all behavioral angles—those who were plain clueless, those who were cognizant of their limitations but not sure how to improve, and those who knew better but simply didn't care. I've trained and coached bosses in the clueless and seeking categories. I've also rejoiced with those who made a commitment to their personal development and who soared to success as head and heart connected leaders. I've also fired my share of those "who cares?" bosses whose poor interpersonal skills negatively affected business results.

Some organizations' owners do understand the importance of leadership development from a head and heart perspective; others are more concerned with the bottom line than investing in the future of their employees or simply are culturally focused on primarily head-oriented items and give lip service to the heart practices. As a coach and consultant, I partner with both individuals and wise owners of organizations who understand the importance of selecting the right leaders and then training them for head and heart success.

Wright

With the recession of 2007 hopefully behind us, why is your head and heart message so important?

Perdue

The head and heart leadership connection is very important for a variety of reasons. The recession has indelibly altered the lifestyle of many people. The nation, even the world, has witnessed the aftermath of unchecked financial greed and its lack of concern for its affects on others. For the first time, there are three generations—all with different viewpoints and approaches—working side-by-side in the workplace. People in all walks of life ask, "What happened to values, to civility, to caring?"

The desire for inspirational leadership in business is unquestionably on the uptick. *Leadership through the crisis and after: McKinsey Global Survey results,* published in September 2009 during the financial crisis, revealed: "The kinds of leadership behavior that executives say will most help their companies through the current crisis, such as inspiring others and defining expectations and rewards, are the same ones they say will help their companies thrive in the future."

Everyone within an organization already understands what specific work he or she must do and the boundaries in which he or she must do it. So, this is the opportune time to take advantage of shifting ideals and get refocused on relationship-building and connections at work to restore values, civility, and caring.

Individuals who aspire to be head and heart character-based leaders can be the water (drawing a metaphor on the Lao Tzu quote I referenced earlier) wearing away the sole focus on profits, undisciplined growth and pleasing investment analysts. They can lead the change for creating a new business model based on the three P's: people, principles, and profits. They can bring compassion, courage, and caring to the business boardrooms, cubicles, shop floors, and conference rooms across the land.

Wright

Why should individuals and businesses care about bringing the power of heart to business?

Perdue

A head and heart approach to leadership is just plain good business, in addition to being the right thing to do. Study after study details the positive economic affect of creating a work environment where employees feel connected to each other as well as to their organization. A Towers Perrin Talent Report, *Understanding What Drives Employee Engagement* (2003), demonstrated that companies with employees who were highly engaged beat the average revenue growth in their business sector by 1 percent, while companies with low engagement fell behind their business sector's revenue growth by an average of 2 percent. That's a significant margin of difference in bottom line affect.

Also, companies must consider the costs of all those employees who leave an organization because of a bad boss or poor work atmosphere. A DDI study, *Employee Engagement: The Key to Realizing Competitive Advantage*, sites corporate executive board findings from a worldwide survey of fifty thousand employees in fifty-nine firms. This study showed that employees with low satisfaction are four times more likely to quit than those who are highly engaged. Turnover is expensive, so increasing employee satisfaction by using a head and heart approach can dramatically reduce those costs.

This is the perfect time, as we reset our values and our economy, for individuals—and organizations—to step up and take ownership for their behaviors, making a commitment to bring a balance of logic and emotion into the workplace. Doing so is a colossal personal challenge, but the win-win proposition that results brings a huge individual and collective payoff.

Wright

What's the downside of companies not using both head and heart practices to run their business?

Perdue

The downside of continuing to focus exclusively on head-oriented items, particularly profits, is loss of productivity, turnover, and lack of employee connection to the organization. It's a perpetuation of the "me first" command and control business mindset.

In January 2010, The Conference Board released its latest job satisfaction survey. Only 45 percent of those polled reported being satisfied with their job—the lowest rate since the survey began in 1987. Given that head-only business practices have dominated in the workplace during those twenty-three years, these statistics are the "canary in the coal mine," signaling the need for bringing the power of heart into business.

Every employee is a human being—a unique individual with thoughts, feelings, desires, hopes, and dreams. Owners of corporations typically want only the thoughts and actions necessary to get the job done. As a former colleague once stated so wistfully, "Management doesn't want me to think or feel, just to do what they tell me to do." But, as human beings, we bring our emotions, our wishes, and our humanity with us to work. We can't just forget our dreams and simply carve out our brains and our hands, working like an unfeeling robot for eight or ten or twelve hours a day. Life with soul doesn't work that way.

Here's how one individual described his boss: "He made every decision and oversaw every detail. Nothing—absolutely nothing—happened without him being involved. Meetings were held every morning to review sales from the previous day. Heads rolled if the numbers weren't met. We were all scared to death of him and frightened that every day would be our last."

Not a very positive work place, right? It was neither productive nor profitable. This all-head-oriented leader was replaced with someone who brought a head-and-heart orientation and spent the next year rebuilding the organization.

The business world does not have to be cruel and heartless to be profitable.

Wright

Okay, let's say I'm a leader who likes your idea of bringing heart practices into the workplace. Where would I start?

Perdue

David, becoming a head-and-heart connected leader requires you to first make a personal commitment to understand, and then be able to manage, your own thoughts and feelings. Lao Tzu, the ancient Chinese philosopher, said it best: "Knowing others is intelligence; knowing yourself is true wisdom. Mastering others is strength, mastering yourself is true power."

The *Harvard Business Review* wrote that the "reluctance to explore your inner landscape not only weakens your own motivation but can corrode your ability to inspire others." Before we can connect with others, we must first identify, and then manage, our own strengths and weaknesses. Once there's that level of mastery, it can spread throughout the company, its teams and departments—the entire organization.

Psychologist and author Daniel Goleman's work with emotional intelligence is highly instructive for individuals seeking self-understanding. As Goleman noted in his book, *Vital Lies, Simple Truths*, that "The range of what we think and do is limited by what we fail to notice. And because we fail to notice that, we fail to notice there is little we can do to change until we notice how failing to notice shapes our thoughts and deeds."

Getting in touch with what we fail to notice—about ourselves and others—is a crucial first step in becoming a head-and-heart connected leader.

Once aware of how you operate as a head and heart-oriented leader, use that personal knowledge to establish relationships at all levels within the organization. Really connect with your employees, colleagues, and peers. Understand what motivates them. Really listen to your internal and external customers. Act on their feedback. Establish mutually beneficial and meaningful head and heart interactions with your suppliers, vendors, and in your community. Operate from the premise that people, principles, and profits are all equally important and that you won't sacrifice or abandon one for the other.

Wright

Using both your head and heart in your personal and professional life sounds like the right thing to do. How do you make it happen?

Perdue

You make a personal promise to making it happen, and hold yourself accountable for making it so. As Mihaly Csikszentmihalyi, Hungarian psychology professor best known for his notion of flow (that feeling of being in the zone), said, "The ability to give objective feedback to oneself is in fact the mark of the expert." However, one must be willing to do lots of introspection and self-exploration to become self-aware. Being self-aware is foundational to getting that connection between head and heart right.

I like to ask leaders: *"Is there a heartbeat in your spreadsheet?"* and see how they react. A few have a short, snappy comeback about the ridiculousness of my question. Many, many more pause, reflect, and say, *"You know, that's a good question. I haven't stopped to think about that, and maybe I should."* So that question is a great way to start the self-introspection process.

I use the seven C's to help leaders on their journey to using and balancing emotion and intellect, analysis and intuition, as they become head and heart centered leaders. These elements are: character, connection, communicate, capability, compassion, courage, and commitment.

Through reading and self-assessments, some individuals can identify their personal strengths and weaknesses, and then learn how to self-manage. Others benefit from working with a coach or mentor who can facilitate the self-discovery and self-management process. You must understand and connect with your own "C" factors *before* you can connect with and lead others.

Wright

Who or what has influenced your thinking about the power of heart in business?

Perdue

Unfortunately, many of the bosses I've had in my career weren't good head-and-heart-connected leaders (and I was not alone in holding that view!). Most of those individuals were well-intentioned but misguided, lacking understanding and/or training that would allow them to be effective leaders. A few of those former bosses were just plain mean-spirited and self-absorbed—the perfect what-not-to-do leadership role model!

But then I met George Newton. I had been hired as the head of the Human Resource Department for a family-owned food processing company in a small Midwest town. The first person I met on my first day of work was the male head of security who greeted me with, "So, you're the one who took the job that should have gone to a man with kids. Hope you and all the ones like you are happy with what you're doing."

With a first-day welcome like that, I needed a boost. I soon found one in my new colleague, George Newton, who had been passed over for the job awarded to me. He had devoted his entire work career to that company and had every right to be resentful of me, but he wasn't.

His smile was warm that first day; and his words even warmer. "I'll help you learn the ropes within the organization," he said, "and I will introduce you to people in the community. Together, we'll make this work." And we did.

Wright

How did that early experience with a head and heart leader shape your career?

Perdue

What impressed me then, and still impresses me today, is how generous George was in his teaching with everyone within the organization. His challenges were pointed yet tactful. He took the time to connect. He remembered people's favorite desserts and always offered up titles of books to read. He truly led from both the head and heart, even when it wasn't popular to do so.

George helped me and others succeed. My first lesson as a leader in corporate America wasn't to "eat 'em up and spit 'em out;" but rather, to embrace, teach, mold, and watch success grow. It was a powerful experience. I made a commitment that I would always be there to teach, to share, and to listen—to those on my staff as well as others in the company and the community.

Wright

You've written a book about the power of heart in business. Would you tell me more about it?

Perdue

David, thanks for asking about my book. It's a leadership fable (like Patrick Lencioni's "Five Dysfunctions of a Team") about the rise, fall, and rise again of a reinvented leader, Neal Holland, whose story is like so many other business executives who have to learn the hard way that being human is not only a better way to live but a better way to do business.

Neal, the book's central character, represents many bosses—individuals so caught up in corporate achievement that they fail to connect with themselves or with others. I think most of us have had a boss like that—all work, no play, not even a "good morning" greeting but rather a brusque "where's that report I asked you to work on last night?"

Neal (dreadful boss extraordinaire) receives his unexpected—but heralded by others—comeuppance, getting sacked for poor business results combined with deplorable people skills and unchecked self-importance. Blind to his own shortcomings, he initially refuses to acknowledge that his leadership style is preventing him from finding another job. It takes quite a series of incidents before Neal finally concedes that *he*—not the economy, not other people—is the problem.

With help from a supportive circle of new associates who teach him about the seven C's (character, connection, communicate, capability, compassion, courage, and commitment), Neal emerges as a self-aware and understanding boss who uses his head *and* his heart to connect with employees and colleagues, creating a workplace where both positive bottom line results *and* relationships are valued.

Any manager or business owner who is seeking to reinvent himself or herself as an inspiring leader, or anyone who has had a crummy boss and swears to treat his or her people differently when he or she, in turn, becomes a boss, will relate to Neal's sometimes positive, sometimes difficult experiences as he transforms himself from a tone-deaf, take-no-prisoners boss into a self-aware and engaging person.

Wright

What final thoughts or advice would you like to share with our readers?

Perdue

I can't stress enough that the point of being a head and heart focused leader is that the workplace can be kinder and gentler *and still make money*. A head and heart connected leadership style produces a better work environment as well as positive bottom line results. It's a win-win outcome that shouldn't be missed. And, the added bonus is that practicing the seven C's—character, connection, communicate, capability, compassion, courage, and commitment—doesn't cost a penny!

Wright

Well, how interesting, especially since I've been running companies for so many years. On occasion, I stubbed my toe on some of these things you've talked about; but hopefully, most of the time I've been a heart and head leader without knowing how to define it. That's good.

Perdue

That's terrific to hear that you've been a head and heart connected leader all these years!

Wright

I really appreciate all the time, Jane, that you have spent with me answering these questions. It really has been enlightening. I've taken notes here so I can go back and change some of my leadership style, thanks to you.

Perdue

Thank you, David. I appreciate your kind and generous words.

Wright

Today we've been talking with Jane Perdue who is a consultant, coach, speaker, facilitator, and author whose career includes twenty years of executive level leadership. Jane works to inspire others to embrace possibilities at the intersection of the art of leadership and the science of business. As we've found here today, she believes that leadership isn't a role; but rather, a mindset and a heart direction, where purpose, passion, power, and performance connect.

Jane, thank you so much for being with us today on *Yes You Can!*

Perdue

David, thank you, and I enjoyed speaking with you today.

Jane Perdue is a consultant, coach, speaker, and author whose career includes twenty years of executive level leadership, with fifteen of those years spent as a Vice President for Fortune 100 companies. As she so humorously states, she earned her business chops by managing twenty-five-million-dollar budgets and thousands of employees, developing and executing strategy as well as creating and implementing numerous leadership development programs.

In 2007, Jane followed her heart and founded The Braithwaite Group, a small female-owned professional development and consulting firm that's poised at the intersection of the art of leadership and the science of business. Her company works with leaders to help them achieve the exquisite balance between head and heart business practices. Jane works to inspire others to embrace possibilities beyond what they think, dream, or believe is possible.

She believes that leadership isn't a role; but rather, a mindset and a heart direction where purpose, passion, power, and performance connect. She brings a sense of fun, adventure, and limitless possibility to leading people, achieving common visions, and being the best her clients can be.

Jane Perdue

2301 Kiln Point Drive
Mount Pleasant, SC 29466
843-810-6777
thebraithewaitegroup@comcast.net
www.thebraithewaitegroup.com
http://lifeloveleadership.blogspot.com

CHAPTER FIVE

Health & Fitness:
Essentials for Success

by Bill Zuti

David Wright (Wright)

Today we are talking to Bill Zuti who is a senior consultant with The Success Associates. In addition, since 2007, he has been serving as the Associate Dean of The College of Education and Human development, Radford University (Virginia). At present, he is a Professor in the Department of Exercise Sport and Health Education, where he helped develop the programs in health and fitness. Bill has written or co-authored six books and forty professional and research publications. Over the years, he has given countless presentations and speeches on all aspects of physical fitness, health, and wellness. He has also worked with corporations and medical and human service organizations.

The phrase "yes you can" is an expression of a positive attitude. Dr. Zuti believes, as many others do, that we are capable of accomplishing so much when we believe we can do it. This book focuses on the positive and it is the premise for success. All of the chapters provide excellent guidelines to success. In this chapter, he states that it is not possible to achieve or enjoy success if a person is not healthy and/or physically fit.

We'd like to welcome Bill Zuti to *Yes You Can!*

Bill Zuti (Zuti)

Thank you very much. It is both a privilege and a pleasure to be involved in this project.

Wright

Why do you say a person must be healthy and fit to achieve success?

Zuti

I think the simplest way to make my point is to ask this: Have you ever gotten sick when you had a project to complete and you were so frustrated because you were still capable of functioning, but not really able to do your best work? You knew you had all this work to do—you knew you had something to get done—but you were ill and nothing seemed to reach your standard of quality. Well, the point is, if you are not healthy and fit, you are not going to achieve the ultimate success of which you are capable. You must keep your body healthy and fit in order to function at your peak and achieve success.

Wright

There are thousands of things out there people are hawking, all sorts of wares—vitamins, gadgets, and so forth, but what must average people do to keep themselves healthy?

Zuti

The health fitness industry is a huge market and we are bombarded with information from all forms of the media. A common problem is to know what one needs to do to maintain one's optimal level of health and fitness.

For the vast majority of people, keeping healthy and fit just comes down to a relatively simple few things. I am going to summarize ten categories and all of them are essential. These are like building blocks or a chain—all are essential to having the system work properly. Do not misinterpret those you do not think are important and feel that you can skip the first four or five. The simple analogy is like a chain—you have to have *all* the links functioning at their best. These ten things are general and some seem easy to achieve. Some of these items we say we do, but in reality we really don't. We intend to do then, but— or we only do them in part (you get the idea). Achieving success is your goal and you must be honest with yourself. There are no shortcuts, so don't cheat yourself.

We will start with number ten, which is to relax and enjoy yourself. You have got to get enough rest and get enough recreational and leisure activities. The best know catch phrase for this is to "laugh, love and live." This almost seems incongruous, because we usually equate success with hard work. We think of the overachieving workaholic as the ultimate role model. In fact, those who are truly successful master relaxing behavior and know its worth.

The number nine is related to your job or profession. Successful people love what they do. Many people do not love their job. They should look forward to the challenges and opportunities it brings. A well-suited career should provide more than money—it should also give the individual personal satisfaction, intellectual development, and a sense of accomplishment. So if you are not getting these, then your job will wear you down over time and can affect your health. If you work primarily for money and you become ill, you will not be able to enjoy it.

Cleanliness is next and it is something most of us take for granted. We have little contact with people who are not generally clean. We know that unsanitary conditions can exist and we make every effort to avoid these. Recently, much attention has been paid to contagious diseases. People are encouraged to use preventive behaviors, particularly washing hands to help keep from contracting or passing colds, flues, and other such conditions.

The next one—number seven—is safety, and immediately everybody thinks of driving safety, which is an obvious one. However, we also need to think about safety in our homes and workplaces, specifically as it relates to falls. This is particularly important as people get older; falls are a very serious problem. We always want to think about safety in regard to our children. Most people realize that if you get injured, you have to recover and this often results in loss of strength and endurance.

Number six is the problem of drugs. When most people hear the word "drugs," they immediately think of illegal or illicit drugs. In reality, there are many people who are not healthy because they have a tendency to overmedicate. They think if the doctor prescribes two, well, four is better. This misuse occurs for both prescription and over-the-counter medications.

Smoking and tobacco use have markedly declined over the last few decades. Smoking is the unhealthiest thing you can do that is still legal.

Alcohol use is next. And most people know it should be consumed in moderation. The specific example of one or two glasses of red wine daily is actually a health benefit. Some have carried this step further with the use of resveratrol, which is the element in red wine that is considered so beneficial. Obviously alcohol consumption taken to any extreme is a serious problem and one with which we need to deal. (Supplemental note: Resveratrol is sold commercially. The recommended dosage is five hundred milligrams daily. It is usually listed as Trans-veratrol or Transmax. The Internet supplier we know is Biotiva.)

What I have talked about up to this point are things that are part of general health or what can be referred to as "wellness." These seven items will, over time, affect your health and well-being, but are often less direct or acute. The next group is the top three; they include stress, diet/weight management, and exercise. These are often considered to be more important because all of these will directly affect your health and fitness severely enough to reduce your effectiveness.

If you are not managing your stress, there is a pretty good chance that you are going to develop some type of illness or disorder. Stress is linked to a variety of diseases. Some of the researchers who work in this area have expressed the opinion that as much as 70 percent of our illnesses can be attributed in one form or another to stress. Most of us experience stress in two general categories. The first is job or work related and the second is at the personal level. Unfortunately, we cannot concentrate on one to the exclusion of the other because they both have a tendency to work together against us. Where the combination effect exists, and the person is having trouble with his or her career and personal life, it seems there is no way to recover.

We all experience some type of stress on a regular basis. Most people compensate, adjust, and/or manage these problems. However, when multiple stressors are encountered, there is not enough opportunity to reduce these levels and it has a profound effect.

Next on my list is diet/nutrition and weight management. This comes very close to the top of that list because right now we are looking at statistics that range from 30 percent to in excess of 40 percent of the population are dangerously overweight. The excess accumulation of body fat is affecting the overall health and lifestyle of those affected. The broad sweeping effect goes from orthopedic problems to increased risk of heart disease. Diet and nutrition experts debate which types of diets are most healthy. The heart healthy people recommend a low fat diet. As a result, the food industry has produced a vast assortment of "low fat" products. The problem that seems to have occurred in doing this is the addition or increase in sugars and starches. It seems that some portion of the population is not capable of metabolizing these properly. As a result, these people accumulate excess quantities of fat. It is up to the experts to resolve this. Nonetheless, maintaining proper weight is essential to good health and fitness.

Of course, number one on my list is exercise. This is the one behavior that is absolutely essential for good health and fitness. When we use the term "exercise," we use it interchangeably with all types of exercise—sports and physical activity. You do not have to participate in a formal exercise program such as getting up and going to a gym every morning. But you do have to be physically active, and that is the key. You cannot be healthy if you are sedentary.

Wright

You say all of these are necessary, and I happen to agree with you. All ten are very specifically important to me personally, but exercise or physical activity for most of us is the key behavior. Why is exercise so important?

Zuti

Let us consider the fact that human beings are animals. I know that we usually distinguish ourselves from the animal kingdom, but if there are plants, animals, minerals, etc, then we are definitely in the animal category. All of our development and design was intended for activity, and the body has to have physical use. The body is absolutely dependent on regular movement and exercise.

The design of the body systems is unbelievable. It has never been equaled in all the technology we now have. It is the ultimate positive feedback loop system. If you use a body system, the body maintains and nurtures that system. If you do not use a body system, it takes the resources from that system and moves it to the one you are using. So anything that we don't use will waste away or atrophy. What you do use is supported and reinforced. What you use gets better and stronger, and what you don't use gets smaller or less developed. I think most adults have experienced this if they have broken whatever bone and had to wear a cast for weeks. When the cast first went on it was tight and if the skin underneath began to itch it was difficult to scratch because there was very little room between the cast and your skin. After several weeks or two months in the cast, you could insert your finger and scratch. The reason you could do that was because the muscle had not been active. That part of your body had already begun to atrophy or waste away. So we have to use the body to maintain our optimal level of health.

Wright

You say that exercise is important because we have become so sedentary. When we become more active, does this reduce our risk of illness? If so, which illnesses specifically?

Zuti

Absolutely, it does. You have just heard my explanation of the system that the body uses to maintain itself and why we cannot be sedentary. The simple rule is: you cannot be healthy if you are sedentary.

All bodies are a little different; we are unique but similar. Everyone looks different, and that is how we can tell one person from another. The same is true for our physiology—we are all similar, but unique. As a result, everyone's learning, training, medical treatment, personality, and so on are all different. Our fitness and health will also be unique.

Differences are attributed to heredity, age, gender, etc. When we consider illness and diseases, it is important to look at how the body systems work. Recovering from injury or disease, we can look at how we heal, how we grow, and how we develop. Obviously, a young child grows very quickly and very well. Then the question is what happens to our growth and healing as we age? How is this affected by age and heredity? And, of course, what role does exercise play in all of this? The key is "physiological age." This is how old and/or responsive our bodies systems are. How well do we fight disease, how quickly do we heal, and how rapidly do we respond to training? People who exercise maintain their body systems, so they seem younger than their chronological age.

There is an old definition of physiological middle age and this surprises a lot of people. This was proposed by the scientist who is considered to be the grandfather of exercise physiology. His name is T. K. Cureton. He said that physiological middle age is twenty-seven. Well, if we use this as a standard, from birth to twenty-seven, we heal at a specific rate. If you then look at a person who is fifty-four his or her growth and development and healing would be twice as long as a person who is twenty-seven. Someone who is eighty-one would take three times as long to heal, recover, or train. Thus, there is not much difference between the healing rates of young people whether they are active or not. However, as we age, this distinction is increased. A sedentary person over the age of fifty will take significantly longer to heal than if he or she had been active, fit, and healthy. Everyone will slow with time, but people who maintain their bodies will be younger on the inside.

When exercising, you stimulate the circulatory system, which helps your heart, lungs, and other vital body systems. The more you exercise, the better your chance of avoiding obesity and the easier it is to manage your weight because you're burning more calories. Because you exercise, your blood flow is increased and this stimulates your lymphatic system. When you stimulate your lymphatic system, your resistance to disease is better. All of these factors come together to enable you to reduce your risk of disease.

Wright

Other than the obvious here, I know I need to exercise much more than I do. How much activity or exercise is necessary to reduce the risk of disease and improve health?

Zuti

There are simple guidelines, but clarification and elaboration are necessary so people understand what and how to become and fit and healthy.

The first thing is to be sure you are healthy enough for physical activity. If you are over fifty, have high blood pressure, high blood lipids, and/or known heart disease, see you physician before starting.

Most people need to do about twenty to forty minutes, three to five days per week at a reasonable level of intensity. Now, that doesn't have to be done all at once and it doesn't have to be done in a formal way like in a class or at a fitness center. For most healthy people, there are general recommendations. People should work within these levels and do as much as they can. People probably need to do a little bit more than they are now doing. Only about 20 to 22 percent of our population is getting enough regular physical activity.

Wright

You are not saying that this activity needs to be rigorous as much as we just need to do it and be involved in it.

Zuti

Exactly, and that is the point people need to understand. You just need to admit that you can do more. You can do it at anytime and anywhere.

The next thing is how to know if you need to increase physical activity, develop more endurance, increase muscular strength, and reduce body fat. The most common motivation to begin an exercise program is if you have excess body fat. This is a simple thing to determine. Reach down and pinch your waist right above your hip bone, just above your belt, directly underneath your armpit. Now hold that layer of skin and fat with the thumb and first finger of one hand and put your middle finger of the other hand over top of it. If that layer of fat is thicker than your middle finger then you are carrying too much fat. Obviously, if you've got to put your wrist on there to match, you have really got a problem.

The next thing to determine is if you are weak. Do you have trouble doing normal daily activity such as lifting grocery bags or picking children up? Another way to tell is if you are tired or not sleeping well. Do you just generally lack energy? Believe it or not, people who are physically active actually have more energy and sleep better. Then, of course, do you have constant stiffness and soreness? If you do, you are not using your muscles enough; they get stiff when they are not used.

Wright

I used to exercise a great deal when I was in my "second youth"—from my thirties to my forties. I would eat like a horse, the more I would exercise. It was amazing; it was almost as though my body was just replenishing everything it possibly could. Now, unfortunately, I still eat like a horse but my physical activities have lessened.

Zuti

The natural response of the body is to maintain itself. That mechanism is what has allowed humans to survive as they went from feast and famine. The only problem is we no longer have famine. We just have this unbelievable abundant supply of food. A compounding problem is that food is available almost instantaneously. When you get hungry now, it takes you probably less than two minutes to eat. You either go to the refrigerator or, if you're at the office, to a vending machine. If you are out you can go to a McDonald's or some other fast food restaurant. The trouble is we still have the same systems as primitive man. Before modern times, when people got hungry they had to hunt for perhaps a day or two before eating. It took a while to go out and kill a saber tooth tiger, roast, and eat it.

Wright

If you've been to my home, when my wife's on a diet it is feast or famine!

Zuti

I know; we do the same thing, and that is one of the successful tricks in the reduction of eating, but you have to keep the healthy food around—the things that you do want to eat. But you have to rid your house of the things you don't want to tempt you or keep them in a place where they are not visible. In our house, the big vices are ice cream and peanut butter, which are common ones for many people. If you want to keep a little bit in the house, then keep it in the outside freezer so you have to go all the way to the garage or all the way down the basement to get to it. This isn't as good as the exercise primitive people had, but at least it's a few more steps.

Wright

It also makes it a little bit tougher to get to.

Are there precautions I need to take before starting or increasing exercise?

Zuti

Absolutely, and the organizations that have promoted and published guidelines or precautions include The American Heart Association and the American College of Sports Medicine. These two were the ones who originally pioneered the work with exercise and cardiac rehabilitation. Now, they actually have guidelines for people and those guidelines are very simple. If you are under the age of forty and you don't have any significant risk factors, and the people in your family haven't died before the age of fifty from heart disease and similar risk factors, then it is probably okay to start exercising. If you are under forty and have no health risks, don't worry about it too much, just start easy and you will be fine.

Everybody else is probably going to have to see a physician for a checkup. See a physician if you have a history and risk factors. Risk factors are abnormal electrocardiograph, abnormal blood-work, which includes cholesterol levels and other blood variables. Blood pressure is a big one, and is easily checked. You can walk around the malls, drug stores, and see units that can give you a reading of what your blood pressure is. Blood pressure should be less than 120 over 80 millimeters of mercury. If you are above 140 over 90, either one of those above, during a resting blood pressure, you definitely need to see a physician before you start. Of course, anybody who is in a high stress job is in the "see-your-doctor" category. If you get winded easily—if you walk up a set of stairs and you are huffing and puffing— you need to see your doctor before you start.

Wright

What's the best way to start?

Zuti

The most important thing is the title of this book, *Yes You Can!*, which means you have to have a positive attitude. You have to know in your heart and believe in your mind that you can do this. It is "yes you can" absolutely all the way. You have to believe in yourself and you have to make this a self-esteem issue. In other words, this is important to you as a person.

I analogize taking care of yourself to the classic example of being on an airplane where they say, "Put on your oxygen mask before you try to help somebody else." Well, this is exactly the same thing. If you want to help yourself and you want to help other people, you absolutely have to do this for yourself.

The next thing is that you have to picture positive success. For this example we go to a sports image. If an athlete is trying to get a ball through a goal, the athlete always has to visualize the ball going into the net. If he or she does not picture that first, then it isn't going to happen. This is what we have to do when we start our health programs. So you have to keep positive images in your mind.

Second thing is to start easy and slow. The worst thing you can do is to overdo it. The absolute sure disaster is to decide on New Year's Day that you are going to totally redo your life—quit smoking, go on a diet, and start an exercise program. Guess what's going to happen? It doesn't work because you can't deal with all of these changes at one time. The bundle of sticks to be broken has to be done one stick at a time. Start easy, start slow; progress and develop at an appropriate rate.

The next thing is to walk—don't run. People think that if they're going to get in shape, they've got to jog. Jogging is great for people in their twenties and it is wonderful for children's development. But as you get a little older—by the time you're in your thirties—it is time to be realistic. The body's muscles, skeleton, and connective tissue were never designed for long-term running. Remember, for cavemen, old age was the early thirties. They quit running in their twenties. We as adults develop too many orthopedic and back problems, as well as other similar problems. So walking is the key. Besides, you can go on indefinitely and it doesn't require a change of clothing. All you need a decent pair of shoes. You can walk anywhere, anytime, anyplace, and with anyone.

Now, if you want to get some supplemental positive feedback and quantify what you are doing, get a pedometer. Place it on your belt, set it, and as you take steps it will give you a count of how many steps you take in a day. Now the real health fitness people say you should be taking ten thousand steps a day. Well, that number is equivalent to running ten kilometers or just over six miles. So you may not want to start there. But the point is, get the pedometer, wear it around for a day or two, and calculate the average number of steps you take per day. Then, very subtly, every week try and increase it by 5 or 10 percent. Keep working your way up to a reasonable goal or even to the ten thousand mark.

The other thing to remember is to "just do it." In other words, any additional physical activity is important. For some people, tracking it is critical and provides excellent reinforcement. Like the pedometer with the walking, just doing more activity of any kind, regardless of what it is, will help. One highly effective system is to record all activity in an exercise log. We have ones you can download or print from our Web site, www.TheSuccessAssociates.com. Most book stores sell a variety of bound exercise logs and you just need to decide the size and style. My personal preference is to use the Excel spreadsheet program to record my weight so I can see the graph and the printed to track muscular strength training.

Wright

What are the simple things people can do in their homes?

Zuti

Believe it or not, most people think you have to go to a gym, which we will talk about in a minute, but in reality you don't. You need to consider doing three types of exercise. Number one is exercise for the heart-lung-circulatory system; that is one area of the body that needs to be worked. The second one is muscle strength and endurance, and range of motion and flexibility. Third are exercises to help manage your weight. We must find activities that meet all three of these areas. Again, we will include a few examples here and put more on our Web site.

One of the simplest things you can do for both cardiovascular and weight management is to adopt a dog. If you rescue a dog, you're going to have to walk it. Now when you walk the dog, you are going to have to do this three or four times a day. The very simple thing is to figure out that if you walk about two hundred to two hundred and fifty yards each trip, that gives you one quarter of a mile. I do this four times a day, so that is a mile a day extra I get that benefits both my heart and my waistline. Now, over the course of the 365 days in a year, you will have burned enough calories to either lose or not gain ten pounds.

The same kind of logic about adding more to your daily life can apply to parking your car. I love to go to Walmart and other big shopping places and watch people spend five or ten minutes trying to find the closest parking space to the entrance. What a waste of time, and it does not help their fitness. I always park about halfway down the parking lot. I do it very quickly and easily and then get out and walk from my car and watch these people still driving around looking for a nearby parking space; meanwhile, I am in the store already. Two things: I save a lot of gas and I get extra exercise from that additional hundred yards back and forth, going in and out of the store. The same principle applies to using the stairs instead of the elevator. The general rule is to walk up one or two and down two or three. So those are the simple things for your cardiovascular system and weight management.

For muscular development, it's not difficult to think about the concept of "just do it." This is simple weight training with a gallon of water or milk. A gallon of liquid weighs about eight pounds. If you want to do something for muscular strength endurance and flexibility and range of motion, you can simply lift a single gallon over your head; push it out to the side, and so on. Then, if you want to do more for muscular strength and endurance, simple things such as vacuuming, gardening, and other similar activities are excellent.

You can just lie on the floor while you're watching television and do what we call abdominal crunches or abdominal curls. You just lie flat on your back with your knees bent looking up at the television, then suck your tummy down as close to your spinal column as possible, arch your shoulders up a little bit, reach up and try to slide your hands down and touch your shins. Now those are all very simple things you can do in your home and meet those three criteria we just mentioned.

Wright

Well, what if the people reading your chapter choose to join a fitness center—how can they tell if it is a good one?

Zuti

This is a very important and common question. Again, we have a comprehensive checklist posted on our Web site. The most important things to look for are those common to almost everyone. The first thing you want to do is network. Talk with people who are working out regularly and have been doing it for a while to find out what centers they like. You can check with the Better Business Bureau, Chamber of Commerce, and the Internet to get more information. This will help you narrow it down to a reasonable number of centers as possible choices.

The next things you do are to visit the centers and meet with the managers and possibly staff. When it comes to staff at fitness centers, look for college graduates with reputable degrees in exercise science and certified personal trainers.

Upon entering a center, the first thing to look for is cleanliness. This is a must. You want to make sure you have a fitness center that has a regular maintenance program that includes using disinfectants and/or disinfectant wipes. The active ingredients will have an *ammonium chloride* base or similar ingredient. Obviously, read the label. It is possible for centers to use wipes that are cheaper and clean, but do not disinfect. Look at the shower stalls and floors, look at the locker rooms. Be thorough in your inspection.

The next thing is usually location. Most people are not willing to travel more than fifteen minutes to a fitness center. The obvious reason is that if you travel fifteen minutes there and fifteen minutes back, you have already got a half an hour of time consumed. If you spend an hour at the center, you now have an hour and a half invested. Most people cannot spend an hour and a half more than three or four times a week. When you are looking at location, also look at accessibility. Examine the in-out pattern to the facility. It is possible for you to pick one that is on your way to work and this seems great. The trouble is you have got to make a left turn coming out to get to work and there is no traffic light. You have difficulty getting into traffic, which is going to be a big frustration to you. The same thing is true for adequate parking. The last thing you want to do is get to a fitness center that does not have enough parking during peak times. You cannot get a convenient parking place and again you are killing more time.

The next issue is equipment. Decide on what you want, and remember, you need to look at both aerobic (the cardiovascular) and anaerobic equipment (weights and nautilus). Aerobics exercises obviously include the whole series of items such as treadmills, steppers, elliptical, bikes, rowers, and arm-cranks. The key is to make sure that they have enough of what you want and the type you want, when you want it. Nautilus equipment should include at least ten stations. It is important to note that free weights are not usually used by the average person who's interested in health, fitness, and wellness. Body-builders use heavy squat racks, etc. Fitness participants will need some hand weights and those are for range of motion and lightweight exercises. Mats and mirrors are a given.

Now the next thing you might want to look at includes programs and group exercises. Some people want to work on their own and others really like the classes. The advantages of the class are the guidance of an instructor and a group of people who will provide social support. The availability of equipment or classes is critical. It does you no good to go to a fitness center when you cannot get on the equipment that you want. You will need to actually visit the center during the time you're going to work out.

When choosing a center, you have two options: national or local. National centers, like Curves and Gold's are great because you know what their programs are, you know how their facilities are designed, and they operate on an established standard of excellence. Local centers (locally owned and operated and not part of a franchise or chain) can be excellent and many cities and towns have very good ones. However, you must be careful because you don't have that national name behind you. The advantage to local centers is that they usually offer programs and services consistent with the community and the needs and interests of the people they serve.

Fee structure is also important. Be careful you are not charged for things and add-ons that you do not need or want. Read the contract; don't be suckered in by bait-and-switch tactics.

The other things I like to add are years of service and other services offered. You want a center that is going to be around for a while. The other services are not really related to health/fitness, but they can affect the decision for some people. Some enjoy a spa, pool, steam, tanning, nails, hair, or any of the other kinds of services enjoyed as extras. These are like dessert at the end of a meal.

Wright

Well, Bill, in closing, we know these changes can be difficult; what are some of the things people need to do to be successful?

Zuti

They must make this a 100 percent commitment. The next thing is that they have to incorporate this into their daily life. In other words, if you say that on Monday, Wednesday, and Friday at 7:00 AM you are going to the fitness center, you must do it until it becomes part of your daily life. You must develop this activity into a habit.

The next thing is that you must have social support. There are two levels of social support. Number one is your significant other and the second is an exercise partner or group. Your significant other, husband, wife, boyfriend, or girlfriend has to support your efforts. Without this support, it will not work. In most cases, either you will give up either the exercise or the relationship. In a case of couples with children, this is even more critical. Since someone must take care of the children, some couples use an alternating schedule. They both do it in the morning; one of them does it Monday, Wednesday, and Friday, and the other one gets the kids ready for school and then the other partner does the alternate Tuesday, Thursday, and Saturday.

The second aspect of social support is almost as critical—the exercise buddy or group. I have been a very fortunate person because I have been able to find outstanding exercise buddies. There are two reasons for an exercise buddy or group. The number one reason is to be there. I know that if I miss exercise, my exercise buddy is going to ask me where I was and say he missed me. So, I feel an obligation to be there because he wants me there and because I help support him. The other reason is that it helps pass the time. When the two of us are there we talk, joke, console, commiserate, and support each other. Because we are together and talking about the Academy Awards or politics or the weather, the forty or fifty minutes we spend on the exercise equipment passes more quickly.

A caution I must give you is to avoid injury. That is part of sticking to doing one thing at a time and not overdoing it. You do not want to push too hard and hurt yourself. One of the biggest reasons people drop out of exercise programs is because they push too hard, get hurt, and then it's very, very difficult to come back.

Next is to maintain life balance—don't go to one extreme or the other. I often joke about people who become what I refer to as "healthier than thou." They become such zealots that they go over the top with this and they neglect job, family, and friends.

I have already mentioned this, but it is worth repeating: make sure that you do one thing at a time—don't try too much too soon.

The next item is to follow your plan. Develop a long-range plan so you know where you are going to go, what you are going to need, and do. You might work this out with the help of a consultant or personal trainer. You can do the research on your own, but develop a plan so you know where you are going. Yes you can be healthy and succeed. We know very well that yes you can reach a goal if you follow the plan.

Of course the last thing is a positive attitude. The "yes you can" attitude must be there. If it is, it will carry you, but you have to do it. The yes you can attitude makes it possible for you to be successful, achieve your goals, be healthy and fit, and enjoy your life.

Wright

Well, I think that pretty much sums everything up. I thank you for your time and for answering these questions. Thank you for being with us on *Yes You Can!*

Bill Zuti is a senior consultant with The Success Associates. In addition, since 2007, he has been serving as the Associate Dean of The College of Education and Human development, Radford University (Virginia). At present, he is a Professor in the Department of Exercise Sport and Health Education, where he helped develop the programs in health and fitness. Bill has written or co-authored six books and forty professional and research publications. Over the years, he has given countless presentations and speeches on all aspects of physical fitness, health, and wellness. He has also worked with corporations and medical and human service organizations.

The phrase "yes you can" is an expression of a positive attitude. Dr. Zuti believes, as many others do, that we are capable of accomplishing so much when we believe we can do it. This book focuses on the positive and it is the premise for success. All of the chapters provide excellent guidelines to success. In this chapter, he states that it is not possible to achieve or enjoy success if a person is not healthy and/or physically fit.

Bill Zuti

"Understanding Health, Fitness and Wellness as part of Success"

The Success Associates
8217 Sawgrass Way
Radford Virginia 24141
540-639-5592
bill.zuti@thesuccessassociates.com
www.thesuccessassociates.com

CHAPTER SIX

Leadership—Securing the Future

by Cy Charney

David Wright (Wright)

Today we are talking with Cy Charney, President of Charney and Associates Inc. A leading consultant in the area of organizational performance, he has developed a variety of unique interventions to help organizations in both the private and public sectors become leaders in their fields. The challenge of leadership is perhaps the greatest now than it has been for decades. Organizations are reeling under the pressure caused by a combination of plummeting revenues and budgets, fast changing market conditions, declining morale, and rising demands from customers. Maintaining a sense of purpose and hope for the future while building the talent pool are some of the attributes of effective leadership. This chapter will describe the competencies of effective leaders who are able to make sense of the complexities of organizational life and inspire their employees to strive for excellence. It will provide the benchmarks that allow readers to evaluate their own abilities as well as discover new strategies for personal growth for improvement.

Cy Charney, welcome to *Yes You Can!*

Cy Charney (Charney)

Thank you, David.

Wright

So how would you define leadership?

Charney

There are many, many different definitions of leadership and I have three that I consider to be really important. To some extent, each one of these has a place in any organization, but it also depends on the challenges of the organization at that particular time as well as where they are in their growth cycle.

Probably the most popular definition of leadership is that it is the ability to get people to achieve goals willingly—goals that they never thought possible. If you're a leader, you're an individual who looks to the future, identifies opportunities, and inspires others to go to places that perhaps they hadn't thought of as being possible.

My second definition is that leadership is the ability to influence others. This was Ken Blanchard's idea coined a while back. I like that definition because, when you consider what you're doing on a day-to-day basis, you realize that you're managing change and you're influencing people. It suggests that not everyone is a leader; you can be a manager, but if you don't have the ability to influence others, then essentially you're not really being a leader. Anyone in an organization can be a leader if he or she has the ability to influence other people in the organization.

My third and favorite definition is that leadership is about developing other leaders. This suggests (and it's really important in the context of today's organizations) that the focus of any leader must be to replace himself or herself. Why is this important? Because about 40 percent of all managers across North America are likely to be retiring in the next ten years. These are the Baby Boomers who are difficult to replace as there is a shallow pool of developed leaders who are following them. So we need to be looking at the next generation of employees to specifically identify those potential leaders who can replace the folks who will be retiring. Developing other leaders is a very important aspect of leadership.

So there are a variety of ways to look at leadership, all of these being important.

Wright

So how is leadership different from management?

Charney

Well, both of them are really important, but to some extent you need both. Management is about getting things done at the present and leadership is more about focusing on the future. So when you think about managers—those who get things done on a day to day basis—people rely on them, they take responsibility for daily performance, they measure performance, they direct and monitor processes closely, and they are judged by immediate indicators of performance, such as daily production. So they're much more narrow in their thinking and in their actions.

Leaders are somewhat different—they are focused more on the big picture, they think more about the future, they think strategically, and they are integrators, which is why they do things on a more strategic level. In many organizations, it's common to find leadership more important as one moves up the organization's ladder. Management is perhaps more important when you are in the lower echelons of the organization.

Leadership is not about today, it's more about tomorrow. The indicators that measure the success of a leader are more macro in nature. You would look at things like growth, innovation, learning, and other measures of future success to determine whether one is a successful leader. You would also look at the leader's ability to create other leaders as measured by, for example, the number of people who have been promoted internally.

Wright

One hears a lot about coaching and mentoring; are these concepts different from leadership?

Charney

No, they really are subsets of leadership, and they tie in nicely with the definition that I mentioned above that leaders develop other leaders, not followers.

So let's take coaching as the first example. Coaching is about showing employees that what they do *and* who they are, matters to you. If what they do matters to you, and you're a good coach, then you have high expectations of people, you set challenging goals with them, not for them. You also measure their performance, and follow up, providing them with a significant amount of encouragement and feedback. A nice metaphor for coaching is a sports coach because an effective coach is able to spend most of his or her time in the dugout or off the field, allowing the players the latitude to execute the plan. The coach can spend more time in the dugout if he or she has trained the team, set goals, monitored performance and has the confidence to allow the players to perform effectively without detailed guidance.

Good coaches not only direct the play, which is the content, but they also have a good appreciation of each player as a unique and able contributor. In other words, your approach has to be balanced. The goal is to get high performance from people and to establish quality relationships with each member of the team. At the end of the day, how you know you've been successful is that you have been able to achieve extra ordinary results that come from an empowered team that have the confidence to play the game (make decisions). They know that they will be recognized for their achievement *and* held accountable for failure.

And what about mentoring? Mentoring is more about the future of the individuals in the team and is an important aspect of leadership too. It's about building (investing in) the human resource. This is the duty of line managers, not the human resource department, to build the competence and confidence of people.

What good mentors do is to spend time developing people, helping them to grow. They do so using a variety of strategies, such as meeting on a regular basis, discussing the future with them, involving them in problem solving and strategies to overcome obstacles. Mentors also develop people through challenging assignments. These strategies are not easy. They require time and patience. It requires a leader to be generous, because you're giving people of your time. It requires great patience because the leader needs to spend time listening to those you mentor, helping them to reach their own conclusions. This is best done by asking powerful open-ended questions to help people arrive at and "own" their own solutions. That's how people learn best—by finding their own way and learning to think independently.

Wright

So would you tell our readers, what is your favorite theory of leadership?

Charney

Again, there is no one favorite theory, but I like to think of two theories that really work well and can be combined.

The first one has been around for many years. It's a situational leadership model. What it suggests is that your leadership needs to change depending on the competence and the maturity of your people, your team, or even your organization. So when the individual or the team is not competent or mature and they don't take responsibility, or are not ready for responsibility then your behavior is more of command and control. So, this leader will instruct and use rewards and punishments to get people to do what they want. They monitor closely, and give lots of feedback.

As people become more competent and mature and show improvement, then the leader would change their style to become more participative and empowering. (The vast majority of people want to become competent and mature, and they like to do the right thing.) This will motivate them because when you engage them in the process they feel very self-assured and they have a sense of pride in what they're doing. This enables you, in many ways, to get to the dugout.

The situational model is best conducted by leaders with high emotional intelligence—the second theory. Emotional intelligence is about interpersonal skills, it's about the humility, and it's about the ability to connect with people—to see the best in people. The situational model only works well when people have the ability to use their emotional intelligence. They know when to back off and when to show trust in people, and they know when to be passionate and optimistic about the future because that's when it is possible to delegate effectively.

Wright

So how would you evaluate one leader as more effective, say, than the next?

Charney

Well, at the end of the day, the reason we create organizations is to meet the needs of our stakeholders. The most important stakeholder is the client, customer, or patient. So at the end of the day, the leader who provides the greatest benefit to all stakeholders is the most effective one. But we need to have a balanced approach, of course. While we are there to serve our clients and customers, the other two stakeholders are also important—the shareholders or management, and the staff. If your staff are not happy and motivated, then of course your clients are not going to be satisfied—unhappy employees produce unhappy clients and customers.

Some of the measures that relate to good leadership also relate to the human component. The kinds of things that are measurable include the number of mentoring relationships, the number of promotions from their work area, staff turnover, grievances, absenteeism, and so on. Comparing these to other parts of the organization or other organizations can indicate that one leader is more effective than another.

These are some of the objective (numerical) ways of judging leadership effectiveness.

Wright

What are some of the major challenges facing leaders today and how should they be solved?

Charney

I think the greatest challenge we have today is our economy, which is in a tailspin. What is really difficult to manage is change. People are concerned, they're frightened, and not sure they will have a job. At the same time, when our revenues are dropping, we're having to trim fat wherever we can. Sometimes this will involve jobs. A good leader needs to face these challenges and understand why people are possibly resistant to change. They need to be empathetic when the reasons are justifiable and good, and to understand them. Most importantly, they need to know how to create an optimistic future and engage people wherever possible so people will buy into changes and challenges. But the need for optimism about the future is very important. Always focusing on the negative, of course, puts people into a mental tailspin making the situation worse.

Wright

There are so many successful people all of whom seem to be so different. Are there some attributes that they all have in common?

Charney

Well, there probably are many, but some that occur to me are people who are incredibly dedicated, and who have great passion for what they do. They're very driven and they have concern for all the stakeholders. Very importantly, they build trust. How do you build trust? To me, building trust is like investing at a bank—when you work with people, treat them well, value them and nurture them, each of these behaviors becomes a deposit of goodwill. The more money you put into the bank (the more you nurture trust), you can, at some other time, call on people to return the favors. But you can't put money into the bank and build that account of trust without being consistent. Good leaders, of course, are also very frank and not afraid to point out deficiencies. But they do so professionally always focusing on the issue rather than the person. They have confidence in their subordinates and expect the most of them. They also know when to make decisions themselves and when to involve their employees.

Mistakes occur regularly in all organizations. Good leaders allow people to learn from their mistakes and ensure that their (the employee's) self-esteem is maintained by focusing on solutions and issues, worrying less about finding someone to blame.

Finally, I think one of the great differences is that great leaders are visionaries—they are able to communicate their vision, they're passionate about their vision, and they engage and motivate other people to get onto the bandwagon with them.

Wright

What are some of the core competencies of successful leaders?

Charney

I'll make it simple by narrowing down to my favorite few. Some organizations have a dozen or more, making it difficult to remember them all let alone practice them all. More sophisticated organizations differentiate and define specific competencies for each level. The higher you go, the more strategic they are, and the lower you go, the more technically focused they are.

A competency I like is the ability to have high expectations of others, to trust others, and to instill hope in others. Another is to have the ability to model the behavior that you expect of others. It's walking the talk. Everyone knows that, like good parents, you can't say "do what I say, not what I do."

Good leaders have very well defined values that guide their behavior. These values are known to everyone, so leaders' behavior must be very consistent.

I also like the idea of authenticity—you're not trying to be something that you're not. You're down to earth and people understand you as someone who could be a neighbor, you're not trying to role-play something that you're not.

One of the most important things that I have come to appreciate over the years is humility. I think that many of the great leaders are humble in that they are more willing to listen to others and willing to attribute success to those around them. I love the metaphor of sitting on a bench; where should one sit? Some people like to sit in the middle; they want to be the center of attention. But humble people are happy to sit on the side and create space for other people. They don't dominate discussions, they don't dominate meetings, and they're happy to listen to other points of view.

Perhaps one of the last competencies is the ability to establish close relationships with people. It's hard to be a leader if you don't really like people and if you can't ingratiate yourself with them. Good leaders have an ability to connect at a psychological level with people and so attract followers like a bee to honey.

Wright

Are there some core competencies that are more important during these turbulent times?

Charney

Without question, there are. Again, when we think about difficult times, we need to think not about the past, but about the future. So effective leaders today are those who have a clear vision about the future. They're optimistic, happy, and enthusiastic about what can be done. So they engage people whenever possible in problem solving and decisions. And they don't shy away from problems but look at them as challenges, often thinking out of the box. They don't have their heads down but they have their eyes forward. It's like driving a car—you're not looking through the rear view mirror, but you're looking down the road, trying to anticipate road blocks, and, most importantly, trying to remove those roadblocks. Good leaders can multitask, they don't get too stressed about the challenges of today, and they're always optimistic and happy about the future.

Wright

So you talked about the next generation. How would you go about hiring the next generation of leaders?

Charney

Well, there's an old saying, the way that you do that is the way porcupines make love—very carefully! So when you hire people, mistakes can be very costly. You want to hire people who have great attitudes. You can always give people skills and technical ability, but great attitudes are hard to train. In fact, I don't think you can train people to have great attitudes. You should be very careful how you bring new people into an organization. Put potential future leaders—your high potentials—through a variety of tests to ensure that you select the best. I call this a hurdles approach. You want firstly to have a look at their resumes, then to interview the most appealing and qualified candidates very carefully, using behavioral interviewing techniques. This is done by providing the interviewee with various scenarios that they are likely to face and ask them how they might have coped with these in the past. Also, have a number of other people in your organization assess the "fit" of the individual into your corporate culture. You should also check references carefully, and where possible get evidence that supports the responses given by the potential new-hire. You would also want to test them on a variety of psychological instruments to see if they fit the mold and are likely to demonstrate the behavioral competencies that you are looking for. You may also want to observe their behavior in an Assessment Center where you could observe their behavior and interactions with others in a variety of challenging situations.

By taking the time and trouble to evaluate candidates properly, your chances of choosing the wrong person are very much reduced. When people actually get the job after a thorough process, I think they appreciate being selected and are more likely to stay with an organization.

Wright

If there was only one secret to successful leadership, what do you think it would be?

Charney

Well, I'm going to surprise you; it's a word that I have started using more and more as I teach leadership. It's the word "intimacy." I think that creating psychologically intimate relationships with people is really important. Employees don't want to feel that they are a number. In fact, I've come across so many organizations that refer to their people as FTEs (Full Time Equivalents) or even Billing Units!

These name and labels are very demeaning. Employees want to feel important and they need to feel that both their boss and the organization values and cares for them. Intimacy is also demonstrated by empathic listening when an employee has a concern. The more intimacy between boss and associate the more trusting the relationship and the more likely it will become a partnership characterized by warmth, trust and mutual support.

The idea that *management by walking around* demonstrated caring, doesn't wash. You actually have to stop, talk and listen when you're walking around. A leader needs to take the time to learn about each person—who he or she is, their background, interests, dreams and concerns. An effective leader works hard to maintain *meaningful* relationships with people. That gives one a significantly enhanced ability to influence people which is why I see intimacy as the real secret to success of a leader.

Wright

Why are some leaders able to motivate employees so much more effectively than others? Do they do anything differently?

Charney

I think they do, and again, I think they operate from a very clear understanding about their values—values that they practice daily. They're not operating from one set of values one day and another set the next. Being clear about their values they document them, communicate them, post them for everyone to see and hold people accountable for practicing them. So again we go back to the issue of trust—when you behave appropriately and walk the talk, you develop trust, and a deep connection with fellow employees. Over time, when you behave consistently, with integrity, empathy and with honesty, you are able to motivate and influence all stakeholders. Why? Because people trust you and they know what to expect.

The consequence of values-driven behavior is trust which enables leaders to delegate, empower, and develop the next generation of leadership. Leaders do this not just by verbally delegating and then hovering around like a helicopter, but by allowing people to muddle through on their own.

Delegating and allowing people to muddle through on their own allows employees the opportunity to learn from their experience. And, in the event, of a mistake (hopefully small) these experiences are best treated as learning opportunities.

Wright

Well, what a great conversation. This is very interesting, especially the theories of situational leadership, and participative, empowering leadership—that is great insight. I've learned a lot here today Cy, and I really do appreciate all the time you've taken with me to let me ask all these questions; and I certainly appreciate the answers.

Charney

You're welcome, David.

Wright

Today we've been talking with Cy Charney, President of Charney and Associates Inc. He has developed a variety of unique interventions to help organizations in both the private and public sectors become leaders in their fields. Based on my conversation with him today, I have a tendency to listen and I've learned a lot. I think you as a reader will also.

Cy, thank you so much for being with us today on *Yes You Can!*

Charney

You're very welcome. Thank you, David.

CY CHARNEY is President of Charney and Associates Inc. and the founder of The Leadership Institute (www.theleadershipinstitute.ca). He is a leading consultant in the area of organizational performance especially as it relates to leveraging human resources. His clients include a number of Fortune 500 companies and governments around the world.

Cy is a frequent keynote speaker and a seasoned trainer. He teaches Leadership and related topics at a number of Business Schools across North America.

Cy is the author of seven management books. He has a BA in Psychology, a master's in Business Leadership, and has a Professional Administrator designation.

Cy Charney

CHARNEY & ASSOCIATES INC.
46 Aleis Road
Thornhill, ON
L3T 6Z9
Canada
905-886-5605
cy@askcharney.com
www.askcharney.com
www.theleadershipinstitute.com

CHAPTER SEVEN

Courage and Leadership

by Bill Mayo

David Wright (Wright)

Today, we're speaking with Bill Mayo, co-founder of Fullsail Leadership. Bill is a graduate of the United States Naval Academy and served as Executive Officer aboard ship. He was also a Battalion Commander of a Naval Recruit training center before joining a global Fortune 50 corporation in 1979. He rose through its ranks to be elected officer of the company in 2005. He "reallocated" in 2008 and currently teaches leadership at Eureka College (alma mater of Ronald W. Reagan). Bill is also an author, public speaker, consultant, and corporate board member.

Today, we're discussing his perspectives about the importance of courage to leadership.

Bill, first of all, you say you've "reallocated" from corporate life, not "retired." That's a curious word. Why "reallocated"?

Bill Mayo (Mayo)

Ah, that's a fun question to answer. If you look up the definition of "retire," it actually means to "shrink away, retreat, or quit." I had no intention of doing that at all! The definition of "reallocate" is to "set aside for a special purpose." And in this phase of my life, I wanted to "give back"—something Bill George terms "Phase 3" in his book *True North*.

I'll admit, it took courage to leave the job—the pay and the perks—but you'd be amazed at how many of my peers and those I've worked with throughout the organization confess they envy me. I didn't do it to be envied, I did it to be true to myself and what I envisioned my true purpose to be. If that's courageous, that's certainly not a charge I shrink from.

Wright

I can see why you speak of courage, then. Tell me, do you find businesses today have the right environment and developmental approach with employees to create courageous leaders?

Mayo

This is a complex question to answer without generalizations. Each business is different, of course. But, I generally do believe there is an overemphasis on "management" and underdevelopment of "leadership" in the typical business culture. I've always liked what Ralph Nader once said, "I start with the premise that the function of leadership is to create more leaders—not more followers." Management seeks followers. I can't tell you how many businessmen and businesswomen have lamented in confidence that their firm was "over-managed and under-led."

Perhaps one of the main reasons for that perception is rooted simply in the distinction between what managers do and what leaders do. Management is about doing things right—reigning things in, while leadership is more about doing right things and "letting go." "Management" is defined in Webster's as "the process of dealing with and *controlling* people or things." A leader is defined simply as "someone people follow."

Leadership can be scary stuff, precisely because it is not about control. Leadership is about *inspiration*—inspiring people in such a way that they willingly follow you. When you're "in control" you feel more powerful—safer—more in charge of your own destiny, if you will. When you're leading, and you surrender control to a degree via the faith you're placing in others, well, it can bring a fairly vulnerable feeling along with it.

I look at it this way: A business essentially wants to control risk and assure outcomes. It attempts to control its products, its markets, its distribution, its manufacturing processes, and clearly those who achieve success, as "managers" are those who have demonstrated a consistent track record of controlling those outcomes while mitigating risks.

One merely needs to look to the "chain of command"—those higher up in the organization. They are typically people who have risen through the ranks by minimizing the adverse affects of all those pesky risks associated with running a business.

Having said that, I don't mean to trivialize its importance. Management is a critical element of business to be sure—you cannot run a successful business without an appropriate level of controls. So in many ways, while following a management approach is "safe," my point simply is that it will not yield the most dramatic results. Leadership does that.

But leadership feels much more risky—fundamentally, leadership is not about control. As a leader, you are certain about your vision—what *needs to happen*—but less sure about the "how to's" that assure the outcome.

And yet, true leaders exist. They set the vision for their team, set an example of trust and integrity, and establish a sense of community among team members. They actually rely much more on faith that people will rise to great levels of achievement simply by being empowered to do the right thing in support of the desired state— not controlling them, but inspiring them.

A leader relies upon others to perform in the face of stress, pressure, or risks. This creates a very genuine sense of fear and vulnerability for the leader. Who would want to "lead" when there is such a genuine ambiguity associated with the assurance of outcome? It's much easier to manage assets.

But I've always said people are *not* assets. An asset is a machine tool. And what do you do with assets? You depreciate them, consume them, and write them off. I certainly would *not* want to work in a culture that boasted, "People are our most important assets." Yet many companies boast just that.

Paradoxically, management control somewhat implies an approach that views people as "instruments to do work." In my mind, this actually stifles true empowerment and creativity. Managers can be rigid, often seeking conformance and compliance with processes to achieve the desired end, whereas leadership is nimble, seeking empowerment and liberty to achieve the desired end. Management overemphasizes "coloring within the lines," but breakthroughs come at the boundaries. And perhaps even more importantly, excessive human control creates emotional disengagement among employees.

People want to feel that their role actually supports a greater vision. They want to be a part of something more noble and bigger than themselves. They don't want to merely comply. They want to matter.

And for an authentic leader, people will put self beneath team. They will be less concerned about their limited authority and tightly defined roles, and will be more concerned about overall team performance.

And importantly, the business vision, that "noble purpose" is what reigns supreme, not the position of the manager. In short, everyone leads. People give their heart—their discretionary and emotional commitment—beyond their obligatory compliance. And everyone is committed to the noble purpose inspired by the leader.

In my mind, this is much more powerful and dare I say, *more fun!* It will also yield much greater results.

But I will admit, for the leader, it doesn't always "feel very safe"—it feels "out there." And therefore, in my view, businesses typically don't create this type of environment—and few managers are willing to work on the ragged edge or perimeter of the prevailing culture.

So yes, I generally believe businesses groom more managers than leaders. By being overwhelmingly concerned with controls, they are naturally less concerned with liberating its leaders *or* its employees. Paradoxically, businesses reap what they sow— and management breeds managers. When businesses sow management control as the pervasive philosophy, they will reap a compliant and conforming culture among its employees. While performance of the business might be good, as Jim Collins urged us all, we should strive to stretch beyond "good" to "great."

Wright

It seems as though you are attributing great significance to a people-oriented culture in order for leadership to flourish. How do you address peers or superiors who do not buy in to the people or "soft side" of business and rely more upon a "command and control" approach to accomplish results?

Mayo

Well yes—I do believe that a people-oriented culture must exist for leadership and leaders to thrive, because again, people are not assets—they're flesh and blood and emotional human beings. I'm convinced you can get human performance through management, but just not their *best* performance. Just as I'm convinced you can't "lead" a drill press, you can only manage it.

You can "lead" an emotional human being because you can inspire. You can touch people's hearts. You can connect them to a more noble vision. And this will unleash their true discretionary commitment and unlock their greatest potential. *That's* where true breakthroughs come from.

Tom Peters once said, "All progress is made by people who get pissed off." While I understand he was speaking not of anger but of discontent with the status quo, I don't think discontent is the "secret sauce." I believe true progress comes through inspiration. And that's where a leader plays his or her most important and game-changing role.

I acknowledge that both management and leadership are required. It's not as if I advocate the absence of processes or the absence of measurements. But I think businesses today have runaway metrics and I think they choke people in a fog of irrelevant data. After all, business isn't brain surgery. It's about producing value in a product and providing a service at a competitive price and running an efficient operation to reward yourself with profit for the effort. So the measures needn't be too complicated. Market share—customer loyalty—profitable growth – these are the most meaningful metrics in my view.

I've worked with many a manager who was overly enamored with metrics. And how did I handle it? Frankly, not always very well because it goes against the grain of what I know to be important. But in each case, I've tried to model my authentic behaviors, speak my authentic values, coach in an authentic way, and discuss any feelings of disagreement openly.

When I've reported to these types of managers, I would always respectfully express my viewpoint about what metrics were essential and which ones were merely clutter. I talked about the distinction between doing things right and doing right things. But frankly, if the manager was not dissuaded from his or her approach, I did the best I could to produce results through leading my team authentically and let the results speak for themselves. I did not rely upon all the red/yellow/green metrics charts. And importantly, I provided a buffer for my team when the management criticism was overly focused on colored metric charts.

I led my team by setting a vision, setting an example, and creating a sense of community. And I did not chase metrics. If necessary, I would be open with my team about any disconnect with management, without sounding disloyal.

I have always admonished myself and others to "find something to emulate about every manager you work for—and something to forgive." "Forgive" is the operative word because we're all flawed human beings. I am certain that, despite my best intentions, I will disappoint someone sometime. I'm just as convinced that there is good in everyone, and disagreements did not have to mean disloyalty.

Wright

What about young managers today who "see the light" of the distinction you describe and now want to make the turn and become leaders. How do they get started?

Mayo

I think it must begin with self-awareness—not just of this distinction between leading and managing, but about the person you are at your core. It's been called having a loving tolerance of who you are, and a loving tolerance of who you are not. This is critical for a leader because this awareness can help set the right people in place on the leadership team.

It ultimately comes down to personal beliefs, convictions, principles, and what I call "leadership credos." Essentially, if you have a set of firm personal credos that are in harmony with who you are at your core, you will be in intimate connection with your purpose and will have an excellent moral compass with which to lead others.

Wright

You use the word "credos"—will you give us an example?

Mayo

Gladly. A credo of mine that always causes eyebrows to arch in doubt when people first hear it is "To strive to treat people like dogs." Sounds dreadful, I know. But hear me out.

Have you ever had a pet dog? What do you do with your dog? Let's call him "Spot." First of all, you play with Spot while training him. The importance of "play" and genuine human connection cannot be overemphasized. People relate to people—not processes or controls. Then, of course, you provide Spot with clear expectations. You are not ambiguous and you don't leave it to him to figure out your expectations as he goes along. And, you're clear about boundaries. "Don't make your mess on the floor. Don't chew on the furniture. Don't jump on the bed."

Let's say you come home from work at the end of the day, and Spot has behaved beautifully. What would you do? You would lavish praise—sincere praise and delight— upon him, of course. "Good dog! I knew you could do it!" But what if he disappointed you? You would again provide immediate and clear constructive feedback for improvement. You wouldn't save it for his annual performance review. You wouldn't even "keep score" or derail his doggie career or talk about his poor performance behind his back. You'd give him immediate and constructive feedback for improvement.

And importantly, when you're providing that guidance, when Spot looks up at you with those big, brown, sad eyes, what would you do? You'd likely say, "Ah, c'mon over here." And you'd love him up unconditionally.

You see, we actually treat dogs better than people. So this credo reminds me to give clear expectations, immediate and constructive feedback for improvement, and unconditional love and acceptance. And I say "love" deliberately, which perhaps sounds like a strange word in a business context, but I think it applies.

I hear a lot about being a professional manager—but I'd rather be an amateur leader. The word "amateur" comes from the Latin word *amator* meaning to love. And unless you love your people unconditionally, you'll never hear the truth again.

Wright

Some might sense you're speaking of leadership as a very "touchy-feely" concept. How do you lead with heart and touch people's hearts, while also displaying strong discipline with clear expectations—accountability, which sometimes includes harsh messages or consequences?

Mayo

Great question. And it's important to note that a leader's empowerment and faith in others does not alleviate the leader or the employee from the consequences of accountability. Just as parenting and loving your children does not remove them from consequences and accountability for the choices they make.

One of my credos is the freedom to fail and the freedom to take risks. But the vision must also be to achieve a "better place" and if failure or a stumble along the way occurs, we are all accountable to learn from it. As for "punishment," I guess it's akin to that "tough love" concept we hear about as parents. I have never hesitated to provide direct and immediate, constructive (and yes, sometimes harsh) feedback. But it is always followed up by that unconditional love and acceptance. One exception is that if the mistake was done unethically, intentionally, or it recklessly endangers others. Then, quite frankly, it may be necessary to make some seat assignment changes on the bus. If the vision were threatened by habitual poor performance of a team member, I would not hesitate to make a move. But it would be done with sensitivity to the employee's dignity—and with a deep sense of accountability for what's right for the individual and the team.

Wright

Some might say there's a fine line between courage and stupidity. Does a courageous leader mean a reckless leader—risk-taker?

Mayo

Yes, there is sometimes a fine line between the two. But back to credos—if your values, beliefs, and principles are solid, noble, and ethical, you'll have the right moral compass to steer your ship.

Risk? Of course—all business managers and leaders play a game of risks. An old quotation from John Paul Jones, venerable father of the Navy says, "It seems to be a law of nature, inflexible and inexorable, that those who will not risk cannot win."

But if there's a line between courage and stupidity, then what lurks in the blurry shadow of that line is daring. And daring need not be reckless.

For example, it's pretty daring to be vulnerable—especially in a hyper-competitive and cutthroat business culture. But it's more stupid to be inauthentic. It takes a much greater toll on the spirit and assaults the soul to pretend to be something you are not. And eventually, you will be unmasked.

I might also add that all choices involve uncertainty. I believe that many managers fall prey to the delusion of certainty and an over-reliance upon process.

I think it was Gary Hamel of the London School of business who said, "Conformance to process is the commodity of the twenty-first century—true differentiation comes only from the passion and innovation of your people."

And I'm reminded of Richard Buetow, considered the father of the ISO 9000 process certification movement at Motorola. He said, "You can certify a company that makes life jackets out of concrete as long as they follow prescribed process and have a procedure to notify next of kin." Again, process compliance assures nothing if the processes are wrong. I've been personally more disappointed by faith in process than I've been disappointed by having faith in a good employee. And I believe most of the time customers are delighted it's because an empowered employee stepped beyond process.

It is never right to be reckless in a way that endangers others—but it is equally dangerous for a business to be so bound by rigid process that creativity and innovation suffers. Teddy Roosevelt once said, "In any moment of decision, the best thing you can do is the right thing; the next best thing is the wrong thing, and the worst thing you can do is nothing."

Sometimes, that's a lonely place to be—like being an "imaginal cell" in a chrysalis.

Wright

Just what is an "imaginal cell," Bill?

Mayo

Actually, Norie Huddle writes beautifully of this transformative process in her book, *Butterfly*. She explains how imaginal cells in a cocooning caterpillar hold the vision of the future butterfly. Despite the fact that these cells are first perceived as foreign invaders and are destroyed by the creature's own immune system, the imaginal cells continue to multiply and connect with a strength and force that ultimately and miraculously transforms the caterpillar into a beautiful future state.

Some businesses are in desperate need of transformative change. And they need leaders who have the DNA and the courage to be imaginal cells. "Courage" is the operative word, because it is sadly true that you may be attacked—attacked by those resistant to change and attacked by those who are comfortable in the cocoon of the status quo. But as author Anais Nin said, "And the day came when the risk to remain tight in a bud was more painful than the risk it took to blossom."

Wright

Well, Bill, if you had one rule to develop your courage as a leader, what would it be? And how do you remain true to yourself when operating in an organizational culture that might tend to suppress that authentic and courageous leadership voice?

Mayo

Paris-born author and physician, Somerset Maugham, said, "There are three rules for creating good leaders. Unfortunately, no one knows what they are!" And the thirteenth Governor General of Australia, Sir William Slim, said, "The best training for leadership is leadership." So the best way to develop your voice as a courageous leader is to practice expressing that courageous voice.

Being authentic cannot be taught as much as it can be encouraged and modeled. Finding a mentor/leader within your organization is very helpful. One essential first step, though, is to know who you are. Know what you believe. Articulate and write down your personal credos. The old adage "if you don't stand for something, you may fall for anything" applies. And my advice is to hold yourself accountable to your team by vulnerably expressing what those credos are. Enlist them to help you and to help hold you accountable.

And recognize that many times, our best intentions are aspirational, and we may fail or fall short of living by what we profess to believe. That's okay—it's a journey. It takes practice. And it takes humility to expose yourself in that way to people you're supposedly leading. But the paradox is this: The more vulnerable you're willing to be—the more powerful the influence from your authenticity. People smell phony from a mile away, but there is true power in being human, admitting it, and seeking the help and commitment of your team to be all that you can be.

As for being authentic in a culture that might not encourage it, that's a touchy one, to be honest. But here's my guidance. While it takes genuine courage to be authentic in a corporate environment, the alternative brings even more stress, anxiety, and tension. Give yourself a gift and be authentically who you are—at work and at home. I've counseled young professionals, who are projected to change careers as many as seven times during their working lives, that if they can't be who they really are—if they can't put their unique thumbprints on the organization being authentically themselves— perhaps that organization is not the right place to be after all, which is ironically another potentially courageous realization.

A leader must create an environment where it's safe for employees to lead. Freedom to make mistakes and the courage to try different approaches is important because that's how human beings learn and grow. "Group think" means someone isn't thinking. In today's increasingly competitive global market place, companies *need* people to risk, to be courageous, to think differently.

Consider the lowly honeybee. I've read that they fly to and from a source of pollen and nectar in a straight line. They fly in a triangular formation, but in a straight line. That's where we get the phrase "bee line." Apparently, bees can transmit a sound or frequency to other bees that communicates direction and distance to the source. It's called their "waggle dance." And most all the bees can interpret the dance and join in the formation and "bee line" straight to and from the source of pollen and nectar.

Supposedly, some 18 percent of bees are genetic mutants. And these poor chaps apparently can't follow directions; as a result, they wander off into other paths—other directions. But guess what? Doing so actually ensures the survival of the beehive or bee colony. Without their going off in other directions, the other bees would simply fly to and fro in a straight line until they exhausted the source of pollen and nectar necessary for the production of honey for the colony.

In other words, thank God for the mutants! We, as leaders, have to allow space to take these other directions. To take risks. To "learn" other ways of doing things. If not, we risk extinction.

Wright

Are you just talking then about courage in big things—in the big decisions? Or can you display courage in little things?

Mayo

I'm really talking authenticity, which takes courage. So yes, I'm advocating courage in everything—every choice made authentically, not politically made or made in submission to conformance or compliance pressures. Choices have to be evaluated alongside your personal credos. If you stand against prevailing "group-think," basing your choice on your personal compass, this is in fact, courageous.

There's always a bit of personally imposed tension in a group setting, though. There's that inner voice saying we need to fit in—win approval. Essentially, each of us is three different people in continual conflict—who we think we are, who we want others to think we are, and who we really are.

These can only be integrated through intense personal reflection, peeling back the onion to find our personal credos and principles. It then takes courage to expose these beliefs, risking vulnerability with others—risking rejection, disapproval, and judgment. But the rewards can be astounding.

So yes, courage in big things, little things, and all things because the call to action is really simply this: be authentically who you are in every circumstance. In John Eldredge's book *Wild at Heart*, he sums it up beautifully. "Let the world feel the full weight of your presence . . . and let them deal with it."

Wright

There's always been the debate that leaders are born and not made. It strikes me that this debate could extend to the attribute of courage, as well. Is it possible to "teach" people to be courageous or does one have to be "born with it"?

Mayo

I think people learn by observation, so yes, this is a call to action for all leaders to not only personally model courage and authenticity, but to consciously create a safe environment for others to thrive and prosper with the same behavior. In effect, teaching the value of diversity and the power of authenticity.

I suppose I must acknowledge that some are more naturally comfortable with this than others. But I do not think courage and authenticity are reserved for a unique subset of the world's or an organization's population. In short, I think it can be learned. More importantly, I believe it must be learned to unleash an organization's untapped human potential.

Wright

How do organizations build a culture where courage is accepted and embraced?

Mayo

Organizations are simply people. They are lifeless without people. So essentially, organizations don't create culture, people do. As Max Weber suggests, humans are suspended in webs of significance that they themselves have spun.

This is the fundamental call to action for any leader. This is your "Yes You Can" moment. If you know what you stand for, are willing to be vulnerable, to be authentically who you are, and if you model that behavior for others, you'll recruit other "imaginal cells" and you'll spin a greater web of significance within the organization.

In the long run, this is the transformative power of personal authenticity. And it is truly the "secret sauce" in the recipe for achieving outstanding results for your business, your family, yourself, and ultimately, for the greater good of the world.

BILL MAYO is co-founder of Fullsail Leadership, a personal development company with a mission to touch people's hearts, provoke their minds, and liberate their voices as authentic leaders. His passion to serve is rooted in a track record of achievement in unleashing potential by inspiring people to leave their unique thumbprints on their organizations, families, and the world.

A U.S. Naval Academy graduate, Bill's career spans more than thirty-five years as a Naval Officer and Fortune 50 executive. He is hailed as a courageous thought leader and inspirational voice on leadership. Today, Bill advises numerous businesses as a consultant, event speaker, and corporate board member. He is an author and educator in the Organizational Leadership program of Eureka College.

Bill Mayo

FULLSAIL LEADERSHIP
www.fullsail-leadership.com
Bill@fullsail-leadership.com
309-397-3913

CHAPTER EIGHT
Achieving A Healthy You

by Jessica German

David Wright (Wright)

Today we are talking with Dr. Jessica German. Jessica is a chiropractor, holistic nutritional therapist, author, and lecturer. She is currently in private practice in Colorado Springs, Colorado. As a health and wellness coach, she emphasizes that making small yet critical changes can easily make transformation possible, no matter who you are. She believes that your health potential is *unlimited*, and what is needed is having a reality check before reality checks you. In addition to helping individuals and families in her practice, this dynamic mother of three uses her passion and enthusiasm for health and wellness to educate the public and corporate audiences.

Jessica, welcome to *Yes You Can!*

Why aren't we more healthy and fit?

Jessica German (German)

Start by looking at what we allow to influence us. Television, advertisements, music, magazines, radio, video games, movies, Internet—we are bombarded with misleading images and misinformation that happiness, health, and fitness come in a certain way for a limited number of people. Health and fitness is made to look as if it is found in a bottle, prescription, or surgical procedure. Unfortunately, we value entertainment in this

103

country over health and fitness, and this conveys a message that we are our physical bodies, which is far from the truth.

Let us look at the effects of technology. Cell phones and computers are intended to make our lives more efficient. The skills we must continue to develop for communication and relationships are being replaced by these devices. With the advancements in technology, convenience and efficiency is definitely a benefit, but the expectations are demanding and unrealistic at times, affecting relationships. People value sitting in front of a computer or screen over a genuine one-to-one conversation or relationship. Relationships are what you need in life to grow and expand.

So the first two points regarding the influence of the media and being in front of the screen illustrates both inactivity and misleading information of what claims to be healthy. Don't get me wrong, we are eating as a nation, just not the right foods. We are overfed, yet nutritionally deficient, overweight, and unfit. The majority prioritize everything else over learning how to eat right and exercise.

Another reason is that we think too much—we spend way too much time are in our heads and our thoughts instead of our hearts. Fear, doubt, inadequacies, and excuses, which are found in our thoughts, are easy to live in, therefore, we can justify like no other. Most people think their whole life and don't make progress. Our mindsets either prevent us from achieving the health and fitness we desire, or assist us in achieving the health and fitness we deserve.

Wright

Health and fitness is a big topic, as well as transition. How do they relate?

German

You are right. Health and fitness should be a big part of everyone's life. Transition means a process of change. For many, this seems scary. In my profession, I see many different perspectives on health and fitness. I work with clients who *want something different* with their health or fitness levels, as in more energy, better sleep, weight loss, stress reduction, mental clarity, focus, and a body that is more fit and adaptable. They want to become more in tune with their body and receive information about real health other than what they receive in the media or with their brush with Western medicine.

Their willingness to do something different predetermines their results. Exercising and eating right is not the hard part, *making the decision* to do this is the difficult part for most people. So wanting better health and fitness combined with the willingness to do the work is the transition connection. One must transition his or her thinking and learn how to be healthy and fit despite the media and other influences we just discussed. I believe the key here is realizing that there is nothing out there to get, to have, or to do that will fulfill you or make you happy—what you desire already exists within. It is necessary to make the decision to *feel* how you want to be, and your actions will align with your true intentions. They already are, so why not create it and live the way you keep wanting to.

Wright

I agree. What must we understand so we can make this decision?

German

You must step back and observe how you have been going after what you want. In regard to health and fitness, there is not one person on this planet exempt from eating right and exercising. I truly believe that when you take a vast interest in your own health and fitness, you learn so much more about yourself and what you are capable of, and this is the ideal investment. You either want to be healthy and fit or you don't.

When I give recommendations, people are either excited to have a deeper understanding of what they can do regarding their health and wellness, or it brings out resistance and skepticism. Resistance occurs because when we are faced with something "new," we are simply challenging our own beliefs of what we know, understand, and are familiar with, even though deep down something better and different is what we are seeking. We become resistant when we do not know what we are capable of doing; it is the initial uncertainty that brings up beliefs. The *idea* of changing something in our comfortable lifestyle habits can keep us close-minded and experiencing the same results. Again, it is not the action itself that blocks transition, it is the *idea* of doing something different that scares us. The goal is to decide to be a part of your health and fitness to further recognize that inner direction that says, "Yes I can."

Buried deep within awaits your personal acknowledgement that what really matters is how you want to feel rather than what you think you want. I have found that choosing a process that values how you want to feel propels you to make better decisions.

Wright

So you are saying that transitioning into a better health and fitness level is initially more mindset than action?

105

German

Absolutely. You always have a choice to improve. Improvement is growth, and settling for what is comfortable is the opposite of growth.

For example, let's say you "hope" to paint the living room someday, get that new haircut, or landscape your yard. You can see these areas every day and keep telling yourself that someday you will get to it. When you arrived at the day that you actually completed your task, what had to happen first? You had to make a decision that it was time, the right thing to do, and once you "made up your mind," *then* the action came easy, right?

Each of us does this day in and day out, unaware. When it comes to improving your health and fitness levels, you see yourself in the mirror every day, and you say, "Someday I hope to have more energy, get to my ideal weight, tone my body, and increase strength and flexibility." But to reach this, you must first *decide* that it is important enough for you, that you value your health enough, that you want a healthier and fitter future, and then you approach this as permanently shifting your lifestyle for the better.

It is like playing the Boggle game for the very first time. As you shake and settle all of the letters into place, it appears to be impossible, but once you make up your mind to focus, have the intention to play and learn, what happens? You come up with many possibilities that you did not think were there, and you learn it as a new and fun game. It is a similar approach with learning how to take care of your health; it may seem impossible, but each time you shake and settle the letters—each time you take a step forward—it becomes a meaningful and fulfilling process of continually tapping into your own capabilities and unlimited possibilities. Results will say it all. You always have a choice. You can either set the game aside and stick with your current results, or you can be the game and play as your real self, experience a higher quality of life, more joy, more endurance, and more opportunities of growth and freedom. You always have the choice to say "Yes I can," and "Yes I will."

As a holistic practitioner, I find that people who really value their health understand they are not their physical body. Therefore, I find those who believe they are their physical body, accomplishments, or other material possessions, do not truly value their health and fitness.

With my experience, I can help connect the dots with each client, meaning I know everything in your life affects your health. The idea of changing eating and exercise habits is also about transition—transitioning into a healthier body or into a more fit body requires what? Change. The desire to be on a different level of health or fitness requires more than just wanting or hoping or wishing that it will happen. The whole idea of wanting to improve and reach a better level in itself is change in motion, and this ultimately stems from how people feel about their body. How many people do you know who say they want to lose weight, be fit, and be healthy? You can fill up your fingers and toes counting these people, and I can guarantee that most of them have been saying this since you have known them, and they always will, unless what occurs?

Wright

Change.

German

Yes, or better decisions.

Wright

Will you address how someone can make a decision to want to change?

German

"Life is change. Growth is optional. Choose wisely"—Karen Kaiser Clark. With this type of change comes conscious responsibility, and this can limit people. If more would understand that what the word "responsibility" really means, besides commitment, is that growth and desired results are produced, the word "responsibility" would be much more attractive.

The opposite of responsible is blame, usually found embedded in excuses, and it is easy to delay what must occur. To become responsible brings out our leadership qualities. We all have common fears of "what if" that can hold us back. Change is obviously occurring at all times—faster and faster actually—and to truly change your health or your fitness level, you simply have to make a decision. Remember that a decision to do something different is always available.

You and only you create your results. If you want the same results you have had all along—the ones that frustrate you and always leave you wishing and wanting—then don't expect different results if you are not willing to *do* something different. If you truly want a healthier body, you have to make a decision to change so that this transition can occur. Changing how you feel about your body is a powerful way to begin.

When people say they fear change when it comes to their health, what they are really saying is that their energy is focused on "I don't want to do something different. I like comfort. Don't make me change anything," although that is what they really want, more importantly it is what they really *need!* I hear all kinds of stories and excuses. I had my own, believe me. I have also realized that the process of change is actually about becoming more of who we really are. Change is not found by following steps alone. As you embrace an unconditional self-acceptance, this locks in a newly connected commitment for how you choose to live and new habits, reactions, thoughts, behaviors, and routines simply fall into place.

A common excuse is, "I don't have something," whether it is money, resources, or time. Many times I hear indirectly, sometimes directly, that "someone" close to them is to blame. If someone is truly telling you that you can't do something to better yourself, this really needs to be handled. Detaching yourself from that negative person may be necessary, but it may simply be your own disempowering beliefs of feeling unworthy that give you that misperception, which is another excuse. I have been there, done that. It is like when you get a speeding ticket or show up late to an appointment—it is your responsibility, no one else is to blame. Our own heads get in our own way very easily. I absolutely believe that as we experience our own life's journey by accepting what is, better decisions follow, resulting in a healthier life.

Wright

I can see how we can easily limit our own progress. How do you suggest we transition our thinking as you stated earlier?

German

Looking at your beliefs around health and fitness in a new way will give you a deeper understanding of why you think the way you do. My initial beliefs about being fit and healthy were what I saw on television, in movies, or magazines. Living in a highly visual society, I was caught up in the shallow misconception that looking a specific way meant healthy and fit.

This message is ingrained in people of all ages. The additional pressure on children and teens into adulthood to "look good" affects performance in every area, schools, relationships, work, business, sports, and finances.

Another trap I lived in was I compared my results with unrealistic expectations. I minimized my successes, suppressed my dreams, and maximized my faults. I had the universal underlying beliefs that I wasn't good enough or deserving enough to be fit, healthy, and have abundance.

A *huge* tipping-point for me was when it sunk in that the *results* in every area of my life stem from my inner thoughts and consistent underlying feelings. My health and fitness levels, finances, relationships, spiritual growth, and *everything in my life reflects my beliefs based upon how I feel*. When I realized this, it was humbling and intensely liberating at the same time. I was even coaching clients to eat healthy and exercise to *feel* healthy and fit, not to spend energy by worrying about how they looked, but I wasn't even in alignment myself! So when I deeply realized that only *I* control my thoughts, feelings, meanings, and reactions, my life has continually been shifting for the better—in all areas.

Feeling and *knowing* that you are capable of creating profound health results in your life can override your thoughts of inadequacy. This is so much easier. It takes the pain and work out of trying to be perfect and releases you from procrastination, which limits you to the same cycle of pain and living small. By making the decision to become healthy and fit, you will experience true energy, enjoy yourself, and really see the results you desire because you are free to dream and create your life here on this earth.

Wright

How does one begin?

German

The first step to achieving the results you want with your health and fitness, whether it is weight loss, more energy and endurance, or increased strength, is to define it in terms of how you feel right now. Take a few minutes and write down these areas on a piece of paper or in your journal: Health, Energy, Physical Endurance, Physical Strength, Eating Habits, Hydration, Stress Handling, Sleep.

The bottom line is this: If you want to *be* healthy, you must *think* healthy. If you want to quit smoking, you must think like a non-smoker. If you want to lose weight, you must think fit. If you want to be out of debt, think financially independent. You must recognize that when you *think anything*, you have personally defined it on your terms, formed from the dominant feelings that drive you.

Let us go further. What is your definition of health? What do you think your health should look like? This is important for you to define because on a level you don't necessarily recognize, you have set standards for yourself regarding your health.

Go back to the list you just created. I want you to define each area as 1) where you are currently in each area, and 2) how you think each should be. Start with your current definition of healthy and fit. What is healthy? What is being fit to you? Then define the other categories as well. If you want to see change in your overall health and fitness, you must invest the time to do this.

Wright

I can see how this would bring up real beliefs.

German

Yes, because it is about examining where you are right now—the starting point of a new awareness. What typically shows up with this exercise is either resistance to do this or "Wow, I get it," and it becomes fun. This is awareness. This is the ah-ha that helps you kick habits to the curb that are not serving you or getting you closer to the health and fitness that you really desire and deserve. This is tapping into your inner strength and aligning with it. This is the shift from thinking "I will never be this or I will never have that" into "I will do this and I can do this"!

How do I know this? From my own struggles. From allowing my own limited thinking to hold me back for too long. From having high- pressured, personal definitions of health and fitness that I felt propelled to meet, although I was not even aware that these were driving me. These were unrealistic and unreachable rules about what I had to do, therefore, I felt pain and feelings of failure because I wasn't meeting them. My battles were in motion because of the defining limitations I held myself to day in and day out without recognizing them. I would blame this or that, procrastinate or avoid healthy habits and not know why. Now I know why. Any limitations I have had in my life I put there all by myself, and they emerged from feelings, which reinforced thoughts that weren't serving me.

This applies to you as well. This is why I am encouraging you to look at your health and fitness in this way. I know a lot of people can relate to this. It does not matter what level of health you are in right now, you have thinking that must shift for you to grow, not only to achieve health and fitness results, but to do so with joy and fun. We all need more fun in life! For some, this is slowing down and squashing the illusion of perfectionism. For others it is stepping up and aligning with a new momentum that serves you. I believe it is both ends—a different pull for each individual.

However we slice it, the bottom line for each of us is to think about how we think and feel. When looking at the chain of creating results, this is the first to occur. There is incredible power in your thoughts and feelings, so it is vital to become aware of the expectations that you subconsciously told yourself you must live by with regards to health and fitness. This applies to every area, including relationships, finances, career, hobbies, etc. Thinking about your feelings is also where you will find your beliefs, values, and hidden intentions. When you are aware of this, you can easily reduce and eliminate your excuses and experience your desired results. For the sake of this interview, we are focusing on how to make changes in your health and fitness, although you can see how this can be applied to *any* area of your life.

Now that you have taken the time to reflect how you have defined your health and fitness, you see how important your thoughts are. If you were like me, you cried and laughed a bit and realized you need to make some changes. The next step is already in motion, and this is the *how you feel* part of getting results. Like me, your neighbor, or anyone else on this planet, you just need to clean it up.

If you looked at how you defined something, and found you want to change it, you have just tied an emotion to your thoughts. Good for you! We actually do this all day long; now you can be more aware of this activity, and it will serve you tremendously. For instance, this is the stage where you buy or don't buy things, where you eat or don't eat something. How? Most people act from emotions, which is fine, but if you have a history of purchasing meaningless and useless gadgets and items, find yourself being taken advantage of, overeating, buying and eating the wrong foods, not exercising, and constantly in arguments because you spend too much, this is a sign you need to handle your emotions better.

An example is when I hear a client tell me that he or she has twenty-eight diet books, thousands of dollars of home workout equipment, top of the line juicers, memberships to several athletic clubs, and the client still "wants" to lose weight and get fit, but is not using one of them because a, b, c and x, y, z.

What these excuses really boil down to is that the individual's perception of what it takes to be healthy and fit is disempowering. I hear it all the time. People really do have good intentions to be healthy, but their current feelings about something in their past or something they made up for their future limits them and they choose to keep wanting what they don't have.

When you are stopped in your tracks on your own path, what you will typically see is procrastination, excuses, drama, your story, keeping busy with meaningless tasks, etc.

Look back at how you defined the key topics earlier. Now, if you attached feelings to these definitions, I can guess there would be words popping up such as disappointed, hopeless, frustrated, angry, jealous, clueless, competitive, invincible, addicted, or possibly a way to escape or cling to your drama so you have an excuse. You can see this can go to either extreme, as can everything. I know they can each be redefined. To do this, you must add how you want to feel when you are healthy and fit. So you *must get clear* about what you want with your health and fitness. Remember, you just spent time recognizing where you are—your starting point. Now is your chance to uncover your negative feelings that you work so hard to hide, and create what you want.

If you are feeling negative or intense emotions, it may be your past that you are remembering, and you are not your past. Please do not define yourself by your physical body or your house, vehicle, bank account, or diplomas. Your biceps, abs, hair, tan, or cup size do not define who you are, either. Your physical body does reflect the choices of your past emotional handling, stress adaptability, nutritional and toxicity status, levels of discipline, and more. How to improve your feelings regarding your health and fitness, whether you need to tone it down or bring it up, is to simply add gratitude and appreciation for your journey. *Redefine it as your way of feeling good about yourself right now, thankful that you have a choice to exercise or eat right to feel healthy, and have an opportunity to learn new things that can dramatically change your results.*

Once you have redefined and felt what you desire for your health, eating habits, hydration, physical endurance, energy, strength, sleep, and stress handling, the next part is *critical!* This is part where you actually *take the steps* necessary for change. Make your goals and set your new action steps. If you do not know what steps to take, there are plenty of ways to research, so get resourceful!

You must have a plan. This is where most people fall off. It is easy to *think* about what you want and *feel* how good it would be to be healthy and fit, but *you* must *do* something different. As Jim Rohn said, "You can't hire someone else to do your push-ups for you." You know what foods you choose to buy as comfort or convenience foods; these must be replaced. Eating healthy is actually very tasty, and the benefits are amazing. Make time to relax, to write your goals, invest in a coach, whether it is a holistic nutritionist or practitioner, life coach, personal trainer, someone who is experienced living healthy and fit. Be sure you choose someone who walks the walk; do not trust your health to someone who has just read about nutrition and fitness or simply knows about it. Remove yourself from stressful relationships and environments—you deserve happiness. You are worth it! Remember, you are in the driver's seat with your health. As Tony Robbins says, "There are no failures, only results."

Wright

This absolutely makes sense, so why is it difficult for people to make all the steps happen?

German

Indecision is one. We want "A" in our hearts, but our head really likes us staying in "B," so we may start a new habit or program and then stop, sinking back into normal routines, or, never start. It is easier to be comfortable in routines, and you really have to step out of your comfort zone and make that new level your new routine to get any real change.

And we do this. For example, moving to another state or starting a new job is uncomfortable at first but soon becomes the norm. I believe that when it comes to our own bodies, when we are real and listen to our hearts, our health and fitness becomes easy. What you eat and choose to do with your body is entirely up to you. All the decision-making and committing is up to you. If you are attempting to lose weight or increase your strength and energy, more than likely, you have been at this for quite some time, and you are getting the same results. This is insanity. Remember that the definition of insanity is doing the same thing over and over and expecting a different result. This all stems from the thought process way before results emerge.

We also need to realize that what we value and believe in most shows up in our decisions. Do I choose to set goals or watch television? Do I choose to forgive or bury my anger or hurt? If I want to be fit and healthy, do I choose to consistently eat healthy foods or do I consistently eat cookies and frosting and hope to be fit one day? Do I choose to get out of bed early and exercise, or do I sleep in and say I will start tomorrow?

I will bet that each of us has carried something with us that we have wanted to change for years, possibly our sleeping, energy, weight, or addictions. To go deeper to the cause of what is holding you back, ask yourself these: What is getting in my way? (Excuses.) What am I constantly distracted by? (Stories.) What am I really attached to? (Drama.) These are the emotional pieces in the jigsaw puzzle of your life. Once you find them, take them out, replace them from your heart, not your head, and you will see a new picture—one that inspires you to take all of the steps and become the fit and healthy being you deserve!

Wright

This is very empowering information. How do you stay inspired?

German

I have come to understand there is a big difference between motivation and inspiration. I have personally attended many motivating lectures, workshops, seminars, and events intended to motivate people into the business, body, or life of their dreams. I know you can relate when I say I was "pumped up," really excited, took tons of notes, or had a brief thought of "I should try that," then walked out, and in a few minutes the new material or motivating vibrations disappeared. The notes were piled or filed somewhere, and I was back to my reality. I tried to tell myself that it was still in there somewhere, and *when I get more time,* I will revisit what I learned. Not going to happen. Being motivated is like buying a pair of your favorite jeans on sale or a caffeine buzz—the feeling fades quickly or lasts for a short amount of time, you snap back to your old routines, and you justify settling for what is comfortable.

But, I have also attended many seminars, events, and workshops that *inspired* me to pursue more—a lot more, actually. To be *inspired* is tapping into your own natural state of personal power and source of creativity. We discussed how to do this in the other book project I participated in with you, *Discover Your Inner Strength*. "Inspired" means you have recognized your inborn desires to grow and contribute, resonating with your natural "Yes I can."

Inspired individuals lead a totally different lifestyle than those who need to be motivated, I can relate to this completely. Motivation is an outside game—you think that something out there will bring you success, and this focus leads you to more pain and frustration. Now do not get me wrong, I still believe motivation can affect people in a way that helps them make a better decision or think a bit differently. But most people need to *feel* the jolt to take action, and quit seeking "out there" to achieve. Inspiration is an inside game, and this is where you *feel* the jolt. Think about when you hear, see, or read something that really resonates with you—that feeling you experience. The key is to be aware of what are you excited about, interested in, and passionate about. In other words, where do you put your focus and attention, your time and finances? Are these activities or organizations about growth and expansion?

For the sake of becoming healthy and fit, I believe that when you follow what inspires you rather than what distracts you, you will redirect your energy to improve your vitality, health, and fitness levels. It is invigorating and powerful to feel in control of your own energy, and the amount that you have tied up in frustration, anger, and hopelessness is necessary to convert to forgiveness, gratitude, and appreciation.

Take an inventory of your current health and fitness right now. How do you see your health and fitness in a year, five years, or ten years if you continue to do what you are doing now? It is up to you to want a better level; the steps are actually easy. The decision is in your hands, and once you commit to a healthier life, the steps become habits like brushing your teeth, sending an e-mail, or making a phone call. How healthy and fit do you want your future to be?

Look at all of the amazing individuals with disabilities and impairments who participate in daily exercise or intense athletic activities from swimming, running, skiing, wheelchair races, and more. These individuals, despite their challenges, clearly demonstrate the Yes I Can attitude!

One of the most inspiring legacies for me is that of Art Berg. He was severely injured in a motor vehicle accident that resulted in his being quadriplegic at the age of twenty-one. He didn't let that hold him back. He became a world class wheelchair athlete, was involved in full contact wheelchair rugby, and raced 325 miles in Utah under challenging conditions. This just names a few of his amazing accomplishments. He became a widely known motivational speaker and if hearing his accomplishments and possibility mindset doesn't inspire you, I don't know what will!

Wright

If you could ask a question or two that you believe would affect the overall health of this nation, what would it be and why?

German

Excellent question! I will boldly ask this, "What would you do without medication and pharmaceuticals? What would you need to change in your life? What would you have to do differently?" I ask this because of the profession I am in and the awareness I have of this way of thinking.

Look at the health of this country, it is not positive. As a holistic practitioner and a mother, I am highly concerned about the illnesses and conditions in children that are on the rise—obesity, diabetes, depression, anxiety, major allergies, skin problems, autoimmune conditions, and more. Medication is not the answer for health. I believe medications are for emergencies, accidents, injuries, or trauma and they should be used appropriately. We live in such an impatient society; it is ridiculous how easy it is to take a pill to mask symptoms and suppress emotions, and this encourages addiction. When kids are started on medications, as they currently are, they grow up with the mindset that if you feel sick, tired, depressed, nervous, sad, too happy, or whatever else, you urgently need to go get a medication, spend hundreds to thousands of dollars on multiple tests, or agree to have something surgically removed.

The sensible approach that worked for thousands of years before medications is to take care of your body, eat healthy, exercise, pray, meditate, and listen to your body. Your body has a magnificent inner wisdom that heals from the inside. God blessed our Earth long ago with natural plants, herbs, and food that have the abilities to help the body heal.

I want to share what Dr. Royal Lee stated in 1952, "One of the biggest tragedies of human civilization is the precedents of chemical therapy over nutrition. It's a substitute of artificial therapy over nature, of poisons over food, in which we are feeding people poisons trying to correct the reactions of starvation." The problems of our health today could drastically shift if *this* was the information continually broadcasted on the nightly news. Our health and fitness levels of this country would dominate if morning and daytime talk shows constantly projected all of the health related stories and amazing recoveries that thousands and thousands of people make with alternative practices and healing therapies. This is not a new concept for those who practice a holistic approach, but it is not the message people are seeing or hearing through the media, is it? Eating healthy, exercising, and handling your emotions is your best health insurance.

I have to share with you that we still have three fast-food burgers from a well-known chain that we purchased *more than eighteen months ago* for an experiment. The burgers look the same as when we bought them—no mold, no decay—it is the same old fake food. We did this as an experiment so we can share this with clients, friends, and our kids as well. Neither the meat nor the bread show any signs of breaking down anytime soon. I know others who have two-, three-, five-, and eight-year-old burgers with the same appearance. This is exactly the point. This country is trying to survive on nonfood, loaded with preservatives, sugar, and chemicals to last longer, and turning to medication to cover up the symptoms of starvation. Processed food delivers absolutely nothing empowering to our health. This is why, if you really desire better health and better fitness, you must become an active participant in your own health.

Wright

As a working mother of three young children, would you share what your successful habits are with our readers?

German

Of course! Let me start out by saying that I had many years living at suboptimal health, having low energy, several health challenges, feeling overwhelmed and in a state of uncontrollable chaos. Finally I had had enough. I chose to become a student again. This time, the subject was my own game of life. I became an eager and fast learner. I began learning how to take control of my life, starting with my health. Now, during the initial process, I was faced with my own beliefs that were limiting me. I had to take on my own resistance and skepticism. I also learned who really supported me during this process, and I had to disconnect from those who did not support me.

It is fact that as you strive to grow and improve yourself, the people in your life who feel insecure and scared will try to stop you. This is why the "Yes I Can" mindset is so important—you must stay the course and choose to be your own leader. So my current lifestyle was learned through personal experience, from trial and error, taking my own steps, one at a time, on a continual path of growth and deeper understanding. I rolled up my sleeves because I *knew* I had to *do* something different, and *now*, not someday. I am so grateful for the challenges I have had and the mistakes I made because those have brought me to deeper appreciation about my own life, immeasurable opportunities of experiences, growth, and the ability to contribute what I have learned. One by one, I stomped out the old habits and created *new* lifestyle habits. We all share so many of the same daily activities and responsibilities, we wear many hats, and we can feel stretched at times. So as a working mother of three young children, these are some of the habits that currently help me stay proactive with my health and fitness. I will gladly share them with you:

Plan and Prepare: I am in control of what I eat. If I have a meeting over a meal, work through lunch, kids have a game, conference, program, or extra activity, I plan ahead. I typically pack my own lunch. I will call and pre-order a specific meal. I eat before I leave and I always bring my own healthy snacks. I take the time to plan before that day arrives, so I am prepared that day when it does.

Communication: With kids, it is essential that they are acknowledged and know they are very important in the family. Observation. Encouragement to explore their feelings.

117

Choices. I want to know what is going on at school, their activities, challenges, highlights, and friends. I schedule time to be with each of them. I communicate about chores, responsibilities, and when I will be working late or at a workshop, letting them be involved in each day. Communication is essential with relationships.

Have fun: Laugh, dance, sing, be present, and keep your spirit alive. Be goofy because smiles and laughter are contagious and healing.

Meals: Plan. I find that it really takes little time to plan out the week, and this habit frees up time when mealtimes arrive. Kids are actively involved with helping plan the meals—even their cold lunches. They love to design one dinner a week. They grocery shop, help make lists, and are eager to help and prepare meals. They see how vegetables are predominant in our meals, and they accept it. That is what they know. I also keep several grocery lists on hand, along with reusable grocery bags. The goal is that kids learn to make good choices with how to eat, what to avoid, how to recycle, and take care of the environment.

Food: Eat *real* food. I only buy what I want to eat and feed my family. I do not buy things that would tempt us to eat unhealthy. We eat fresh, organic, or local vegetables and fruits, raw nuts and seeds, lentils and beans, grass-fed meat, and fish. We use whole grains and avoid the *whites*—no white sugar, flour, potatoes, pastas, etc. We do not consume preservatives, additives, sodas, corn, corn syrup, processed food, pork, soy, or dairy (I grew up on a dairy farm!). If it is not in its natural state, we avoid it. Foods that are in their natural state provide energy, decrease cravings, and promote detoxification. Do we sometimes enjoy pizza, ice cream, or a food on our "no" list? Of course we do, but those foods are considered a treat to us, not a way of eating.

Hydration: Water. Water. Water. Organic herbal teas. I add lemon, lime, chlorophyll, or my favorite greens to my water daily.

Exercise: My goal is to exercise daily—cardiovascular or strength training. For my body type, I learned that I respond better if I do cardio at different times of the day than when I strength train. The reality is that I am exercising four to six days a week, sometimes three, sometimes seven. My point is that I am no longer attached to a certain number of workouts, or amount of time—that drove me insane. I schedule it, and if I see an opening other than what is scheduled, I take it. It's like when you are looking for a parking space—if you find one earlier or later, maybe it is not as ideal but it'll fit, you take it! I choose to not force working out into my day anymore, and I vary my workout. I have a mini-trampoline at home. I have a membership at a local gym where I strength train, emphasizing core strength. I enjoy running, so when there is an opportunity for me to get out, I do.

I also love to hike and be out with the kids. They enjoy hiking, biking, soccer, football, anything that keeps them active. This is our lifestyle. I feel that as parents, we need to help our children exercise daily so they develop this habit at an early age.

Meditation: I take twenty minutes before the day begins to quiet my mind and connect. This brings focus, direction, and tremendously helps me create my day.

Flexibility, adapting to changes, being open-minded: I am able to put myself in other people's shoes—observing and continually working on being present

Rest: I listen to my body. If I feel I am stretching too far, I welcome rest, and recover quickly.

Intentions: I set goals weekly, monthly, and yearly. I also have my big intentions written down to review often. I am constantly writing lists and having the big picture in front of me. This keeps me clear and on track with the steps I need to take.

Reading/Personal Growth: Every day I read something. It may be a quote or a chapter—sometimes it is several. I believe in forever learning. I read, listen to speakers on CDs, and attend workshops and events to understand, grow, improve, and share.

Journal: Daily I write something, whether it is a sentence, a page, or more. I have gratitude journals, which are very empowering. I have other journals to write family memories, attempting to capture most of the cute things the kids have said or done, and journals for ideas and thoughts.

Pay attention to emotions: I utilize several techniques that help me to better recognize my emotions and redirect them (along with my excuses and justifications) by moving into my heart, and out of my thoughts easier. This is a continual learning process, which has been highly effective for me. I encourage investing time in personal growth strategies, as I believe the emotional piece is key for amazing health.

Environment: I choose to create my environment and keep it as positive as I can. I choose those whom I spend time with and what I will listen to.

Celebrate wins and accomplishments: It is important to acknowledge all the steps. The more you tap into your accomplishments, the more you feed that "Yes You Can" inner strength.

Wright

Would you please give the readers suggestions on how to make their health and fitness their number one priority?

German

Absolutely. Everything in our lives is connected to our health—finances, relationships, energy, creativity, careers, success, everything! If you are not healthy, do you feel like you can contribute to your family, friends, work, networking, or personal organizations? If you are not healthy, can you maintain your duties, finances, focus, or social life? If you don't have your health, how does that affect your ability to have healthy habits of being active and eating right, or have positive thoughts that move you forward? I do believe that you must have your health and fitness as a priority. When you are leading a life committed to being healthy and fit, you rarely get knocked down, you are rarely sick or weak, your stamina and endurance is exceptional, you have a strong connection to your creative source of power, accomplish more, make better decisions, and experience more joy and fun.

"Happiness lies, first of all, in health"—George William Curtis.

As I mentioned earlier, when you fuel your body with real nutrition from complete foods, drink pure water, and exercise, your body is able to naturally release toxins as we are designed to do. When you are truly cleansing, which is a continual process, and able to maintain that normal detoxification process, your thoughts, emotions, decisiveness, vitality, capabilities, and overall well-being improve tremendously, as well as your body's ability to function.

In conclusion, I want to touch on the emotional healing that can take place in each of us. Emotions and memories have a phenomenal affect on our entire body—physically, mentally, biochemically, and spiritually. Look at the amazing and profound wisdom that mind-body experts such as Deepak Chopra have found, studied, and proven on the quantum level. Stored emotions and memories in our bodies impact our health and once these are released, deeper healing can take place.

There is a deep rooted connection in all of us regarding our own emotional weight, and this creates a stressful internal environment, manifesting in symptoms, such as weight gain, hormonal imbalances, and nutritional deficiencies—even if we are eating right and exercising! By releasing these emotional anchors, you can free up your energy to heal. We know that eating right and exercising improves our well-being to better handle our emotions. It is all connected. But, flip this around, and I strongly believe that when someone is able to face and disengage from the memories that are disempowering on their deeper, subconscious levels, this catapults the body's ability to heal beyond thinking.

I am not an expert on this subject of mind-body healing, but I am highly aware of the emotional sabotage happening in each of us, affecting our health. My intention here is to increase your desire to research this subject on your own. Find out what has been studied and proven about how to heal your body on deeper levels, with the approach of learning how you can assist your body to live and thrive.

I personally plan to forever study about how the body heals naturally using the organic resources of the Earth, and our inborn capabilities that God created within each of us. I believe each one of us is responsible for learning, applying, experiencing, and sharing. We all deserve life and love at its fullest, all beautifully guided by our Spirit. This is your journey—have fun creating the life you choose!

Dr. Jessica German is a chiropractor, holistic nutritional therapist, author, and lecturer. She is currently in private practice in Colorado Springs, Colorado. As a health and wellness coach, she emphasizes that making small yet critical changes can easily make transformation possible, no matter who you are. She believes that your health potential is *unlimited*, and what is needed is having a reality check before reality checks you. In addition to helping individuals and families in her practice, this dynamic mother of three uses her passion and enthusiasm for health and wellness to educate the public and corporate audiences.

Dr. Jessica German

Health Unlimited
Colorado Springs, CO
719-649-4455
drjessica@holisticnutrition4u.com
www.holisticnutrition4u.com

CHAPTER NINE

A Special Interview

by Jim Rohn

David E. Wright (Wright)

I join the millions of people whose lives were changed by the teachings of Jim Rohn and remember him for the wisdom he unselfishly shared with people all over the world for more than four decades. I always looked forward with excitement to our conversations because I knew that he would be interested, engaged, and always informative. He was the perfect conversationalist. Jim Rohn died of pulmonary embolism on December 5, 2009, at the age of seventy-nine. Jim's courage in his final months was a testament to the messages he shared with the world. He was truly an original and I will miss him.

It's my sincere pleasure today to welcome Jim Rohn to *Yes You Can* Jim helped motivate and train an entire generation of personal development trainers, as well as hundreds of executives from America's top corporations. He's been described as everything from "master motivator" to a "modern day Will Rodgers," to a legend. Jim has been internationally hailed over the years as one of the most influential thinkers of our time. His professional development seminars have spanned thirty-nine years. During his lifetime addressed more than six thousand audiences and four million people worldwide. He has authored seventeen books as well as dozens of audio and video programs. There simply are not enough superlatives when introducing Jim Rohn.

Jim, thank you for taking time to visit with us today.

Jim Rohn (Rohn)

Hey, my pleasure.

Wright

Before we dive into some pretty deep subjects, I know our readers would appreciate an update on your focus at the time of this interview.

Rohn

Well, I'm still involved in world travel—from Asia to South Africa, South America, to Europe, across the United States—which I've been doing for the last forty years and enjoying it very much.

Wright

I've belonged to a political discussion group called Great Decisions, for the last fifteen years. Every year we discuss conditions in Africa and every year we come away with our hands in our pockets, saying we don't know what can be done about it. Is it as bad as we believe?

Rohn

It's a complex continent and who knows what it will finally take. You know, there are some good signs but you're right.

Wright

The problems are just voluminous.

Rohn

I have lectured in all the major cities in South Africa. I've gone there several times over the last twenty years. When I first went they still had Apartheid, now that's all gone. There are some good signs that recovery is under way and I love to see that.

I first lectured in Moscow in Russia, starting about ten years ago and fortunately that was after the walls came tumbling down—they were changing from communism to capitalism. I've made about five lecture tours in Russia in the last ten years, teaching capitalism and personal responsibility and entrepreneurship. It's exciting to go back and see so many of them doing it. They still have a long way to go—there's still push and pull between the old ways and the new ways.

Years and years ago when I went to South America, every country had a dictator. Now they're all gone, for the most part. So there are a lot of improvements that have been made around the world but there is still a long way to go.

Wright

Do you appreciate the United States when you come back?

Rohn

No doubt about it. This is the place where you can start with so little and still you can start with pennies and make your fortune with some good advice and coaching and a bit of training and personal responsibility and a whole lot of courage. That's extraordinary.

Wright

I spend a lot of time with professionals from all types of industries and I often give career advice when I'm asked.

Would you mind looking back over your career and sharing a story or two that demonstrates some relevant success principles? In other words, to what do you attribute your success in life?

Rohn

I met someone when I was twenty-five; his name was Earl Schoff (this is in most of my recordings and writings). I worked for him for five years. He died at the early age of forty-nine, but during those five years I worked for him, he gave me really a lot of the fundamentals—especially the economic and personal development principles—that revolutionized my life.

When I met him I had only pennies in my pocket, nothing in the bank, and creditors calling once in a while saying, "You told us the check was in the mail." That embarrasses me.

I think what triggered my search to find him was what I call "the Girl Scout story." I was at home alone and heard a knock on my door. I go to the door and there's this Girl Scout selling cookies. She gives me this great presentation (it's the best organization in the world). She goes on and on and she describes the several different flavors available and that the cost is only two dollars. Then she politely asked me to buy.

125

No problem, I wanted to buy—big problem, I didn't have two dollars. I can remember today that embarrassing moment—I'm a grown man and I'm twenty-five years old; I've had one year of college, I've got a little family started, I live in America, and I don't have two dollars in my pocket.

I didn't want to tell her that, so I lied to her and said, "Hey look, we've already bought lots of Girl Scout cookies, we've still got plenty in the house we haven't eaten yet.

She said, "Oh, that's wonderful! Thank you very much," and she leaves.

When she leaves, I say to myself, "I don't want to live like this anymore. I mean how low you can get, lying to a Girl Scout? That's got to be the bottom, right?

I called it "the day that turns your life around." Everybody can look back at some of those days when you made a unique decision at a particular time and you were never the same again. That was one of those days.

Shortly after that I met this incredible mentor I went to work for—Earl Schoff. Using the things he taught me, I became a millionaire by the age of thirty-two.

It doesn't take much if you get the right information and put it to work and are willing to accept refinement, keep up your studies, and engage primarily in what we call "personal development"—becoming more valuable. For economics, personal development makes you more valuable to the marketplace. Personal development also makes you become more valuable as a father, a mother, a parent, a friend, a business colleague, and as a citizen.

Personal development is the subject I have talked most about seeing how valuable you can be to yourself, to your community, and to those around you.

I've got a little economic phase I use that says, "We get paid for bringing value to the marketplace." And the first part of that is the value you bring such as a product, but the biggest part of what you bring is how valuable you become through personal development. I say, "To climb the ladder of success, work harder on yourself than you do on your job." If you work hard on your job, you can make a living, if you work hard on yourself, you can make a fortune.

I learned those very fundamental ideas when I was twenty-five. Fortunately I discovered them at twenty-five rather than at fifty-five. Fifty-five is okay and seventy-five is still okay but gosh, it's good to learn them at the age of twenty-five when you can really put them to work. These ideas revolutionized my life and they formed the foundation of what I've shared now all these years in so many forms.

Wright

I've only heard the name Schoff twice. You just mentioned it and when I was in junior high school in seventh and eighth and ninth grades, one of my mentors was a coach named Schoff. He was a real mentor. This guy was just a fine, fine, man.

Rohn

The same man, Earl Schoff, influenced Mary Kay (the lady who started Mary Kay Cosmetics) and me back in 1955–1956. Those were the early, early years. Mary Kay went on to become a superstar. What he shared with me just transformed my life.

Wright

You're known throughout the world as a personal development expert. In practical terms what does that really mean?

Rohn

Well, there's a phase that says, "Success is not something you pursue, success is something you attract"—by becoming an attractive person. Currently I'm sharing it like this: to really do well you need multiple skills. If you've just got one skill, it's too risky economically. For example, a guy has worked for a company for twenty years and the division he works for goes out of business. He's lost his job and he tells us he's in financial trouble. The reason is that, even after twenty years of working, he only had one skill. If he had taken an accounting course or some other course two nights a week he would have had another skill to market. There's so much available out there that can increase your value to the marketplace.

I started learning these extra skills: finding good people, sales, finding a product I could believe in, and talk about its merits until somebody said Yes, then follow up, and get referrals. Then I learned to build an organization. I then learned organization—getting people to work together. I needed to learn to get a team and work together. Then I learned recognition—I learned to reward people for small steps of progress.

The biggest skill I learned was communication. I got involved in training, showing people how the job works, and then I got involved in teaching. I taught setting goals, personal development leadership, and communication skills. My theme for that was, "You need both job skills and life skills," because just learning how to set goals revolutionized my life.

Then the ultimate in communication is learning to inspire—helping people see themselves as better than they are, transport them in to the future, paint the possibilities, and then use your own testimony. Say, "Hey if I can do it, you can do it."

So you're starting with pennies, you're behind, the creditors are calling; but that's not really what's important. What's important is the decision today to start the journey of self-improvement. I think that theme has been paramount in all of my teaching and training during the last forty years—work harder on yourself than you do on your job.

In leadership, I teach that to attract attractive people, you must be attractive. So it's a constant pursuit of self-development and personal development.

The theme during my career, teaching and training during the past forty years is: communication, managing your time, managing your money, and learning to inspire.

Wright

You know, I have my own opinion about how difficult it is for people to change whether it involves a health issue or dieting, for example. Do you believe that people can really change and why is change so difficult?

Rohn

Give easy steps. For example, if you want to change your health and you say, "I've got to do something that will make me healthy. My momma taught that an apple a day was healthy," why not start there?

If you don't start with something simple, you can forget the rest of the complicated stuff. Sometimes it's good to do it with someone else. I've found in all my entrepreneurial business projects during the last forty years, it's more inspiring to say, "Let's go do it," than to say, "I'm going to go do it." Get together with someone and say, "Let's get healthy, let's exercise, let's go to the gym, let's climb a mountain." The "let's" is what's very powerful. A lot of things are pretty tough to do all by yourself.

Wright

In the past there've been some major scandals in corporate America. I know you've counseled many high profiled executives throughout the years. Is there a leadership crisis in America? What do you think has contributed to this kind of moral failure?

Rohn

No, it's always been such from the beginning of recorded history, when there were just four people on earth. You know there was the great scandal of brother who killed brother (Cain and Abel). So it's not a current phenomenon—it's not a twenty-first century phenomenon. Even the Old Testament records good kings and bad kings—those who "did right in the sight of the Lord" and those who led the people into idolatry. You know, it's just not unusual.

My best explanation is the "great adventure" started ages ago, according to the Storyteller. God created all these angels and then gave them the dignity of choice, and a third of them decided to go with Lucifer and make a run on God's throne. They didn't win, but it started what I call "the adventure of the Creator and the spoiler." And then I further describe it with the concept that the adventure of our life seems to be that opposites are in conflict and we are in the middle. But this is what makes a great adventure.

Illness tries to overcome your health, but if you work on your health you can overcome your illness. If, however, you let up the least little bit, sure enough, illness creeps up and takes away some more of your health.

Regarding liberty and tyranny in the world, for a while there was more tyranny than liberty. Since the walls came down in Berlin I am hopeful that there will be more liberty than tyranny in the future.

But whether its politics or whether it's corporations, it doesn't matter, the temptation is always there the drama is always there. Should we do the right thing or would it be okay to cross the line? I use the following illustration sometimes: When I was a little kid I saw a cartoon of a little boy. The little boy had an angel—a little angel—on one shoulder, and a little devil on the other shoulder. Both of them were whispering in his ear. The little devil said, "Go ahead and do it, it will be okay."

The little angels says, "No, no, it *won't* be okay."

The little devil says, "Yes, yes, go ahead, it's okay; nobody will know."

The little angel says, "No, no, no!"

That little cartoon appeared back when I was a kid. It describes the concept of opposites in conflict and that's what makes an adventure.

There wouldn't be positive without negative it doesn't seem like. And you couldn't win if you couldn't lose. If you took a football today and walked out to the stadium and we followed you and in the football stadium you took the football and walked across the goal line, would we all cheer and call it a touchdown? The answer is No, that's silly. It's not a touchdown until you face the three-hundred-pounders. If you can muscle past them (they want to smash your face in the dirt) and if you can dance by the secondary, on a special day, we call it a touchdown, and maybe you win the championship.

That's the deal—opposites are in conflict. We're tempted every day, whether it's the little things or something big and major. You come to the intersection and the light is yellow and it starts to turn red. Some little voice may whisper to you, "Go ahead, you're late—you can make it." But if you try running that light you may wind up dead. If you say, "No, I'll be more cautious," then you live a little bit longer.

So it's not that we're not involved in this push and pull. It happens at the high echelons of corporate America. Little voices whisper in a collective way around the boardroom, and the board members decide to cross the line. They think, "It looks like we can get by with it—we can put it off shore or we can play some games here and we'll be okay" or "If we want this stock to grow and necessity demands it, we probably skate the line a little bit." That happens in the poorest of homes and it happens in the riches of homes. It happens in the boardroom and it happens on Main Street and it happens in the back alley. So it doesn't really matter where it is, temptation is always there. But that's what makes the adventure—to see if you can handle the temptation and do more right than wrong—have a longer list of virtues than mistakes—then you win.

Wright

I once read an article you wrote about attitude. In it you said attitude determines how much of the future we're allowed to see. This is a fascinating thing to say. Will you elaborate on this thought?

Rohn

Well, it's attitude about four things:

1. *How you feel about the past.* Some people carry the past around like a burden. They continually live and dwell on their past mistakes. They live in the past (i.e., their past failures) and it just drains away all the energy they could apply to something much more positive. We have to have a good healthy attitude about the past. The key on that is just to learn from it. Hey, here's where I messed up, I've got that corrected now, and I'm going to make the changes for the future. We call that "drawing on the past" as a

good school of experience to make corrections in errors in judgment or whatever put you in a bad place.

2. *How you feel about the future.* We need to look back for experience but we need to look ahead for inspiration. We need to be inspired by the goals we set for ourselves and for our family, the goals we've set for friendship, lifestyle, becoming wealthy, powerful, and influential, and as a unique citizen, those goals that get us up early and keep us up late, fire up the fuel of our imagination, and how can we accomplish them.

3. *How you feel about everybody.* You can't succeed by yourself. It takes everybody for each of us to be successful. Each of us needs all of us. One person doesn't make an economy; one person doesn't make a symphony orchestra. So you have to have that unique sense of the value of everybody and that it really does take everybody for any one person to be successful.

4. *How you feel about yourself.* This is the most important one. At the end of the day evaluate yourself: "I pushed it to the limit, I did everything I could, I made every call, I stretched as far as I could." If that's true, then you can lie down and sleep a good sleep. Solomon wrote, "The sleep of the laboring man is sweet . . ." (Ecclesiastes 5:12). This describes people who put in the work—who work hard either with their hands or with their mind or with their ability to communicate, whatever it is—so at the end of the day they feel good about themselves. Nothing is more powerful than high self-esteem. It builds self-confidence, which builds success.

Those five attitudes really do give you a promising look at the future. But if you're always being pulled back by the past or distracted because you find it difficult to manage your life with people you have to associate with, that's tough. And the better you can handle that and realize the law of averages says you're going to be around some good people and some bad people, and you're going to be around some ambitious people and some not so ambitious, the better off you'll be. You've got to learn to take it all in stride.

Then knowing that you're on track for better health and you're on track for becoming financially independent. You haven't quite got it solved, but you're on track for the management of your time and your money. And your attitude toward that really creates high inspiration that the future's going to multiply several times better than the past.

Wright

I don't normally like to frame a question in the negative but I thought it would be interesting to get your prospective on mistakes that people make in life and in business. If you had to name the top three on a list of mistakes people make that kept them from succeeding or living a fulfilled life, what would they be?

Rohn

Well, number one mistake economically is not to understand that people can make you wealthy. And all you have to do is just figure out how to do that. For example: Johnny mows Mrs. Brown's lawn and she pays five dollars. One day it occurs to him, "If I get my friend Paul to mow this lawn, Mrs. Brown would pay five dollars. I would give Paul four dollars and keep one for myself because I got the job." Instantly Johnny has now moved to a higher level of economics that says this is how you become wealthy.

A little phrase that philosophically and economically changed my life is: "Profits are better than wages." Wages make you a living but profits make you a fortune. You don't have to be General Motors, you don't have to be high in the industrial complex society to understand this concept; that's why it's so powerful to teach capitalism, how to buy and sell and how to sell and buy.

I've got so many stories of people I've helped in my seminars who started with pennies and now they're rich. That's the key—learning how to employ other people. First do it yourself—learn how to do it yourself—then find a need someone has and get someone else to render the service, and then someone else and then someone else. Teach them the same, and the principles of economics and capitalism. The knowledge of how to go from having pennies to gaining a fortune is so simple.

When I taught it to the Russians they couldn't believe how simple it was. I said, "Capital is any value you set aside to be invested in an enterprise that brings value to the marketplace hoping to make a profit"—that's capitalism. They couldn't believe I could put it in one sentence.

Wright

I can't either.

Rohn

I teach kids how to have two bicycles—one to ride and one to rent. It doesn't take long to make a profit. If you're halfway bright, if you get just a little advice to give you a chance to start, you'll make it.

I see capitalism in two parts—one is capital time, the other is capital money. If you wisely learn to invest capital money you can make a fortune. And then together with that, if you can learn to invest capital time you can also amass a fortune. You set aside time to be invested in an enterprise.

I started that part-time when I was twenty-five years old, all those years ago in 1955. I took about fifteen to twenty hours a week part-time and invested it in a capital enterprise. By the time I was thirty-two I was a millionaire. It didn't take much money because I only invested $200, which I borrowed. That was my capital money, but the other was my capital time. Once I learned how to invest both and then learned how to teach and train and inspire other people to do the same, it totally changed my life.

I don't have to worry about social security—I developed my own social security. It's interesting that they're not teaching that today when social security is such a main topic. We've got to let our young people put aside some of that withholding and put it in a personal account. How about teaching them how to be financially independent? Who's doing that? John Kennedy said," Don't ask what your country can do for you . . ." Don't ask what the social security program can do for you . . . Why not ask what you can do for your country—or social security? Could I mow Mrs. Brown's lawn and collect five dollars and do it part-time? Then could I get someone else to do it and then someone else to do another job, and finally work my way from the pennies in my pocket to the fortune that I could have because this is America—the land of opportunity?

It's startling how simple it is in concept and how really easy it is in practice; but the results can be phenomenal. I got such great early results that I never did look back, from age twenty-five until today.

For me it's fun to teach it. I've been teaching it now for all these years and I've got some testimonials where I helped people start, just like I started with pennies and now they're rich. It's just exciting.

One of the great exciting experiences is to have your name appear in somebody's testimonial: "Here's the person who found me, here's the person who taught me, here's the person who wouldn't let me quit, gave me more reasons for staying than for leaving. Here's the person who believed in me until I could believe in myself," then they mention your name. I call that big time, and you can't buy it with money. You have to simply earn it by sharing ideas with somebody that makes a difference in their life. And I love to do it.

Wright

This is the definition of great mentors.

Rohn

Yes, I love to be that. Hopefully my books and tapes and my personal appearances have done that throughout the years.

Wright

I'd like to go back to the issue of personal development and change. Considering the issues most Americans face in this modern era with all of our technology, where would you advise most people to focus their energy if they could only change one thing about themselves?

Rohn

I'd advise them to start figuring out to how to learn another skill, and then another skill. Then it would be good to learn another language. People who know more than one language receive good pay. Some of my business colleagues who speak three or four languages make three or four million a year. Not that this is a guarantee, but that's just an idea for self-improvement. Learn something beyond what you know now because it could be something that you can cash in on, maybe sooner than you think.

Wright

Not to mention the fact that you're talking for the first time to another whole culture and look what you could learn. I've always been fascinated by the Chinese culture.

Rohn

I would also suggest that people develop wise use of their time and then wise use of their money. I teach kids to not spend more than seventy cents out of every dollar—ten cents for charity or church, ten cents for active capital (e.g., the two bicycles, one to ride and one to rent concept), then passive capital of 10 percent. Let someone else use it (you provide the capital that will pay you dividends, increase in stock or whatever). I call it "seventy-ten-ten and ten." Then I teach not to buy the second car until you've bought the second house. Cars won't make you rich but houses will make you rich. I love to teach that.

A lady called me from Mexico not long ago and said, "Mr. Rohn, I'm now shopping for my third car because I just finished paying for my third house." She started listening to my training ten years ago. She not only uses it, she teaches it. Down in Mexico she makes about $40,000 a month, which is just staggering.

But it's fun—it's been fun for me over the years to have stories like that. I use my own story as an inspiration not only for myself but also for the people who listen to my lectures. And then it's fun to watch people actually grab hold of something and turn it into success.

Wright

Jim, it's been a sincere joy having this enlightening conversation with you today. I really appreciate and thank you so much again for taking the time to be with me.

Rohn

I appreciate it also and I thank you for calling.

Jim Rohn was a philosopher, motivational counselor, business executive, and best-selling author. He has been recognized as the greatest motivational speaker of all time. He was one of the world's most sought-after success counselors and business philosophers. Some of his most thought-provoking topics include: sales and entrepreneurial skills, leadership, sales and marketing, success, and personal development.

Jim Rohn conducted seminars for many years and addressed more than six thousand audiences and four million people worldwide. He was a recipient of the 1985 National Speakers Association CPAE Award. He authored more than seventeen books, audio, and video programs. Rohn has been internationally hailed over the years as one of the most influential thinkers of our time.

Revealing contemporary success secrets in a way that is both accessible and practical, Jim ignited enthusiasm and a can-do attitude in all who heard him speak. He approached the subjects of personal and professional success by asking four questions: Why? Why not? Why not you? Why not now? He answered these questions and revealed practical, perceptive secrets for success and productivity. His special style, laced with witticisms and anecdotes, captivates listeners. Among his most thought-provoking topics include: sales and entrepreneurial skills, leadership, sales and marketing, success, and personal development.

Jim Rohn

www.jimrohn.com

CHAPTER TEN

Jesse's Life Challenges Answered From Above with "Yes You Can"

by Dr. Jesse LaPrade

David Wright (Wright)

Today we're talking with Dr. Jesse LaPrade. Jesse has been a successful agricultural professional since 1974. After earning a PhD in post-harvest plant pathology from the University of Florida, Jesse has made numerous agricultural research discoveries, most dealing with the naturally occurring animal toxin, afloxatoxin. Jesse spent more than thirteen years in the agricultural industry with Union Carbide Agricultural Products Division and the France-based company, Rhone Poulenc. He was named outstanding field development representative for Union Carbide in 1980, bringing more than twelve million dollars yearly in sales by finding new uses for registered pesticide products.

Jesse is currently a full-time Auburn University professor and has earned many accolades for his more than seventeen years of service including designer of the national award-winning program, Radon Awareness. He is author or co-author of more than 145 technical journals on radon, indoor air quality, environmental education, global warming, and agricultural safety training and program design. Jesse has delivered more than three hundred technical speeches since 1990. His most precious hobby is painting seascapes and butterflies as well as having been initiated into the Kennedy Center's world-class artist status in 1995. He says, "I am a folk artist without any formal training, if you are interested in my life you can read a lot more on my Web site."

Dr. LaPrade, welcome to *Yes You Can!*

Jesse LaPrade (LaPrade)

Thank you very much, David. I am thrilled to be a part of this opportunity.

Wright

So why did you make the commitment to write a chapter in this book?

LaPrade

"Yes you can" has always been my way of life, it seems. There have been more than thirty "yes you can" incidents in my life, many of which have been life-changing. You will hear about several in this interview but there are many more that I will disclose in my autobiography.

Wright

So what has been your guiding light throughout the years and what drives you to succeed?

LaPrade

My guiding light has always been my love for people and humanity and what drives me to succeed is my innate desire to try and help them improve their lifestyle and overall success in life.

Wright

Has there ever been a major transformation in your life that has taken place in, say, recent years?

LaPrade

Yes, there has, and it deals with my heritage—who my parents were and how I was born. It's really transformed a lot of the way I look at things and the way that I approach life now. My number one motivational factor today came from discovering who my biological mother was, where she came from, and how she fought so hard to give me life. (This highly motivational event will be detailed in my autobiography.)

Wright

Hmm, that must have been a story.

LaPrade

Well it's a story that I am looking forward to writing about. I'm going to reveal my life history to the world. After I told close friends about it, they encouraged me to put pen to paper.

Wright

So what were your early interests? What piqued your interest and motivated you to go on and graduate from college?

LaPrade

As a child growing up through fifth grade I just wanted to enjoy life. I wanted to observe nature and I wanted to learn as much as I could, but I only had certain things I wanted to learn. I wasn't really that interested in people, I just thought that if I learned how biology worked and how electronics and physics worked, I would be successful, or at least I'd satisfy my basic thirst for knowledge.

But then, in junior high school through the eighth grade, my interest was in young ladies. I discovered that many women were different and that was really interesting. In high school I was interested in football, as small as I was. In fact, when I went out for the team in the ninth grade, I weighed 97 pounds, but the school regulation was that players had to weigh at least one hundred pounds to be on the team. The coach said, "I'll help you, Jesse. Go down to the grocery store and get a tag of bananas and make sure it weighs at least five pounds." I came back with the bananas and I ate every one of them. I felt like was about to pop. When I got on the scale, I weighed 99.5 pounds.

"Uh oh," said Coach Guyer. "Jesse, go drink some water, as much as you can hold."

I drank enough water to weigh one hundred pounds and made the team. I played enough to letter in the ninth grade, which I thought was pretty good for a little bitty fellow who thought he wanted to be a football player.

Wright

So what was your biggest disappointment during the years, 1960 through 1968?

LaPrade

The Vietnam War took a lot of my friends from Chatham, and that was an awful disappointment. My best friend had to go to Vietnam and came back in a body bag. That was devastating, emotionally.

I had a hard time deciding what career I wanted to pursue because I had quite a few interests, mostly all technical as opposed to business or the arts. In college, I switched my major at least a half a dozen times, starting with Physics going to Geology, Geophysics, Electrical Engineering, Chemistry, and finally settling on Ornamental Horticulture. My dad was saying, "I wished to heck you'd just take something and get it over with."

I earned a bachelor's degree in Ornamental Horticulture in 1966 from Virginia Polytechnic Institute and State University, but I then faced the dreaded draft by Uncle Sam with a certain invitation to "vacation" in a tropical environment for a while. I really wasn't that impressed with our Uncle's invitation, but I decided to make the most of it if I passed the physical. I decided to "see that tropical paradise" from the air and I volunteered for the Air Force.

To make a long, gut-wrenching story short, I failed the physical, not necessarily to my chagrin. I have found out since that time that this event occurred all because of my genetic heritage. I have experienced severe blinding migraine headaches since I was nine years old. Actually, I also have had Severe Attention Deficit Syndrome as well, although in the '60s it was not well recognized. I just thought that everyone thinks about more than one thing at the same time, no big deal. I have since learned to focus on two or three things at a time instead of six or more, which I am doing right now. Quite frankly, I believe that people who cannot do this are missing out and not using a lot in their thinking ability!

By the way, my only son was diagnosed with this "malady" when he was in the sixth grade. He currently works for the Omni, one of the largest physical work-out facilities in Alabama, no doubt still thinking of several things at the same time!

Wright

So what was your main success during 1968 through 1970?

LaPrade

I met Betty June Davis in December 1968. I fully recognize that as my main success during that time frame.

Wright

I bet she loves to hear that, doesn't she?

LaPrade

Well, now, I don't know if I'd even have the nerve to tell her because that just might give her a "swelled head"! Oh yeah, she knows she's the light of my life. We get along very well. I asked her one time, "What did we ever have in common?

Her answer was, "Nothing, but opposites attract."

"Yes," I agreed, "Chemistry and Physics at work, my dear."

And honestly, it has worked for us for more than forty years.

Wright

So after earning your PhD degree, what motivated you or attracted you to seek a position in the agricultural industry?

LaPrade

The industry jobs were the top level jobs that paid the most money and when I got my master's degree I was supposed to interview with The Dow Chemical Company, which was one of the industry leaders, but I forgot about the interview appointment! I didn't even show up for the interview. The guy who did the interviews called me up and said, "I'll give you another chance. I know how busy graduate students are right now."

I thanked him for the opportunity and I said, "No, I know that your mind is made up since I missed the interview."

I now know that I made an incorrect judgment call; I should have done the interview. But in retrospect, if I had been hired, I would not have been treated to my final training, and that is to earn a PhD degree. After earning my PhD, I wanted to do research because I was leaning in that direction.

I ultimately actually did some pretty innovative things with a toxin called Aflatoxin. This toxin is produced by fungi that will affect all animals that ingest it into their bodies, causing sclerosis of the liver and or other cancerous tumors and lesions. My first grant provided by the United States Department of Agriculture was for $465,000 for a three-year program to study Aflatoxin, a contaminate of field corn being grown in South Carolina.

I was able to characterize fungal infection of field corn in South Carolina, getting two major Phytopath publications from this effort in a span of less than two years. The farmers who grew field corn there were better able to understand how to prevent Aflatoxin contamination after the study was completed. It ended being a rather simple cure for what appeared to be a devastating problem that had cost large farmers in South Carolina millions of dollars from having their field corn rejected at buying points across America.

I worked at the "Pee Dee," Experiment Station in Florence, South Carolina. I had established a well recognized research program and I had also established a field study to evaluate pesticide efficacy that attracted attention of quite a few pesticide industry representatives.

So I was recognized, and company representatives of Union Carbide Agricultural Products Division came and talked to me. They asked, "Have you ever considered going into industry?"

I said, "Yes."

They said, "We want to hire you."

"That sounds good," I replied. "Where is your main facility located?"

Their main facility was in Salinas, California, and I was scheduled to interview there in late August 1976. Now, Salinas is where lettuce is grown year-round. Lettuce is a cold-weather crop. That was about all I knew about the interview site. When I left Florence, it was probably 98 degrees, and when I arrived in California in the middle of the day, it was 60 degrees; I felt like I was at the North Pole! I seriously thought about re-boarding the plane, going back home, and bypassing my second opportunity to work for the agricultural industry! But there was someone there waiting for me when I got off of the plane. He had a sign with my name on it, which somehow impressed me and we continued on to the interview. The next day, the interview seemed to turn into an interrogation. I ended up talking with everybody in the company—I mean *everybody*—and it took all day.

Wright

At Union Carbide?

LaPrade

Yes, at their agricultural-product facility in Salinas, California. You see, Union Carbide is a big corporation and they were located on 5th Avenue in New York. They later moved up to Connecticut, but I didn't go there for the interview—they don't let job applicants see the board of directors before being hired—but I did I meet them later. I was taken to a very fancy restaurant on the coast of California that was less than fifty yards from the Pacific Ocean. Subsequently, I painted several scenes that I saw looking out over the Pacific Ocean, right out of the restaurant window. Hey, the Carbide guys knew how to impress a potential colleague. I didn't have a camera on this trip, but I have been said to have a photographic mind and most of my artwork is from memory. I was just so impressed with the Pacific Ocean that I kicked myself for not going to UCLA when I could have, after earning my MS degree at North Carolina State.

Union Carbide hired me on the spot and they gave me a raise. My new salary was 60 percent higher than what I had been making at Clemson. That was when my life really began in earnest.

Wright

So what were your most memorable accomplishments while you were working at Union Carbide and later with Rhone Poulenc?

LaPrade

Actually, while I was working with Union Carbide, it was easy to excel because I had a lot of experience working with plants and working with pesticides because my dad had worked for Virginia Tech. He worked at an experiment station and always conducted a pesticide test every year. He'd put the test products out and see which ones worked the best. He was one of the first Outsider Researchers who tested the Union Carbide product, Temik. (The term "Outsider Researcher" means a researcher not employed by Union Carbide.) When Dad first evaluated the product, it was formulated as a wetable powder. He sprayed it on apple trees, which is a definite no-no today, because it has an LD-50 of one—it's the most toxic active ingredient of any pesticide. I told my dad about that and he said, "Congratulations on being hired and thanks for reminding me about something that I should not have done!"

But the Union Carbide employees were good people; every one of them would do anything they could for me. Salinas was not where my family relocated because Union Carbide Agriculture Products Division relocated to Jacksonville, Florida, which made it that much more attractive to me.

My wife's family lived in Fort Myers, Florida, where I met June in 1968. We were currently living in South Carolina, where it was a two-day trip, or a heck of a long one-day trip to visit her parents. From Fort Myers, Jacksonville is just an easy one day trip, so we welcomed that move. Our son, John, was born in December 1976.

Union Carbide gave a commitment to hire me, saying that the new facility in Jacksonville would be ready by June 1977. When we made the move, John was about six months old and still in diapers. Although he was born in South Carolina and is technically a South Carolinian, but he thought that he was a Floridian because those were the people he grew up with, at least until he reached four years old. However, in industry, most employees don't stay very long in any one place.

I accepted a new opportunity when I was still working for Carbide and we all moved to Dothan, Alabama, in 1980. I was awarded the coveted "Outstanding Field Research and Development Representative" award for Union Carbide Agriproducts for 1981, company-wide. I received a new suitcase and a nice watch. I think that the Vice President was actually sending me a message, but it took a long time for me to get the true meaning! Thankfully, I had been an outstanding Field Research and Development Representative for that entire period of time and they recommended that Rhone Poulenc keep me on, after Carbide sold their pesticide business to R.P.

I was one of the lucky ones; many colleagues were not hired by Rhone Poulenc. For instance, my counterpart in Arkansas opened a used vehicle business and after the initial struggle, he made a small fortune and has now retired and passed the business on to his children.

There is a message here for our readers—there are times when we must face reality and take a new route to further our careers. That is what I did when I accepted a position with Auburn University, and I will talk about that before we finish our discussion. There is certainly a lesion to be learned there as well.

Now, back to your current question, David. When I was in Dothan working for Carbide, they only had four or five registered sellable products. They had Seven and Timik, two premier pesticides, and 2,4-D, and 2,4,5-T, two mediocre herbicides (which was later dropped), and several other herbicides and a plant growth regulator, Etheral, which hadn't been fully developed.

I covered all of Alabama, North Florida, and East Tennessee. Most of it was just over in Knoxville, but it was a bigger territory, requiring more travel than was comfortable, particularly with a young child at home. When they sold Union Carbide to Rhone Poulenc they asked me if I would work just in Alabama. I told them I'd be glad to—it was almost too good to be true!

I really did excel for Rhone Poulenc. I found several new uses for registered pesticides, one of which received a new patent that extended the original patent life. I increased sales by over 12 million dollars for the use of Etheral on cotton in the Southeast to be used as a cotton boll opener. It was an instant hit for all big cotton producers in North Alabama, and soon its popularity spread to Arkansas, Texas, and southern Oklahoma.

Wright

What were your most notable accomplishments that you believe you've made while working for Auburn University?

LaPrade

I brought an industry perspective to extension. I don't know what you know about university outreach education programs or the Extension Service, which is offered to the agricultural community through land grant developed schools of higher learning, but in 1876, all states were encouraged and received funding to establish colleges where agriculture would be taught. These colleges were funded to provide agricultural training to citizens who could not attend the college because they were busy farming and most had families.

The Alabama Cooperative Extension Service grew out of that effort, as was the case with most other state colleges, now called universities. County agents were put in place in most or all counties in Alabama at about the turn of the twentieth century. County agents typically hold a bachelor's or a master's degree in Agriculture or a related field. Because farming has become more complicated throughout the years, most Extension administrators have seen a need to supplement the knowledge of county agents and other county personnel with specialists who hold a PhD degree or the equivalent and with significant experience to assist the agents and other county personnel within certain disciplines and subject matter.

I am one of the specialists for the Alabama Cooperative Extension System at Auburn University located in Auburn, Alabama. Now, to answer your question. I was really honored with having been selected as coordinating one of the ten top environmental programs in the nation through extension in 1999. The program was Radon Awareness and Mitigation and I served as Program Director from 1995 through 2000. I got to go to Reno, Nevada, to present the program. My wife and I drove up to Lake Tahoe, California. It was Mother's Day when we got there. It was beautiful; it was a little crisp that day. We rented a car in Reno and drove over the mountains. It was such different and beautiful scenery than we'd ever seen before. The Reno and Lake Tahoe area isn't quite as glitzy as Las Vegas. June liked Reno and Lake Tahoe and she was really enjoying the trip.

The next morning we looked out the window and it had snowed. This was in May, the day after Mother's Day, in 1999. We were planning to look at Lake Tahoe because we had never seen anything remotely similar to that area in the Southeast where we had both lived all of our lives. The snow was a definite deterrent but, I said to June, "Oh let's try it. I grew up in Virginia, and have experienced driving in snow before." I convinced her, so we drove all the way around Lake Tahoe and I took some pictures. One of the most impressive scenes I saw was the one that I painted after returning home. I titled it "Lake Tahoe Looking West At Mid Afternoon." The mountains are in the background with snow and all the snow trails and skiing trails visible. That painting is currently on my Web site, in the "private art, not for sale" category.

Then, the next morning I thought I'd get up very early before the meeting started. I planned to take a picture of a sunrise scene, but the sunrise was not spectacular that morning. I waited until the afternoon and, since our hotel was on the east side of the lake, I did not have to go very far to see about the most beautiful sunset I have ever witnessed. This was the most beautiful scene that I saw on the entire trip. I painted what I saw when I returned home and titled it "Lake Tahoe At Sunset." It is also on my Web site in the same category as "Lake Tahoe looking West At Mid Afternoon."

I sent a small version down to The University of Florida, to a colleague, Dr. Carol Lehtola, as a gift to her for assisting me with the Farm Safety education program that I have been coordinating since 2001. Carol told me that she plans to take it to the University museum and see if they will want a free Gisele of that scene to add to their collection. I haven't heard from Carol lately or the University of Florida Museum.

Wright

So have you ever owned a business?

LaPrade

Oh, I've owned many businesses. The first business I ever owned was when I was working as a county agent in Naples, Florida. They had me doing specialist work as a landscape design and landscape guru who would help people who had problems with their landscape. I also served golf courses and commercial nurseries. It was a really good job, it just didn't pay very much. I had met June and we'd gotten married and I started a lawn care business. A fellow had come to me and had said, "I live in the Naples Country Club community. I just hired this guy to come by and mow our grass all summer and most of my neighbors are off in Canada and they don't know it but he isn't mowing anyone's grass. What can you do to help us?"

"Well," I said, "maybe I can find somebody who will take over. Maybe I can help the guy and see what's wrong."

I called him up and found out that he was a one-man operation with a lawnmower in the trunk of his car. When it didn't run, he didn't do anything—and it didn't run most of the time. But he billed customers anyway.

"That's going to get you in trouble," I told him.

"What the heck," he replied, "maybe you should get somebody else to do it." And I told him I would try.

He was the only person who would do that back then so I told him I'd start a lawn care business and he said, "Okay, go on and do it."

I took over about a dozen of his accounts, and told them what happened. They were pleased and I told the county agent. I didn't want to be fired for working for myself when I was supposed to be working for The University of Florida. My supervisor told me that if I worked on my lawn care business after hours it was fine with him.

I hired a couple of kids who would come and actually do the mowing. I had a truck they could use to carry the equipment and I showed them how to work the equipment. Business started booming, but it really went haywire after a little while. My first employees got jobs elsewhere, and I started running into equipment problems and more personnel problems.

"You're doing a little too much extra work here," the County Agent told me. "You'd better cut back."

"You know something," I said, "I'm making more money at this small business endeavor in one month than I make in six months for the county Extension Service." That was when my boss told me how he was bringing in extra income working as a consultant for Naples Tomato Growers, which I thought should be a part of his regular duties as County Agent Coordinator for Lee County, Florida. Anyway, we finally saw eye-to-eye—our university salaried job did not pay enough to live on even reasonably well.

I later did some consulting work for a large nursery, Palms Nursery in Naples, Florida. I did that on the side and kept my job initially but I soon retired from the

Florida Extension Service. I did landscape maintenance and got considerably more equipment and customers.

The business booms when the stock market is up and retirees have plenty of money, but when it's the other way around you really have to go hungry or find additional customers. So I decided that with a master's degree, I'd better go back to college if I was going to get my PhD degree, and that's what I decided to do from there.

I sold the landscape maintenance business for $34,000, which included the truck, the equipment, and some chemicals. It was worth the selling price because accounts receivable were in excess of $68,000 per year. All of the tangible products such as truck, and lawn equipment fertilizer, etc., with initial cost to me was approximately $26,000, but since the business had a potential of bringing in enough net profit to pay for the entire business in six months. That made it worth more than simply my original cost, and the buyer agreed.

I can think of at least ten other businesses that I have owned during the last forty-five years. I have owned a greenhouse business and a nursery business, a hardware business, a farm consulting business, a craft business, an energy efficiency business, a radon mitigation business, a painting contractor business, and there have been many others, including a small engine repair business. Some of these businesses have done quite well, netting more than $100,000 per year and some have been short-lived. One business mistake cost me more than $200,000 over a four-year period. That was the only franchise business I have ever owned. Most of these businesses were owned while working for the agricultural industry or a major university. The more time that can be spent by an owner pursuing success, and the more interested the owner is in the product or service being sold by the business, the better the chance for success of the operation. The time factor mentioned above limits a part-time owner's ability to succeed and will challenge one's psyche.

I know more about starting and growing a business now. I was taught in the "school of hard knocks" and, as we all have heard, it is a dear teacher. I think that "dear" in this context means expensive. I have learned a lot from past mistakes. I have never made the same mistake twice in any of the businesses I have owned; however, all businesses are different. I try to learn to spot potential problems and either head them off or cash out as soon as possible.

When I have sold any business I own, I have always told the prospective buyer what problem(s) I am facing so a decision on whether to buy or not can be done intelligently. My strengths and weaknesses are different from any other business owner. I try to find a good fit when buying a going business. If the new owner knows what to expect, he or she can have a chance to succeed and what he or she should have, must be superior to what other owners have. I must be absolutely convinced that my product will do what I say it will and it is the very best available at the retail price or I am not interested in pursuing that business.

I am looking forward to retirement when I may get enough time to pursue my most attractive desires for new businesses, such as opening a disco and offering dancing lesions, thus increasing the number of customers. I have often wondered what a disco club that does not sell hard liquor might be like, in terms of net profit. A license to sell whiskey in a night club is much more expensive than one that sells only beer and wine. I wonder how many patrons come to a disco mostly to dance and if they could do without hard liquor altogether.

At least, I am not shy! I have tried many unique ideas for business offerings. My video inventory business never had any clients! I now own a very high quality professional video camera. I suppose that is one of the advantages of starting a new and perhaps risky business.

Wright

So what do you think is your most personal accomplishment throughout your entire life?

LaPrade

Well, I have to go back to 1968. I think that meeting June is really my most outstanding accomplishment. These two events are the most meaningful and rewarding accomplishments in my life as well as finding God and Jesus.

Wright

So on the flip side, what about your most unforgettable failure?

LaPrade

It was my divorce from my first wife, Betty Sue, because I didn't see that coming. I knew we weren't getting along but I just didn't have time to spend with her when I was in graduate school at Raleigh, North Carolina State University. At Virginia Polytechnic Institute, I majored in Ornamental Horticulture and most of my electives were in production horticulture, which did not prepare me for advanced bio-chemistry, microbiology, or advanced botany courses. I had to try to make up for that at North Carolina State. I worked from sunup until midnight five days a week and I worked at least eight hours on Saturday. I went back to work Sunday after church for a few more hours of catch-up work.

Betty Sue was getting around and meeting new people, while I was struggling with graduate school. I just hope she met somebody she loves because I never heard anything more from her after the divorce. My only thought about her now is that I hope that she has what she wants and she is happy. I do plan to provide more details about our separation and contacts after we separated in my autobiography.

Wright

What do you hope and plan and expect to accomplish from this day forward—what's on the horizon for you?

LaPrade

I want to complete my autobiography. I want to write about my life's experiences because there have been so many things that have challenged me throughout my life. There have been many surprises; but I never backed up from a fight—I never did. You see, when I graduated from high school I had C's and D's. I was in a class of brilliant young people, but I wasn't. There were twenty-five in my class and I graduated either 23rd or 24th in the class. But I never studied either, never took a book home. I just loved sports and chasing girls; I had a good time.

There were several vocational career instructors assigned to assist our graduating class. Some of those people from some outside state agency came in and looked at our grades. They gave us a special test. They told me, "Jesse, we can't fully figure out what you should and shouldn't do after graduation."

"Why is that?" I asked.

"Well," came the reply, "if you try to go to college you're going to be very disappointed. You've got some talent to learn and you could go to technical school, learn electronics, or you could go in the military. These appear to be your best options."

Well, the military was out as far as I was concerned; I had no interest in that. I did go to technical school when I first graduated from high school. The school was located in Washington, D.C. In the summer of 1961 I attended and learned basic electronics and electrical motor technology, but knowledge about electronics was limited to vacuum tube circuitry and wired circuits, which is not all that applicable to current electronics theory today.

I later earned a degree in general contracting, with hands-on work in plumbing and electrical wiring—house wiring and commercial wiring. That only took one quarter for me to complete. I wanted to take it and move on, perhaps trying college after I had completed training for a trade.

When I attended trade school, I wasn't really that pleased with the caliber of people who were around me. I thought the other students were low class and I thought I should go to college. I asked my brother if he thought I could make it in college. He told me, "Hell no, you can't make it in college."

You see, my brother got his bachelor's degree in chemical engineering. He earned A's and B's, and then he went to Washington D.C., where he attended night classes at George Washington University. Before I knew it, he got his law degree, passed the Virginia and D.C. Bar exam on the first try, and right now he and his wife live very comfortably, holding property in Washington, D.C., Miami, Florida, and San Diego, California. Some of his property is income producing rental property. He and his wife have done very well.

I had thought throughout my life, up until I was fifty-three years old, that John was my biological brother. I found out that I was adopted by Lucy and John Lovelace LaPrade because their child had been still-born. I learned this in a letter from my dad that I read on December 24, 1993.

I couldn't ask, "John, are you really my brother?" A hint that we weren't related was the fact that I've never had asthma. Everybody in the LaPrade family had asthma—my mother, my father, my brother, and my sister—but I've never had asthma. I always had blinding migraine headaches and they've never had migraines. My blood type is B negative and nobody in the LaPrade family has that blood type. My biological mother and biological father both had B negative blood type.

My brother, John, challenged me when he said that I could not complete a college training program. I just had to prove him wrong! We ended up betting fifty dollars that I could get accepted in a college somewhere and that I would successfully earn a degree. That was the first bet that I won from my brother. My brother has always been special to me, and the letter from my dad did not change that at all!

The LaPrade family was kind to me for the most part, and I am very grateful to have been allowed to be a part of it. Oh, Lucy overdid a whipping that she gave me once—or maybe twice. I do appreciate being disciplined; it has helped me survive others' attempts to discipline me throughout the years. I may have committed murder if someone I did not know had treated me the way Lucy did when I was about eleven years old. If it hadn't been for Lucy, I could have spent most of my life on death row. I do think that is worth something. From a positive standpoint, Lucy always wanted me to have everything necessary to survive, and she did her best to make sure that I got *all* of everything she wanted me to have—particularly her whoopings.

Wright

Well your life story is going to be really interesting to read when it comes out; I can't wait to get it. I really do appreciate all the time you've spent with me to answer these questions today. This is going to enlighten a lot of people and maybe help people make decisions to stick it out as you did such as going from someone telling you, you can't go to college and coming out with a PhD degree. That's something in itself.

LaPrade

I went to my first high school class reunion in 2006. Now, I don't know what I expected to see. I thought I'd see a bunch of young people. I hadn't seen them since I graduated. I could recognize them all but they looked rather old.

"What's happened to you all?" I said.

"Well, it's been a long time," said Carlton Hayden.

I soon found out that there were three of us out of twenty-five graduates who went on to earn a PhD degree—Jesse Lee East, Ellen Bryant, and me. Ellen is married now and I do not know what Ellen's husband's surname is, but Bryant was her family name.

Now, Jesse Lee wanted to compete with me in school, but he didn't want to compete with me on the football field; he didn't want to have anything to do with football.

I took chemistry and the high school coach taught it. I wanted to impress the coach that I could learn. I got an A, and Jesse Lee got an A. The coach taught biology as well, and Jesse Lee and I both got an A. But I didn't care for math or French. I could give less of a hoot about those two subjects, but English came natural. So I got a B or C in English all the time. I hated history with a passion. Right now, I thoroughly enjoy watching the History Channel. I guess it has a lot to do with how a subject is presented and how much visualization is involved. In my autobiography you can read about how I was able to bargain my way with the head of the Department of Horticulture at Blacksburg VPI to substitute History of Art instead of taking the second quarter of Western Civilization. The department head's name was Dr. Wesley Judkins. I definitely owe the gentleman a debt of gratitude! Western Civilization was a monumental stumbling block for me that Dr. Judkins eliminated for me.

Now, Ellen and I got to know each other better while we were in grade school at Chatham. We used to see each other during recess, which by the way was my favorite subject. Ellen told me one day that I looked like a cute monkey. Now, nobody else at Chatham had ever told me that. As I now reflect back on those good old days, I can actually see the resemblance in the mirror that Ellen told me about; only, today that is a definite compliment. At my age, to look like a cute little monkey sounds right darn good! It now appears that Ellen may well have been the most observant person in Chatham or that maybe a lot of folks look somewhat like our true ancestors. As they say on FOX news, "Now that you have the facts, you make the call."

Wright

Well, Jesse this has really been great. I really do appreciate your being with us here today.

LaPrade

I enjoy you folks. You're doing a lot for the community. You're doing a lot for all of us who want to reach people and help them. In fact, I have a little special program that I'm going to do for the Methodist Church, which I joined back in September. It is a little bit about my life and how I came to God and Jesus. It's going to be a chapter in my autobiography. I have a photographic mind. I don't remember words on paper—don't misunderstand—and I can't remember a road map that well. It's only the things that made a difference to me in my life, and there have been a lot of those events fully committed to memory in living color!

Wright

Today we have been talking with Dr. Jesse LaPrade. Jesse has been a successful agricultural professor since 1974 after earning a PhD in Post Harvest Plant Pathology from The University of Florida. He is currently a full-time Auburn University professor and has earned many accolades for his more than nineteen years of continued service.

Jesse, thank you so much for being with us today on *Yes You Can!*

LaPrade

Thank you sir and good luck. I am looking forward to being a part of the book, *Yes You Can!* I look forward to reading it and just revel in all of the great experiences and wisdom offered by so many great and talented professionals who are writing a chapter as well!

 **Dr. Jesse LaPrade** has been a successful Agricultural Professional since 1974, after earning a PhD degree in Post-Harvest Plant Pathology from The University of Florida. Jesse has made numerous Agricultural Research discoveries, most dealing with the most potent known naturally occurring animal toxin, Aflatoxin. Jesse spent more than thirteen years in the agricultural industry, doing amazing accomplishments for both Union Carbide Agricultural Products Division and later for the French-based company, Rhone Poulenc. Jesse was named "Outstanding Field Development Representative" for Union Carbide in 1980 and went on to gain fame as their most effective Field Development Representative by bringing more than twelve million dollars yearly in new sales to the company by finding new uses for registered pesticide products.

Jesse is currently a full-time Auburn University Professor and has many accolades to show for his more than seventeen years of service to academia, including having designed a national award-winning educational program, "Radon Awareness." Jesse is author or co-author of more than 145 technical journals on subjects ranging from radon, indoor air quality, environmental education, global warming, and agricultural safety training and program design. Jesse has delivered more than three hundred technical speeches since September 2, 1990, when he began his Auburn University career.

Jesse's most precious "hobby" is painting seascapes and butterflies and was initiated into the Kennedy Center's "World Class Artist" status in 1995. Jesse says "I am a folk artist without any formal training. If you are interested in my life, from birth to this day, you can read a lot more on my Web site."

Dr. Jesse LaPrade

Renaissance Folk Art and Motivational Speaking
150 Benwood Circle
Auburn, AL 36832
334-209-0544
jesse@seascapesbyjesse.com
www.seascapesbyjesse.com

CHAPTER ELEVEN

Deliberate Lives:

Navigating Life's Transitions

by Dawn Robertson

THE INTERVIEW

David Wright (Wright)

Today we're talking with Dawn Robertson. Dawn has more than twenty years experience helping organizations and the people in them deal with changes and transitions—large and small. As Founder of Strategic Change Resources, she guides senior teams to work with strategy, focus, and culture. She is a graduate of Oxford HEC's Master program in Consulting and Coaching for Strategic Change. She has developed a road map for deliberate transitions based on her researched thesis. She is a sought-after coach, facilitator, and speaker who has worked for global companies in more than fifteen countries with clients from more than thirty countries.

Dawn, welcome to *Yes You Can!*

Dawn Robertson (Robertson)

Thank you, David.

Wright

So what differentiates people who navigate life transitions with ease and confidence from those who do not?

Robertson

Well, I've been asking myself this question for years, in multiple forms. In my search for understanding the *whys* of transitions, I wanted to unearth and identify what separated people who are able to move through these psychological changes with ease and confidence and to gain an understanding of what makes them tick. How is it that some people seem hardwired to move through transitions with a type of easy grace?

Before we begin, I think it's necessary that we clarify what we mean when we use the word "transition." Many people use the words "transition" and "change" interchangeably. William Bridges, who wrote the seminal book, *Transitions,* in 1979, states that change is situational, while transition is the psychological underpinnings of change—either one we are currently going through, or one we are anticipating. It is the contract we have with the situation or the person involved in change that is actually the transition. Dealing successfully with these psychological aspects of change is an internal journey into new territory and, like most significant journeys, requires courage and perseverance. I think that's an important differentiation.

Very little literature on the topic of transition exists, and what is available, such as Bridges' work, is not research-based. Hermina Ibarra's work, although research-based, is about self-initiated career transitions, and doesn't address my question.

Based on my research, which involved almost seventy people, I've learned that people who are able to navigate easily through planned or unplanned transitions know a lot about themselves. They are "Life Navigators" who live deliberate and authentic lives. My research revealed that they are consciously aware of:

- Who they are
- What they stand for
- What their aspirations are and have been
- Their goals and what will move them forward
- How to see things from others' perspectives
- Knowing that they always have choices

Whether their transition is one they have wished for or one they hoped they would never have to face; one they've been excitedly planning or one they've worried about; one they have looked forward to or one that came out of the blue; a work transition or a personal one, they are clear about and can answer the following questions with little or no difficulty:

- Who am I?
- How did I get here?
- What do I want?
- What have I learned?

These are people who look at life through lenses of optimism, appreciation, happiness, and well-being. They are connected to family, friends, and their community, savor life's experiences, and face challenges head-on on with determination. They live deliberately grounded in the present while always looking to the future, balancing ambiguities daily.

Somehow, at an early age, these Life Navigators began the process of establishing goals—ones that they may or may not achieve. They are self-motivated and have a vision of who they might become and how they might get there. They may not have either means or access, but their visions seem to be enough to move them forward.

More than any other factor that has surfaced in my research, successful transitioners believe that *they always have a choice*, no matter what. Much like individual studies in survivor research, what separates those who survive and thrive when going through transitions from those who don't is the ability to look at a negative experience of loss and turn it into a positive outcome and learning experience. Harvard professor Tal Ben-Shahar believes that having goals to focus on and aim toward helps people move forward, and forward motion is essential to navigating transitions.

Wright

So how does the type of transition influence successful transition navigation?

Robertson

A driving goal for my research was to identify key elements of successful transitions and to create a road map to help people move through their transitions with ease and confidence.

What I've learned is that the process for dealing with transitions depends on whether the transition is planned or unplanned, and not so much the type of the personal versus work. The differentiator is whether someone initiates the transition—deciding to go back to school, to get married, to change careers, to move—or whether the transition is imposed or unplanned, as in losing a job, death of a loved one, or a breakup that wasn't anticipated. This difference between a deliberate, self-initiated transition and an accidental, other-imposed one is quite significant. It can be compared to the difference between jumping off a cliff and being pushed off a cliff. Both the time and emotions involved differ when processing and living through planned and unplanned transition. Recognizing and knowing the difference between the two types is critical to addressing the transition and planning appropriately.

Let's look at how time influences both planned and unplanned transition.

For planned transitions, time is elastic, stretching to meet the individual's needs. In a planned transition, a significant amount of time is spent up front in a musing phase with a sense that something needs changing. There may be a feeling of discomfort, unease, or a yearning for something different that sets the planned transition in motion. This phase may begin on an unconscious level and last anywhere from six months to several years. Once consciously aware of this desire or concern, Life Navigators begin addressing their transition process in two specific ways:

First, they begin to reflect on who they are and what they stand for. They can spend weeks or sometimes months answering questions that center on the issue of, "Who am I?" These questions might not be shared with anyone or might be shared with someone close and trusted. To be most effective, the questions and answers need to be recorded in some way—notes to self, tape-recorded, or witnessed by a close and trusted ally. The answers do not have to be long; however, they must be truthful and based on deep self-knowledge. All successful Life Navigators do this—and they seem to find a method that works best for them.

Second, Life Navigators recognize their autonomy. As soon as they are consciously aware of their desire for change, they take ownership of the internal and external process and assume responsibility for where they are taking their lives and how they show up while doing so. They recognize that they have put this process of change in motion and are willing to devote their time, energy, and resources to explore the multiple options and opportunities that face them. They leap willingly into their future.

For those who are going through unplanned transitions, time is completely different. People who are pushed into transition and thrown off the cliff have no time to prepare.

There is no time for unconscious contemplation or for deliberate explorations of any kind. Those in unplanned transitions move straight into survival mode. There is no time for anything other than protecting themselves while hurtling into the unknown.

What differentiates those who do well going through unplanned and unsought-after transitions is that they, too, ground themselves by starting with autonomy, owning their situation, and answering the question, "How did I get here?" While they do take time to deal with the shock of the situation and mourn what was, they consciously regroup and plan how to move forward relatively quickly. They use the initial time in freefall to begin learning from the experience and to craft a narrative or story that they immediately begin telling themselves and trusted others.

Wright

So what attributes or competencies are essential to deliberate navigation?

Robertson

Life Navigators, those people who move through their transitions with ease and confidence, share many commonalities; however, the starting point is always the same. They ground themselves in autonomy and recognize that they have choices in how they deal with life. My research revealed that deliberately moving through transitions, either planned or unplanned, requires competency and skills in eight areas. While each is important, autonomy—the intrinsic belief that you, as the person going through the transition, have a choice—stands out as a fundamental. It is almost a prerequisite for navigating transitions. Without this belief in choice it is hard to focus on the future.

Survival literature reveals that no matter how dreadful the conditions, those who survived believed that they had choice about how they focused their energy and their mind. Is it any wonder that the bedrock skill for successful transitions is autonomy? The other seven of the eight attributes leading to navigating transitions are:

1. *Comfort with ambiguity*—the ability to deal with the unknown by constant recalibration
2. *Empathy*—the ability to understand and share others' feelings
3. *Future orientation*—a willingness to spend time envisioning the future
4. *Goal-setting*—the object of a person's ambition or effort
5. *A learning mindset*—seeking to gain knowledge through reflection, study, or experience

6. *Self-awareness*—conscious knowledge of one's character feelings, motives, and desires
7. *Self-motivation*—internally driven to do or achieve something based on one's own enthusiasm or interest without needing external pressure

Each of these attributes is critically important and operates with the other seven as a cluster of competencies, yet without the concept and imbedded belief of autonomy—a deep belief that each of us has a choice about how we show up in life—the other seven cannot function properly.

Wright

So how do values affect transitions?

Robertson

The ability to live a deliberate life starts with unraveling personal values from parental values. Parental values lead to parental expectations, which are often internalized by children without conscious thought. For Life Navigators, an early differentiator seems to be making a conscious choice in electing their personal values. It doesn't seem to matter if parental values are adopted wholly, or if they are a variant of those elected values, or if they are rejected in favor of some other set of elected values entirely, it is in the choosing that people gain autonomy. It is the choosing that puts individuals in charge of their own lives and causes them to create their own expectations.

While this critical decision point can be embraced at any time, it gets harder as people get older. Letting go of one way of being is a serious undertaking that requires focus and effort, and may be too big an adjustment to make voluntarily and independently. Some people may be hardwired to make this choice early because of their drive and desire to learn. Certain brain types (those more curious and interested in conceptualizing about the future) may make this choice early because of a predisposition toward learning. For all others, it takes determination and significant inner work.

Deliberate Life Navigators are able to describe their personal values using crisp, precise language. They are aware of how their values influence their roles and identities and, whether inspirational or aspirational, they use their values to build their lives. Values are linked directly to their personal goals, guiding principles, and decisions during transitions. They create transparency in their lives by acknowledging their personal values and making visible their belief system that allows them to make choices and decisions more intentionally as they move forward.

Wright

So what are the underlying aspects of living a deliberate life?

Robertson

While the importance of autonomy cannot be overstated in describing what is necessary to leading an authentic, deliberate life, three additional components are critical to moving through life deliberately, with confidence and ease. They are: making time for reflection, tending to life's key relationships, and matching personal intent and action. Let's take a look at how Life Navigators address each of these components.

Making time for reflection

This may be the most difficult for people who are used to action. The Conference Board has cited the need for executives to reflect more in order to lead their complex organizations. With our myriad of digital/electronic devices, very few people take a *timeout*—send themselves to a place of contemplation and review, or for exploration and rehearsal. Without such *timeouts*, we ricochet from thing to thing, mostly in a less than purposeful way. Yet, without reflection there can be no learning. With the skill of reflection, people expand mental and emotional flexibility, build comfort with ambiguity, and practice empathy, which is developed from looking at situations and experience through other people's perspectives.

Reflection is a place for practice—where pre-plays and replays come alive and enrich our ability to connect with others. My study of the *whys* of transition led to exploring self-development, socialization, and role identity, as well as the aforementioned personal attributes and happiness theories. All contribute to the understanding of how Life Navigators function. What they all do consistently is take time out for reflection. They make this choice because they believe reflection creates room—room to grow, room to be, room to deal with life's issues, large and small. What reflection means to each Life Navigator is highly personal, defined specifically and consciously—deliberately selected because it meets their individual needs.

Tending to life's key relationships

In my research, every person indicated that valued others were involved in some way throughout his or her transitions. Deliberate Life Navigators pay attention to their relationships. They are clear about what relationships mean—they see them as two-way connections. They keep relationships alive, not just when they need them, but as part of how they live their lives. They have friends, family, colleagues, neighbors, paid professionals, and counselors—trusted advisors from whom they seek advice and, in turn, advise. They are generous with their time in sharing their skills and ideas, and support others going through transitions without judgment. They celebrate others' successes; they listen and commiserate when things don't go as planned.

When going through their own transitions, these deliberate navigators ask for and receive the help they need. In the past, they have been there for others and now reach out to many of the same people, moving from being the supporter to being supported. Being vulnerable is another aspect of their personality that they openly display. Trusted advisors or valued others provide support, comfort, hand-holding, perspective, sounding boards, role models, thinking partners, advice, connections, and laughter. They witness the changes Life Navigators are making and living through. While all of this seems perfectly logical and just a common everyday way of living, it's surprising how few people nurture and tend to relationships until they are in crisis. What's distinct about Life Navigators is that they tend to their relationships *all* the time.

Matching personal intent and actions

Living a deliberate life requires that people show up intentionally, not accidentally. Being with family, helping in the community, and developing others are some of the ways they really spend their time. They do not give lip service to some stated ideal. They arrange their lives in such a way that the two or three things most important to them are acted upon. Sometimes doing so costs them and keeps them from doing something they would rather do.

They treat time as a valuable resource that cannot be replenished and live accordingly. This activity alone sets Life Navigators apart. Their commitment to do what they say is important to them and does not change when they're going through transition—whether the transition is planned or unplanned or when things don't work out or when things go exceedingly well.

Their priorities never vary. They stay focused on what they believe is important in their lives. Being self-aware and being able to manage oneself are critical to this aspect of living deliberately, as is the recognition that everyone has a choice about how to use one's time. Control belongs to each of us. Individual intentions spring from values and guiding principles unique to each of us, and are core to deliberate living.

Wright

What about the emotions involved?

Robertson

Remember that transitions are the psychological aspect of change, and almost all change is emotional. Certainly all transitions are. That said, it is important to understand that transitions involve the end of something—letting go of someone or something or a behavior or a way of being.

Both planned and unplanned transitions tackle the same range of emotions including: anger, fear, shock, anxiety, excitement, and pride. With the exception of shock, the emotions are the same for both types of transitions, but the sequencing of those emotions is different.

Unplanned transitions start with shock. Without thought and reflection, individuals reacting to unplanned transitions may begin their transition process thinking they have no choice and are victims in some way. If the issue of personal choice is not addressed, no matter the severity of the situation, people can remain in the victim state that is neither helpful nor healthy. Getting stuck in this victim "dead zone" prolongs time spent at the front end of the transition process. While some of this time is spent mourning or grieving for what was, not coming to terms with and moving on from shock and anger prevents the healing process of letting go and moving forward. Life Navigators proceed through this aspect purposefully, with more ease and confidence, turning a negative experience into a learning experience.

Planned transitions start with excitement and are resolutely set in motion either to move away from something or to move toward something future focused, more aspirational in nature—something not known but only glimpsed.

While planned transitions are exciting and determined, frustration and anger sometimes surface when planning goes awry or when the pace of getting to the new is not fast enough. Still, with intentional focus, all of these psychological alterations can be managed with confidence by relying on others, sharing emotions, and asking for help. People move through each emotion at their own pace. Even in unplanned transitions, people feel a sense of excitement and pride as they begin to realize a different future and move toward something new.

Wright

Are there differences in dealing with change and transitions based on age or life stages or gender?

Robertson

The answer is both yes and no. A premise and hypothesis of my research was that differing life stages would affect the success of transitions, believing that how people handle transitions and what they deal with would be different based on age stages. What I discovered is that in each of the five age groups that I studied—22–32, 33–43, 44–54, 55–65, and 66–76—there were some similarities and some differences. Looking at the similarities, the major themes that surfaced across all age groups were:

- All transitions influenced both personal and work whether they were planned or unplanned. The key point here is that transitions cannot be walled off or isolated. There is no quarantine of emotion during transition; emotions related to transitions spill over into every facet of life.
- While the majority of transitions reported in my research were in the past, it is important to recognize the emotional affect of transitions, even after completion. Described in highly emotional terms, the difficulties of the transition were the same for all ages and genders and had two major components: 1) dealing with the new, visioning something in the future for themselves or others involved; and 2) overcoming a piece of the past, dealing with their understanding and definition of who they are, or were (loss).
- As mentioned before, everyone going through transitions had valued others whom they were able to rely on for help during their transition
- The average duration of transitions is about six to eighteen months, although some can last two to five years, especially when they are self-imposed.

Even though my research participants were clustered by age groups, almost all of the transitions they spoke about took place in the years between thirty-eight and forty-eight, with the average age being forty-two.

Gilbert Brim, a researcher who studies midlife, and has been a recipient of the MacArthur Foundation Grant, believes that people know by the age forty-five whether they will reach their ultimate personal or professional goal. In my research, the majority of the participants' career transitions were planned and set in motion by the individuals themselves. There may be an unconscious urge to precipitate transitions that will avoid failure or that will directly address it, proactively.

The main differences that related to age group had to do with transition focus. The twenty-two through thirty-two-year-old group looked at their financial independence/freedom. The thirty-three through forty-three-year-old group looked at who they were and creating a vision for their lives. The forty-four through fifty-four-year-old group realized that they owned the responsibility for their decisions and those that affected their family. The fifty-five through sixty-five-year-old group was dealing with a new life and having new people in their lives. The sixty-six through seventy-six-year-old group was dealing with the day-to-day uncertainty of their lives.

There were also some differences based on gender. Men and women approach transitions differently, or at least report on them differently, both within their age groups as well as across them. Men talk about professional work-related transitions to a much greater extent. Women speak about professional and personal transitions in close to equal measure. Women are more likely to plan their transitions, whether personal or professional, and are also more likely to report on current transitions, while men talk about transitions that have been completed in the past. Whatever the reasons for these differences, men and women would most likely benefit by sharing their transition knowledge and experiences.

Wright

Dawn, do you have any tips or techniques for dealing with the complex problem of transitions?

Robertson

Yes, as a matter of fact, I do. It is called the Transition Navigation Star, a tool I've developed to assist people in creating a personal road map to work through their changes, either personal or professional, planned or not. It is made up of four sets of reflective questions to be answered by the person going through or anticipating a transition. Not for the faint of heart, these questions are designed to create an honest, internal conversation that can also be shared with valued others. While the questions start with the present, they represent the future by asking people to choose how they want to show up as they move forward. The future orientation is critical to successful transitions.

That's what's so important about the Transition Navigation Star—it serves as a virtual compass with its four navigational points assisting in successful passage through each of the four main aspects of transition. Each aspect addresses a pivotal question:

- North: Who am I?
- South: How did I get here?
- East: What do I want?
- West: What have I learned?

Wright

So what's different about this model?

Robertson

Most people facing change and transition first think about what they want or where they want to go. My model has two main differences. One is that my model starts with understanding the origin of the transition. None of the previous models or any research has addressed the difference in timing between planned versus unplanned transitions. Knowing who began the process and the trigger point for the start distinguishes this model from others. The metaphor I have used previously in describing this differentiation is either gleefully jumping off a cliff (picture bungee jumping) versus being pushed off that same cliff.

As people tumble through their planned or unplanned transitions, they land on an aspect of the Navigation Star, which they can use as a guide. Where they land is totally dependent on whether theirs is a planned or unplanned transition. People who leap into their transition and their future land on the northern aspect of a compass, which addresses the question, "Who am I?" For many people, it would be a review of what they have been addressing in the months leading up to their leap. For others, it may be the first time they've actually thought about their values and where those values come from.

If people are pushed off the cliff, they land on the southern point of the compass, which is the balancing aspect to the values of the north. Since people pushed into transition will be dealing with shock as the starting emotion, they need a chance to make sense out of what has happened to them. They need to gather the facts. They need to be able to answer the question, "How did I get here?"

There are two possible paths that can be taken in answering this question. One way is entering into the blame game where people explode in anger or dissolve in tears over what has been done to them. They will need time to sort out their emotions, tell their stories, vent, and clear before moving on.

Another way of dealing with being pushed off a cliff is the way that deliberate Life Navigators do. They begin the process of coming to terms with where they are first. They do not blame anyone. They do not spend time lamenting their loss. While they may get emotional, they do so in a way that mourns their loss without blame. Then they assess the situation, gather facts, and begin looking to the future. They, too, tell their story, but only by looking to the future and owning responsibility for moving forward.

Working through this north/south access is essential to successful transitions. Those in planned transitions start by being clear about how they define themselves internally for their grounding, before they move to the southern point where they will deal with relational self-awareness. Conversely, those thrown into their transitions will have to make sense of their situations first—their grounding—before they can deal with who they are. Many people pushed into transitions lose their identity and must either regain or redefine who they are. This north/south access creates a support beam to the rest of the Transition Navigation Star; it is the pillar that underpins all options to be explored. This deep internal work is the second difference of my model.

Once a person in transition has moved through these north/south aspects, he or she can tackle the question that most people want to start with: "What do I want?" Located on the right (eastern) side of the Transition Navigation Star, this aspect of the model looks at internal motivation. Almost all the research—done by other experts and my own fieldwork—identify self-motivation as the key to successful transition. While there is a belief that self-motivation is a hardwired, intrinsic aspect of personality, I have a contradictory belief that, with focus and effort, it is an attribute that can be adopted to enhance transitions.

With a coach or trusted other as a mirror, people can practice taking a few tentative steps towards their future. With such a witness, they can imagine themselves moving forward into an unknown territory and practice before they try out new ways of being. They gain confidence through building on their initial sense of accomplishment. That is why, if internal motivation is not a natural part of an individual's personality, the eastern aspect of the Transition Navigation Star process is where individuals can benefit the most from the interactions with others going through transition, whether in the same age group or not.

Those in the "What do I want?" aspect of their transition will find it helpful to seek out support groups or networks to share and discuss their evolving ideas. Having a group to go to for support and to use as a sounding board for testing potential hypotheses reassures those for whom self-motivation is new and different. Knowing that everyone in the group is dealing with difficult changes in his or her life provides both solace and courage. Once their confidence is strong enough to take action, they can come back to the group to report progress, reinforcing their new experience and potential skills. Most self-help groups operate with a version of this process, and it is the reason that I believe workshops for transitions will work as well, especially with those in the same age cohort. Of course, seeking out trusted others will work as well, but doesn't provide the wider variety of ideas.

Whether the transition is planned or unplanned, one can benefit from envisioning a new or different future through some form of scenario-planning or storytelling. And it is this eastern junction that has the power to transform lives. The ability to see the future, to dream, to invent another way of being is a gift for people going through transitions to give themselves. And, if people work in groups to explore their future, this forward look is a gift that can be given to others as well. Again, the power here is rooted in choice. Trying on different futures is like having an eraser and a giant chalkboard—draw another future, get some feedback, alter it, or get rid of it. These are great skills for personal transition and great skills for organization-wide transitions.

"What have I learned?" is the question on the western point of the Transition Navigation Star. In moving from the east side of the Transition Navigation Star to the west, we move from a creative brain function to a more analytical one. This phase starts with what has been learned. Essentially, the reflective, western aspect of the compass can send the user back to any one of the other three navigation points to refine and refit their current reality. This is the place of learning.

Empathy, the ability to see the situation from the other person's point of view, is critical to the person moving through change and transition, not just being able to look at what is happening to others, but also having the curiosity to do so. No one going through transition is totally alone. Having the capacity to realize this and explore others' thoughts and ideas about the transition experience keeps individuals from becoming totally myopic about the experience. Empathy, too, resides on the west side of the star.

The east/west access of the Transition Navigation Star is a place where options for choice are entertained. It is a place for possibility, where storytelling and imagining play out as the first step forward. However, if the transitioner has not answered the grounding questions of the north/south access—"Who am I?" and "How did I get here?"—the exploratory work embedded in the question "What do I want?" may not be answerable in an actionable way. The solid base of values and self-awareness is essential to support the new way of being. It is a constraining factor that may need an intervention of support, such as a coach or valued other, to pull or even push the transitioners to do the fundamental baseline work of values and self-awareness.

Wright

Does the Navigation Star just apply to individuals?

Robertson

No, actually it works just as well with organizations going through change. While executives in an organization think they are simply closing an office, the employees are dealing with the psychological aspects of change. They're wondering if they have a job, if they will work with the same group of people, where they will get lunch now that they're not near their favorite coffee shop, and what it will be like after the office is gone.

While we know that organizations change one person at a time, most organizational change efforts neglect the role that leaders play during times of change. Leaders must be deliberate in the way they communicate the changes and in the way they involve and enlist people to come on board. They must give each individual a chance to explore his or her personal, psychological reaction to the impending change. Without this opportunity, people spin and frequently get stuck in reaction mode, blaming others and not taking ownership for what they can control.

This is no small matter, given the complexity of today's organizations, but the cost is stunningly high for not doing so. According to John Kotter, 85 percent of companies fail to achieve needed transformations and, according to *Fortune* magazine, between 50 to 80 percent of change efforts in Fortune 1000 companies fail.

By using the Transition Navigation Star, leaders and organizations can recognize and acknowledge whether the change and its counterpart transition is one that their employees have put in play or one that was visited upon them. Should it be an unplanned one from the employees' point of view, each person will most likely be starting at the south end of the compass. They must be given the opportunity to gather the facts and make choices about how they individually want to proceed. Without this involvement, employees subjected to unplanned transition are left to feel like victims—afraid and worried.

Deliberate leadership recognizes the importance of engagement, and structures interventions and communications for involvement and choice, helping employees make the psychological shift from "not in control" to "in control" with a focus on the future. This is not some touchy-feely idea, but one based on solid research and tied to the concept that up to 70 percent of professional work is discretionary. We are talking about engaging employees during times of change and treating them like the adults they are by giving them choice and increasing productivity sooner rather than later, which makes good business sense.

Wright

Anything else you think I should know about deliberately navigating life's transitions?

Robertson

I believe that if people have a clearer understanding of the *whys* of individual transitions, we can approach major and minor changes knowing how we might act or react. The cost of not knowing is one of distraction and of time. Since there is no way to wall off personal or professional transitions from one another, they overlap and bleed into one another, reducing focus and energy. When we are armed with the right questions to ask ourselves and know how to involve key people in our immediate circle, we can move through our transitions in a shorter period of time with less disruption and greater confidence. And always remember: at every stage in the process of change, we can decide how we want to show up and engage in the situation. It is always a choice—our choice—in living a deliberate life.

Wright

So what is the single most important thing to remember about transitions?

Robertson

We can all be deliberate Life Navigators—people who calmly move through transitions whether they are planned or not. To do so, we must believe that we always have a choice in our transitions, and use our values to guide us every step of the way. We must mindfully select significant others to involve, and make time for and nourish those relationships. By doing so, each of us can move through the immense number of changes that modern life presents with less anxiety, more ease, and more confidence.

Wright

Well, what a great conversation, and based on research, that's great. Sometimes I talk to people with opinions.

Robertson

Yes, this is solid new research, which I believe can make a difference in people's lives.

Wright

I really appreciate the time you have spent with me Dawn. It's been very enlightening. You've given me a lot of things to think about.

Robertson

It's been fun! I appreciate your time as well, David.

Wright

Today we've been talking with Dawn Robertson. Dawn is Founder of Strategic Change Resources. She works with senior teams to develop strategy, focus, and culture. She has developed a unique road map for deliberate transitions based on her research thesis. I don't know about you readers but I'm going to listen to her; she sounds like she knows what she is talking about.

Dawn, thank you so much for being with us today on *Yes You Can!*

Robertson

Thank you very much, David.

Dawn Robertson has more than twenty years' experience helping organizations and the people in them deal with changes and transitions—large and small. As Founder of Strategic Change Resources, she guides senior teams to work with strategy, focus, and culture. Dawn is a graduate of Oxford HEC's Master program in Consulting and Coaching for Strategic Change. She has developed a road map for deliberate transitions based on her researched thesis. She is a sought-after coach, facilitator, and speaker who has worked for global companies in more than fifteen countries, with clients from more than thirty countries.

Dawn Robertson

6 Green Beach Drive
Rowayton, CT 06853
203-831-9001
drobertson@strategicchange.us
www.strategicchange.us

CHAPTER TWELVE

The Co-Creation of Conflict

by Liz Berney

David Wright (Wright)

Today we're talking with Dr. Liz Berney. Liz is the President of Berney Associates, Training and Organization Development. She provides consulting, speaking, training, and facilitation services for clients including Bill and Melinda Gates Foundation, Coca-Cola, Tropicana, Baldridge Quality Program, AT&T, Fannie Mae, John F. Kennedy Center for Performing Arts, the Marriott, MCI, the U.S. Environmental Protection Agency, and the U.S. House of Representatives. Her areas of expertise include conflict management, interests-based negotiation, change management, and team development. Liz has taught for the American Management Association, the Accelerated MBA program at George Washington University, and Executive Programs at the University of Maryland's School of Business and Management. At Georgetown University, she founded, designed, and directed the Organization Development Certificate Program. At George Mason University, she was a tenure track psychology professor. Liz has a BA in Psychology with honors from Yale University and an MA and PhD in Industrial Organizational Psychology from the University of Maryland where she was awarded a Teaching Excellence Award.

Dr. Liz Berney, welcome to *Yes You Can!*

Liz Berney (Berney)

Thank you.

Wright

So what originally got you interested in studying conflict?

Berney

I wrote my dissertation on mergers and acquisitions because I was fascinated with the growing number of these integrations with high failure rates. Most fail because of cultural differences among top management teams that lead to dysfunctional conflict. Yet, senior executives focus most of their attention on financial integration. What intrigued me are the paradoxical intentions upon which mergers seem to be based.

Consider this scenario: The buyer company wants to acquire another company because it offers something different and unique. Perhaps the buyer company is large and bureaucratic, even a little slow-moving. So it purchases a small, fast-growing, new, high tech company to overcome these weaknesses; it can then respond much more quickly to external changes in the environment. Yet, despite this intention, the buyer company often superimposes its old policies and procedures that make it hard for the acquired firm to be responsive to the external environment. The very aspects the buyer firm once coveted in the seller are the same ones it now impedes.

I laugh to myself thinking of the similarity of these dynamics in love relationships—individuals often choose spouses or partners different from them because they find these differences attractive, yet they spend a good deal of time trying to get their partners to become more like them during the course of the relationship.

Wright

So how would you define conflict?

Berney

Conflict occurs when two or more parties—individuals, teams, even organizations—perceive that they have different needs, goals, or interests that cannot be resolved. The word "perception" is key because the parties may make a number of assumptions about each other that are not valid. Parties often create stories about each other that are inaccurate and based on their own view of the world. With these assumptions, the parties make choices, sometimes unconsciously, that lead to either functional or dysfunctional conflict. Functional conflict involves adults listening to each other, checking out their initial assumptions, and then voicing and working through their differences to a mutually agreeable solution.

Dysfunctional conflict involves parties acting "positional" (i.e., each insisting on getting what he or she wants and failing or not wanting to attend to the other party's needs). The fear that they will not get their needs met leads to their acting "positional" and thus unwilling to compromise. Once positional, parties often engage in power battles, making it nearly impossible to reach any kind of mutually acceptable "third way." Power battles are characterized by oppositional and rigid behavior.

Similarly, once partners or spouses engage in a power battle with each other, there is little hope for resolution. The old adage that couples should not go to bed angry is not true—once engaged in a power battle, parties become increasingly positional and rigid, eliminating any opportunity of inventing effective solutions. Better to get some sleep than to escalate the argument! As a matter of fact, Fisher and Ury (the Harvard Negotiation Program) suggest that once escalation occurs, parties should "go to the balcony" (metaphorically!). They should end the discussion for the time being, take time alone to reflect and calm down, and set a time to reengage with the other party to continue the discussion.

Wright

So is it dysfunctional when people argue: "That's not the way we did it before this stupid merger"?

Berney

Yes. Although understandable, rather than focusing on the overarching goal of the merger and its inherent opportunities, individuals often regress to survival mode, clinging to what they have done in the past. They need to reframe their thinking and ask, "How are we going to reach our new goals? What new strategies will get us there?" Clinging to old ways, acting positionally, and insisting on one's own culture prevailing, will only yield the exact opposite of the merger goals—failure!

Ironically, when we fear and resist change, we do the exact opposite of what will benefit us—we regress to our fallback position—how things used to be. We view the world from a child's eyes, as though it were black and white, and then options fail to exist. We polarize and thus are rarely able to step back and see the big picture. At the very time we most need to be open to new possibilities, we regress and contract to earlier stances that no longer serve us.

Wright

Since conflict often results in viable solutions, why do so many people find dealing with conflict so challenging?

Berney

There are a few different reasons. From a psychological perspective, people do a great deal of displacing and projecting onto others daily. They bring anxieties, fears, and stories from their past to present day interactions and displace these onto anything that either reminds them of family behaviors (displacement) or of parts of themselves of which they are none too fond (projection). Once they do this, their capacity for listening, brainstorming, and joint problem-solving is diminished severely. The only way to resolve conflict is for both parties to be curious and learn as much as they can about each other's needs. Listening actively with curiosity also strengthens the relationship between parties because it demonstrates interest in each other, often leading to greater openness from both parties. Buoyed by their understanding and appreciation of the other's needs, both parties are often quite capable of creating inventive solutions to extremely challenging problems.

Wright

So when you go into an organization, are there techniques or methodologies to help them have these kinds of discussions?

Berney

Yes. In addition to providing a conceptual understanding of conflict dynamics, I use diagnostic and strategic tools to help facilitate communication and manage conflict. I find the tenets and strategies from the mediation literature, particularly the Harvard Negotiation Program, extremely useful in both helping to resolve conflict and to provide people with a fuller range of conflict management skills. In particular, Interests-based Negotiation from the Harvard Negotiation Program offers specific strategies to identify individual, team, and organizational interests, as well as strategies for finding joint solutions based on these interests. The keys to interests-based negotiation are listening and empathizing before moving to fact-based problem-solving.

It is important to discern between interests and positions. A position is what someone believes he or she must have, whether it is a new computer or a larger budget. If both you and I want the only orange left in the refrigerator, each position is that we have to have the orange. A position is what a person believes is the only way to meet an interest. An interest underlies someone's position and can be identified by asking, for instance, "Why do you want that? What is most important about that to you?" There are usually multiple interests underlying a position. In the orange example, after asking these questions, we learn that I wanted the orange to eat the inside and you wanted the rind to bake a cake. Even when situations do not dovetail as neatly and easily as this one, once interests are identified, many more options are possible.

Individuals engaged in conflict are often reticent to listen to others for fear that they will be perceived as pushovers. They often assume that in order to get what they want, they have to fight and push and demand. Paradoxically, those very behaviors yield the opposite result. In contrast, when parties are truly curious about each other's needs, they obtain crucial data, usually allowing them to find a mutually acceptable solution.

Wright

Why do so many of us try to change and control others to make them more like us?

Berney

People become threatened by these differences and the potential affect on themselves. They may wonder, "Will I have to make major changes?" "Will these changes knock me off balance?" "Will I lose any power or influence from the change?" It can be threatening to have to change and try new strategies, that's why people often become positional and insist there is only one possible solution—mine!

The only way to move from that narrow and narcissistic view is to expand one's thinking and reframe the conflict—to realize that there are a host of solutions that can meet each party's goals. Listening does not mean accommodating. To paraphrase Fisher and Ury from the Harvard Negotiation Program, parties need to be "soft" on the relationship (listen and empathize) and "hard" on the issues (no agreement is allowed until most interests are met). Never should parties agree to solutions that do not meet the majority of their interests.

Wright

So why do many of us repeat the same patterns of conflict with others over and over? For example, the controlling boss always picks on a passive employee.

Berney

Until we resolve any long-standing dynamic with which we struggle internally, the universe will continually offer us opportunities to address that very dynamic.

Let's say that I don't like conflict and passively agree to help others and sacrifice myself regularly. It is likely that I will attract people into my life who take advantage of others, including me. In this case, I am sending clear signals that I will do whatever others need and ignore my own needs. Enter the demanding, controlling boss. This boss is likely to take advantage of those employees like me who allow it. And this dynamic will continue to occur in my life until I learn to set boundaries and limits and pay more attention to my own needs. In *The Law of Attraction*, Esther and Jerry Hicks suggest that we attract to us those people from whom we most need to learn. So in this example, I unconsciously "invite" controlling people into my life until I learn how to set limits and take care of myself.

As a consultant, I once worked with a group of managers who struggled with a terribly controlling boss. After I interviewed each of them, I found that one of the five group members, whom I will call Steve, wasn't experiencing this same problem with the boss.

I asked the entire group, "Why doesn't the boss behave this way with Steve?" They didn't have a clue. I then asked them to consider whether Steve acted differently from the rest of them. Eventually, group members concluded that Steve, while willing to work hard, would not tolerate rudeness or any kind of abuse. So the boss didn't waste his energy imposing on Steve. Unconsciously, or perhaps consciously, the boss chose to impose on those in the group who appeared less comfortable saying "No." The team members thus colluded with the boss by *allowing* the boss's behavior, thus co-creating the conflict. Why would you ask Susie (i.e., Steve) to try Life cereal when you know that Mikey (the other four managers) will?

There is a great deal of learning possible in these dysfunctional conflicts we co-create. In this case, the managers who failed to set appropriate boundaries were "invited" by their boss to learn how. This boss unconsciously offered them the opportunity to learn a new skill that they had not yet developed.

One can view this scenario in one of two ways. The team members can choose to feel victimized and helpless or they can ask themselves what they could learn about themselves. Once they start setting better limits, the boss is forced to address his own behavior. She or he can learn to manage his or her own aggression and anger rather than dump it on others. So a choice is involved—moan about one's powerlessness or focus on developing one's own skills. Until the managers stop allowing the boss's inappropriate behavior, the boss is likely to continue this behavior. I can promise you that this victim-abuser dynamic will continue to get recreated in different situations for both the boss and the employees until all involved learn to develop their anger management and limit-setting skills respectively.

Wright

I wonder why that is—why do some people seem to attract difficult people in their lives more often than others? For example, the employee that always has an abusive boss.

Berney

Have you heard the expression "You can run but you can't hide?" People may change jobs to avoid a difficult boss; but, ironically, they often attract a similar situation at the new workplace.

For instance, when people end one love relationship without learning what they are supposed to learn about their contribution to the relationship's demise, they often enter into another plagued by similar challenges. In the book, *Radical Forgiveness*, Colin Tipping suggests that the very conflicts in which we find ourselves engaged—at home or at work—offer us the opportunity to forgive radically the party we often perceive as the "instigator." Despite the instigator's obvious faults, she or he offers us the opportunity to learn about ourselves. The forgiveness is "radical" because the instigator is forgiven despite his or her unpalatable and potentially destructive behavior. The forgiveness comes from realizing that the conflict requires us to grow a part of ourselves—be it assertiveness, directness, empathy, or accountability.

The spouse or partner who has the affair offers the couple a wake-up call—the opportunity to refocus on the couple as a unit as well as each person's needs. The affair also provides the opportunity for each individual to reflect upon his or her own contribution to this affair. That is absolutely not to say that the spouse having the affair has no responsibility or accountability. Forgiveness of the spouse's betrayal comes from realizing that the affair has been *co-created*. The betrayed partner's challenge is to move from blame to reclaim his or her own power. We have far more power focusing on what we *can* change in ourselves rather than what we *can't* change in others.

Challenging work situations often offer us the opportunity to develop new skills. For example, let's say that I am often excluded from important meetings at work. Each time

I don't get invited, I could complain to others and feel sorry for myself. Little headway will occur. But if I can wonder how I might have helped create this exclusion, I might learn that people find my behavior overly aggressive. I then have a choice—to temper my behavior and gain inclusion or to refuse to do so and be powerless. We have far more power focusing on what we can change in ourselves rather than on what we cannot change in others.

Many of my clients disagree when I tell them they co-created a problematic situation. They point to the egregious behavior of the other party or parties and tell me that sometimes it really is all the other person's fault. I would argue that these egregious behaviors are never random—we attract them to us so that we can develop parts of ourselves requiring growth. In the previous example, had I not been excluded from meetings, I would not have been challenged to address my aggressive behavior.

Wright

Why do some people hook us, or drive us crazy?

Berney

In two words: projective identification. For example, let's say that I, Liz, see a quality in you, David, that I, too, share. Let's say that quality is stubbornness. Now assume stubbornness is not what I consider one of my more admirable traits! It is much easier and more comfortable for me to focus on your stubbornness than on my own. When projective identification occurs, I overreact to your stubbornness because I see a trait in you that I dislike in myself.

Once I can acknowledge my own stubbornness, I will react less to you. The process is unconscious because, in the moment, I am only aware that you annoy me. And while objectively, your stubbornness is annoying, my reaction is way out of proportion. I'm "hooked." Once "hooked," I've lost my objectivity and hence my power. I can no longer be neutral and calm. Until I can make peace with my own stubbornness and really acknowledge and own it, I will keep projecting it onto others.

Continuing with the example, making peace means noticing my tendency to behave in the same way that you do. Once I can see this tendency, it comes out of the dark (Jung calls this our shadow). The behavioral tendency then moves from unconscious to conscious awareness where there is a choice to change the behavior.

Let me give you an example from my experience as a coach. I coached a CEO who was extremely frustrated with her "demanding" Program Director. She wanted to learn why this person drove her so crazy and how she could more effectively deal with her.

So I started with data collection. I asked the CEO (I will call her Sue) to tell me about her Program Director (I will call her Joan). Sue replied, "Well, Joan comes into my office asking for what she wants all the time."

I asked her to clarify what she means by "all the time." She said this occurred once every day or two. Then I asked her if Joan's requests were appropriate. She said Joan occasionally asked for more money for her budget or a day off after running a large meeting.

The data suggests that Joan's behavior is quite reasonable and that Sue is "hooked."

So I asked Sue, "What about Joan drives you crazy, given her reasonable requests?"

"She acts so entitled," was Sue's reply. "Joan is always asking for what she wants, she's demanding, she's so sure of herself, and she's full of herself."

"Sue, is there a part of you that acts like that?"

"Well I hope not," she replied. "I really don't like that. Some people think I act entitled but I certainly don't. Joan acts much more entitled than I do."

I gently suggested that it is easier to see undesirable behavior in someone else rather than in oneself. Rather than stay aggravated with Joan's behavior, Sue could explore her own feelings about entitlement. Where do they come from? Is it okay to be assertive without being aggressive? Would she like to become more assertive? What are her fears and concerns about that?

By addressing her own feelings around entitlement, Sue is less likely to become "hooked" by Joan's behavior or anyone else's.

Wright

So why is it so hard for so many to give direct and honest feedback to each other?

Berney

People don't tend to feel comfortable giving others direct and honest feedback. Most people are much more comfortable complaining to a friend about someone at work rather than addressing the person directly. This indirectness, referred to as triangulation, only makes the problem worse. It is paradoxical (and human) that managers tell me they can't confront others because they don't want to hurt their feelings. Triangulating by talking to third parties often ends up being far more damaging.

Many clients will tell me they are upset with someone at work but not upset enough to talk to that person directly. Let's say that Jorge is upset with Ming, a colleague who manages a different department. Jorge feels that Ming takes advantage of some of his staff. Rather than deal with Ming directly, he seethes, which his staff notices. Soon after, Jorge's staff and Ming's staff become engaged in conflict. Staff in both departments unconsciously pick up the tension between the department heads. Now, not only is Jorge upset with Ming, but also two departments are no longer cooperating with each other. Had Jorge spoken to Ming directly with his concerns, the conflict between departments could have been prevented.

In order for this directness to become a norm in the workplace, employees need to receive "hands-on" training in which they practice giving and receiving feedback, as well as receive feedback on their own feedback skills.

Part of giving feedback includes two behaviors rarely mentioned in feedback training: 1) listening and being curious about *why* the feedback receiver did what she or he did and 2) the feedback giver's examining his or her own contribution to the feedback receiver's behavior.

For example, when Marge, who likes interacting with others through debate and challenge, communicates with George, who prefers harmony and connection, George experiences her as abrasive and argumentative. George may even assume, from Marge's behavior, that she does not like him.

Conversely, Marge may assume George has no interest in connecting with her since he avoids her whenever she tries to communicate with him.

Both are inferring intention that does not exist. If George asked Marge about her behavior, he would learn that she was trying to connect with him. Her intention was not to be difficult. George's assumption about Marge was based on a story he told himself. George, who prefers finding commonality with others, read Marge's intentions through his own filter and thus misinterpreted her intentions. When George gives Marge feedback about her behavior, he needs to ask her about her intentions without assuming he already knows them. That is not to say, however, that Marge is not responsible for the effect of her behavior. She is!

Wright

So why do some teams continually get stuck in conflict?

Berney

Teams just make the whole equation more complicated because of the larger number of individuals. Since teams are typically composed of members who are different along a variety of dimensions, there are more opportunities for team members to misunderstand and make incorrect assumptions about each other. These assumptions can lead to polarization and entrenchment into one's own worldview.

When team members manage conflict functionally by listening, exploring, and understanding various viewpoints, they become increasingly productive. This task of managing individual differences is central to Tuckman's group stage of "storming." But if team members get locked into positions, they will get stuck and be unable to function productively.

In the same way, a couple must learn to manage differences. When a couple is in the honeymoon stage, differences are rarely present. But eventually the couple moves to the "storming" stage and must learn how to manage differences.

The way for teams and couples alike to move through conflict is to learn strategies to manage these differences, thus broadening their repertoire of conflict-management skills. Once members of a couple or team engage in dysfunctional conflict, they need to step back and take a broader view of the issue, focusing on the goals and needs of the couple or the team. Strategies, including identifying underlying interests, active listening, mirroring, and brainstorming can help move individuals in the team/couple to refocus on the overall unit rather than solely on the individual.

Wright

So how can we understand the sources of conflict in teams?

Berney

First, we need to pay more attention to diagnosing the sources of the conflict before trying to resolve it. Often when employees squawk at one another, their managers assume the source of conflict must be personality differences. While the symptoms may look like incompatible personalities, the source may not be.

For example, the two could be arguing over different interpretations of their roles; without clarification, the conflict will not be resolved. This confusion may very well be an issue for others in the team as well.

Clarifying team member roles, team goals, procedures, policies, and norms can help prevent conflict. If the manager doesn't make roles and responsibilities clear, one team member (Jane) may think that a particular task is her responsibility while another (John) thinks it is his.

More commonly, team members may have different understandings of a project's goals or of team decisions. Patrick Lencioni, in *The Five Dysfunction of a Team*, talks about how common it is for leaders like department heads to leave a meeting after reaching an office-wide decision, only to learn later that they had interpreted the decision differently from one another. Once they realize this, the damage has often been done because they had already shared this decision with their staff members, who in turn were already comparing their department's decision with that of other departments. Once an agreement is reached, it is important to go around the room and hear everyone's version of the agreement and then discuss it until everyone has the same version. Think of how often one's significant other understands an agreement the couple made in a way completely different from you.

In a similar vein, two people arguing may be "acting out" the argument for the group as a whole. For this reason, when I have been asked to coach a "difficult" manager, I am cautious. While this person indeed appears difficult, he or she often voices a need or hurt for the entire group. When these group-level dynamics are at play, focusing the blame on an individual never resolves the conflict. When one person looks like the "bad guy," it is important to check how others in the group feel about the issue too. Often the person scapegoated is the one with the courage to voice the group-level issue affecting everyone.

One should always assume that all team members need to participate in resolving a group issue even when only a few voice concerns. The "hard knocks" way of learning about group-level dynamics is working with the "identified" person or persons, only to find that different individuals in the group are quietly upset about the same issue. An "identified patient" or individual focus allows dangerous scapegoating and, at the same time, fails to solve the overall problem.

Remember getting in trouble complaining to a teacher because your friends "forgot" to back you up? The teacher thought only you had the concern and may have become angry with you. The teacher failed to realize that this was a group-level issue involving the whole class—one that might impede learning. Perhaps the teacher's explanation was unclear and the students, while wanting clarity, feared the teacher's potential anger. Had the teacher realized that this might be an issue for the whole class, she or he would have asked other students individually if any had related concerns. It is imperative to consider a group-level perspective when solving team conflict.

Wright

Would you help our readers with perhaps what new ways of thinking help people and teams learn from and perhaps leverage their differences?

Berney

Some of the most effective strategies in which I have been trained come from Interests-based Negotiation, developed by the Harvard Negotiation Program. The conceptual framework and practical strategies from Interests-based Negotiation center around negotiators being firm and friendly—firm on the issues, friendly on the relationship. Rather than forcefully demanding what one wants, one should use curiosity and active listening resulting in far more leverage in conflict resolution and negotiation. Once one party listens, the other typically returns the favor. After both parties discuss what is important to each of them, they can create space for creative problem-solving to meet both their interests. There are always multiple ways to problem-solve when one moves from what she or he needs to what both parties need.

When I consulted to a small engineering firm that manufactured custom-fit valves, the President was extremely concerned that his Marketing Director was going to leave. The Marketing Director needed cash, and the President had none to provide. The President asked me to help the two of them discuss their underlying interests to find a way to satisfy both of them.

I didn't expect the resolution to be particularly challenging—all I had to do was learn why the Marketing Director needed the cash. I knew the President would be amenable to getting him a loan or providing him with additional resources. The Marketing Director needed immediate cash to quickly buy stock.

While the final solution wasn't perfect, it met most of both of their interests. The President agreed to double the Marketing Director's commission for six months. Even though the Director wouldn't get cash immediately, he would quickly make money because the industry was picking up and his commission was doubled. The President got to keep his Director and, despite his paying him a double commission, he would reap plenty of profits, given the Marketing Director's huge incentive.

Often a facilitator helps move people from their positions to joint problem-solving around their interests. By getting people to step back, listen, identify underlying interests, and focus on the team's goals, the facilitator creates space to jointly identify inventive solutions. Conflicts aren't that hard to solve technically; what's difficult is managing individuals' feelings and reactions.

Wright

What an interesting conversation, and informative as well. I really appreciate all the time you've spent with me and answering these questions. I've really learned a lot and I know our readers will.

Berney

Great.

Wright

Today we've been talking with Dr. Liz Berney. Dr. Berney is the President of Berney Associates Training Organization and Development and she is an Organizational Psychologist who provides consulting, speaking, training, and facilitation services. Her areas of expertise include conflict management, interests-based negotiation, change management, and team development. I don't know about you, but I'm going to listen to her—she sounds like she knows what she's talking about.

Liz, thank you so much for being with us today on *Yes You Can!*

Berney

You're very welcome.

Liz Berney is the President of Berney Associates, Training and Organization Development. She provides consulting, speaking, training, and facilitation services for clients including Bill and Melinda Gates Foundation, Coca-Cola, Tropicana, Baldridge Quality Program, AT&T, Fannie Mae, John F. Kennedy Center for Performing Arts, the Marriott, MCI, the U.S. Environmental Protection Agency, and the U.S. House of Representatives. Her areas of expertise include conflict management, interests-based negotiation, change management, and team development. Liz has taught for the American Management Association, the Accelerated MBA program at George Washington University, and Executive Programs at the University of Maryland's School of Business and Management. At Georgetown University, she founded, designed, and directed the Organization Development Certificate Program. At George Mason University, she was a tenure track psychology professor. Liz has a BA in Psychology with honors from Yale University and an MA and PhD in Industrial Organizational Psychology from the University of Maryland where she was awarded a Teaching Excellence Award.

Liz Berney, Ph.D., Berney Associates

315 Autumn Wind Way
Rockville, MD 20850
301-424-4633
lberney@verizon.net
www.berneyassoc.com

CHAPTER THIRTEEN

Self-Empowerment for

Personal Success

by Heather Wagenhals

David Wright (Wright)

Today we're talking with Heather Wagenhals. Heather is a celebrated columnist, host of *Unlock Your Wealth®Radio,* member of the National Speakers Association and the International Speakers Network, a Certified NLP Practitioner, and a designated broker of HQ Real Estate and Investment, LLC. A native Phoenician, she has two decades of experience in financial services that have developed her Keys to Riches™ Program that teaches people how to fix every area of their financial life.

Recently, she received her official Certified Identity Theft Risk Management Specialist designation from the Institute for Consumer Financial Education and was named one of the Top One Hundred Financial Experts to Listen and Learn From by Accredited Colleges Online.

Heather, welcome to *Yes You Can!*

Heather Wagenhals (Wagenhals)

Thank you so much for having me; it is an honor and privilege to be here.

Wright

So what is empowerment?

Wagenhals

Empowerment has been heard in a variety of contexts. Everywhere you turn in the media, it seems that it is used so cavalierly, like the latest fad catch phrase. I believe its true meaning has been whitewashed. The broadest and easiest definition of empowerment is that it is a process that challenges our current assumptions about the way things are and the way things *can* be.

Now, to narrow that definition a little more, in the sense of how empowerment can belong to everyone else, I have found the following definition from www.visualthesaurus.com: Empowerment is to give qualities or abilities to. We are getting closer to a usable term with this version. I still feel this definition allows for too much interpretation, which ultimately leads to the confusion and misuse of the word that we experience today.

Moving forward on that premise to make the definition more explicit, my definition of empowerment is the process of providing skills, resources, attitude, planning with accountability, flexibility and openness to create new options, ways and ideas, the confidence of others and finally, the belief in one's self.

I made the definition more concrete for empowerment because I felt that the broad strokes and the vagueness of others' definition really didn't fit what I felt empowerment is as a structure, a concept, and a process. I like to be very articulate in my definition of empowerment because of the difference between empowerment and motivation. People often interchange those ideas and words and they do so incorrectly because they're vastly different concepts.

Wright

So what is the difference between motivation and empowerment?

Wagenhals

As a Neurolinguistic Programming aficionado and certified NLP Practitioner, I learned a lot about how the brain operates, and how we create and model patterns of excellence. Motivation from the definition of inner or social stimulus for an action is biological; it is what speaks to someone's automatic drive toward pleasure or away from pain. It's a very primal, very instinctual, and a reactionary place to be acting from.

If you have ever gone through motivational courses, you know that they all have a similar goal. They call people to action and inspire people to move toward an incentive or some thing. When people have motivation, biologically it's either toward pleasure or away from pain. Most people are not very incentivized toward pleasure and don't actively move toward pleasure. You would think that they would, however, most people will only move or take action when they are presented with a painful situation.

When I talk about motivation and empowerment, I purposefully differentiate the two because motivation is so instinctual and empowerment is so much more than a mere fight or flight reaction. This distinction is more valuable. When someone tries to empower you versus motivate you, that person doesn't just give you the reason to do or not to do something. He or she gives you many other elements to ensure your success at whatever that given task may be.

Wright

So why is that so important to you?

Wagenhals

You can go to a slew of motivational seminars and hear professional speakers on the sidelines saying, "You can take an idiot and motivate him or her, but all you have is a motivated idiot." That is why professional speakers don't do motivational seminars—they do trainings. I think they get pigeonholed into that genre.

If you talk to Tom Hopkins, he's a sales trainer, he is not a motivational speaker, but if you are uplifted or motivated, great. Larry Winget, author of *You're Broke Because You Want to Be* wants to be called The World's Only Irritational Speaker®. Every professional speaker has his or her own take on it, but essentially they say the same thing, "This isn't motivational. I'm not here to get you excited about doing what you are supposed to be doing." What they say is, "I am going to give you the tools to do what you are doing better." That is why trainers say, "I am not a motivational speaker, I am a trainer," more often than not.

When I think of motivation from that distinction, what we need isn't more motivation to go do something, because that's automatic, what we need is a process of being successful at a given task. Empowerment isn't just about getting people motivated to do something. It's giving them all the resources they need to complete whatever the task is.

For example, when I do my Real Estate training I could say, "Okay, this week's goal is to sell twenty houses and whoever sells twenty houses this week, I'm going to give you an extra five thousand dollars" (I have now added motivation). The week will pass by and I'll ask, "How many houses did you sell?" and everybody will just give me a blank stare with maybe one of them accomplishing the challenge. Well, I made them excited with five thousand dollars. My Real Estate agents are saying, "Wow, that's so great, lots of money for me, but now I've got to do the work and I don't know where to start." But if I train these agents and I empower them with the resources, information, and skills necessary to go out and get those twenty sales, I will have a greater success ratio than if I had just motivated them.

When I train every week, my goal is to empower my agents with resources, information, and skills to go out and get those closings for the next month. Empowerment is more important than motivation because you can give anybody a job assignment and add incentives, but if you don't give people the elements of the empowerment process, their success is unlikely. That is why we define empowerment specifically in this manner and why this chapter of self-empowerment is different than any other.

Wright

So what do you believe makes up empowerment?

Wagenhals

Great question. I started studying and evaluating the "empowerment process." I asked myself how we specifically lift people up to another level of achievement, particularly in an area they know nothing about and how we get them from that motivation point to action and results. Then, we look at how people can take it from its definition and integrate it personally.

When we talk about empowerment of an individual, a group, a population segment, or a community, it always starts with the individual. I have identified seven different elements that go into the empowerment process. This is a multidimensional social process that someone can utilize as a system that can be replicated over and over again with consistent results.

Wright

So you created and subscribe to the Seven Elements For Self-Empowerment™. Will you briefly describe each of the seven elements?

Wagenhals

Yes. The Seven Elements for Self-Empowerment are:

- planning with measurement of results
- providing of skills
- gathering resources
- attitude
- flexibility to create openness for new options, ways and ideas
- confidence of others
- belief in one's self

The first is planning with the measurement of results/accountability. What is needed is more than just a goal.

I remember when I was seven I said, "I want to be a famous singer," and I remember I drew that in my little diary. I drew a picture of myself with a guitar. I was so excited because I had imagined myself as a rockstar and a famous singer. I didn't have much more than that other than the picture of me and that the written goal. The goal never materialized because I had missed the component of accountability. Accountability would include milestones adjusted based on my long-term goals that I listed, working backward from the end result. Doing this, I could measure my results with a system of accountability where I continually reviewed my progress or I had another person or entity continually reviewing my progress to measure my results at success or failure in relation to my accomplishing that ultimate goal.

Now, as an adult, I'm a writer, radio talk show host and Real Estate broker. So at any point, if I didn't make my goals along the way it was because I didn't have a specific plan. It is predictable.

Jeff Cutler, my investment advisor and fellow professional speaker, shares this about goal planning: "People don't plan to fail, they just fail to plan." One of the specific things that allow us to get from point A to point B or C and beyond is to have a map or a plan. You have to have a plan in order to get where you want to go. Ambling through won't get you anywhere.

For example, if there is a woman and I am to empower her to create a new minority owned business, and minority owned business is the goal, do we just say, "Hey, we are in business" the next day? We don't. There are several steps involved that must occur in a certain fashion in order to get that business "open for business." While some of the order doesn't matter, most of the order will. Some tasks on the list to opening up a new minority owned business are going to be dependent upon others being performed first, in a certain order. So we have to have a plan in order to get there, and we also need the accountability to measure our results—"What did I get done today, where is my goal, how close or how far away am I, what do I need to do tomorrow and the next day, and how much more do I need to go?" We must have accountability.

One of the things NLP talks about in goal-setting is to know what you want and know how you will know when you have it. You must know where you want to go and how you know when you are there. The only way to do that is going to be through the process of review. Just like we do on my *Unlock Your Wealth* radio show with The Keys to Riches, we do a Review, Revise, and Recommit segment where we have to continually check with the plan to see what we have accomplished or haven't accomplished and what we need to do next. Then we make necessary changes and recommit ourselves to the plan. That is why measurement of results is so important as a dimension to the planning empowerment element. How does one know if he or she has gotten there if the person doesn't have a plan? How does one know how much further he or she needs to go or is it, "Wow, am I already there?"

People have to be specific with their planning. It has to be articulate, it has to be written down, and it has to be specific to what they want to accomplish. One's plan also has to have realistic time constricted goals to measure movement forward in accomplishing that goal and one must have accountability for those plans. I will go one further with Cutler's quote and add, "Those who lack accountability for their goals will also lack measureable results."

The second element is the acquisition of skills. If you are going into a new career and it's something that you haven't done, most often your new employer is going to have a training program set up and you're going to have to learn how to acquire these new skills to be able to create the desired results, whatever that new career is going to be. If someone else is empowering you, they usually offer the training program. What you need to do is sit down and organize all seven elements, based on your planning, and determine that you are going to have to acquire certain skills to perform repeatedly and consistently in order to achieve your goals. After you have created your goals, identify and begin with acquiring the skills necessary.

With the wealth of knowledge and information out there through the television and Internet, we can do that a variety of different ways. We can go to a traditional "brick and mortar" school, we can also go to an online course, or maybe we need to go to a specific trade or technical school to get those skills necessary. Whatever the source of learning, we need to seek those educational institutions out in order to perform successfully and learn those skills.

The third element is the gathering of resources. Once we have planned, identified the skills that we need and acquired them, we're going to need certain support items in order for us to be able to use those new skills. For example, if it's a manufacturing process, we're going to need raw materials so we can create our finished product. We need to identify what it is that we need in order to be successful, and gather those necessary resources. Maybe it is equipment we need to execute the task successfully. If it is supplies, we will need to gather those, too, in order to successfully utilize our skills, manage our plans and track and store our results. Without resources, our plans and skills mean nothing without the ability to deploy them, so this is an integral element.

The fourth element is attitude. Attitude is everything. I read an article where they were interviewing a military officer who was talking about training and survival. He was asked, "Wouldn't you rather have somebody highly trained with you if you had to survive in the wilderness?" He answered vehemently, "No, I would take a minimally trained soldier who had the right attitude over a well-heeled soldier that had all the possible training in the world for survival but the wrong negative opinion of the current situation."

One's attitude is the fervor and excitement with which one takes on tasks. I've heard Brian Tracy say, "Your attitude determines your altitude." Given that statement, one has to start with the right perspective. Just because you don't know what you're doing or if this is a new field or maybe you're reentering the workforce or have not been in the workforce at all, it can be a bit intimidating or a little scary. If our attitude is one of eagerness and we are willing to consider new things and go forth and learn, that is going to make the most of our success. This element also plays an important role in the next element, too.

The fifth element is flexibility to create openness for new options, ways and ideas. This one goes along with some of the Neurolinguistic Programming presuppositions and it is one of the four pillars of NLP. Flexibility to create openness for new options, ways, and ideas is so important. An age old saying you may have heard is, "A mind is like a parachute—it only works when it's open," has everything to do with flexibility. It also calls to mind another colloquialism for the definition of insanity—doing the same thing over and over and expecting different results. Whatever it is we are trying to accomplish, we must be open and flexible and willing to accept new and different ways to get to the same goals. Simply put, if what we are presently doing isn't working, change it! And change it quickly, do not waste anymore of our precious time and resources on something that is akin to a dog chasing its tail.

If one says, "I want to change, I want to be this," it must be genuine. Some folks say they want change, if they do, then the things that are suggested to accomplish that particular change aren't options.

People can be notorious for creating options that aren't really options also. They want to "feel" like they have some options, even though they are never going to act on them or if those options just justify current behavior. We have to ask, "Is that really being flexible or do we just not really want to change?" People must be truly open to new ways of doing things—new ideas, new concepts, new technology and be willing to incorporate that in their repertoire. People can be fixated, committed, and focused on their way to accomplish a particular cause or task for achievement, which is a positive quality. But if it's not working and they have racked their brain to make it work in that same fashion, maybe they need to back up and consider other options. That is where flexibility comes in.

For example, we started driving down the road in a certain direction but then there was a rock in the road and we didn't have the right tires to go over the rock so we have to go around it. Some people just get blocked if a rock is in their pathway; they don't even consider going around it to accomplish the same result.

A story I tell when speaking is about doing the dishes. When I was growing up, we had to do the dishes after dinner. We always hand-washed the dishes. We couldn't afford an automatic dishwasher so my brother and I were the dishwashers. My mother said we had to do them in a certain order. It was as if that order was the *only* order and if it got messed up, for some reason unknown to my brother and me, the dishes wouldn't be clean at the end of the process. I didn't see what the problem was with the order in which we were doing them because I thought that they were clean at the end. As long as they all got cleaned, who cares how we did it? Well, my mother cared because she wasn't open or flexible to new ways of doing things; there was just one way growing up, her way or the highway.

So many people get caught up in their day-to-day routine and aren't willing to break out of that routine to create a different result.

I like Henry Ford. He had so many powerful ways of explaining the obvious and sometimes we are oblivious to the obvious. He said, "If you've always done it that way, it's probably wrong." In a concerted effort to try, many will refuse to consider alternative ways to accomplish the same task. If we can just be open to consider alternative ways to accomplish the same task, possibly faster with more efficiency or with more effective results, we may get where we want to go faster.

Change is inevitable. You are not the same person you were yesterday and you are going to be somebody else tomorrow—not radically different, but different. Change is inevitable and people can fight change and be fixed and they will be left behind or they can be flexible and open and move with new ideas and changing times and embrace and welcome change. That will continue to allow them to remain flexible. Things are going to change whether or not you have a choice. You'll be more likely to succeed if you are flexible. That is why it is an essential element.

The sixth element is the confidence of others. The confidence of others gives us external praise, which is something that we all crave. The support knowing that someone else believes that you can do something great is extraordinary. The benefit of this element is two-fold: first it makes you aware that someone believes in you, and second that you are being monitored somewhat. There is a little silent accountability when someone else has confidence that you will do well in your given task.

You may have heard of the statement "against all odds." "Against all odds he broke out of Harlem." "Against all odds this person broke the four-minute mile." "They said it couldn't be done, and then somebody broke the record."

A great example of this is Sir Roger Bannister. No one believed that a person could run faster than a four-minute mile and then one day, Sir Roger Bannister, a twenty-five-year-old British medical student did. Nobody believed he could do it, but right after he did, proving that a human could run faster than a four-minute mile, others were able to run faster and break that four-minute mile record. That is because somebody proved it could be done; others then had confidence that it could be done again. Instead of having to go "against all odds" when you are taking on a new endeavor, if someone else has the confidence that you are going to succeed, that is going to make it so much easier for you. Now you aren't struggling "against all odds."

To enjoin the confidence of others, people must first seek the confidence of someone worthy of supporting them. Then they may share their carefully laid plans, knowledge, skills, the resources gathered, and their excitement and enthusiasm for the project or task. Their winning attitude along with the other elements will be sure to engage the confidence of others. This is where mentoring becomes invaluable. In addition to confidence, this special person can advise them and aid with accountability. A mentor can add to the level of confidence as people will not have to "reinvent the wheel" and will learn from their mentor's mistakes without having to make too many of their own. This element also has a few valuable facets to it.

The last element is belief in oneself. This is the most important component. When people have the support of others, the last struggle they have to worry about is themselves. Belief in oneself is the cornerstone of all of these elements. NLP teaches that we have all the resources necessary to accomplish anything we want. So it's not about capability, it's about belief in oneself. You can have a thousand people believe that you are capable of doing something, but if you personally don't believe that you have the capacity to accomplish your goals, they are probably never going to get there. Henry Ford said, "Whether you think you can, or you think you can't, you're probably right." With the world against you, your belief in yourself will carry you many great places.

With NLP we know that languaging our desires has everything to do with how successful we will be, based on the way we language it. A presupposition of NLP is that we have all the resources we need to accomplish our goals; they just may not be arranged in a way that they are serving us currently. All we have to do is identify where our challenges are and rearrange the resources.

Our value system and hence, belief in ourself, comes from the first ten years of childhood, which is programmed by our parents. The next ten years of our lives are shaped by our peers. During these years we develop our value systems, behavior patterns, and decision-making capabilities. The first twenty years of our lives we've had exposure to all these other people's ways of doing things and right, wrong, or indifferent we adopted them; some work and some don't.

My point is that our concept of our personal value came from other people and if we have allowed other people to say things like, "You can't do that; who are you kidding," our self-esteem and belief in ourselves may not be very high due to the negative programming. If we took seriously statements like, "Our family has always been big boned and you're never going to lose weight," or "You're always going to be fat," and that's all the conditioning you've had it would be hard to break out of that. You would be fighting twenty years of influence from your family and peers.

So we have to meet with ourselves. I call it a "meeting of us three"—me, myself, and I. When you have a little sit-down, you are able to deal with that inner curmudgeon who is always ready to be the first naysayer, to grab and pooh-pooh any new idea, and to shake or cause to falter any confidence you might have in yourself.

When we empower ourselves to accomplish a given task, we must have all of these elements and we must believe in ourselves, specifically that it can be done by our hand.

That is why it is so important to feed your brain with positive things. It is precisely why I do affirmations every day—to keep my inner curmudgeon at my disposal and not be at his every whim. My very first affirmation is, "I am my greatest asset," and, I am. I know that because if anything in life is meant to be, it's up to me. Nobody else is going to do it on my behalf. I can beg, borrow, and steal and hope and pray that somebody else makes something happen for me, but if I truly want it to happen, I must do it myself.

We must believe in ourselves. Until we come to that point where we can be free from the influence of others—especially our inner curmudgeon—we must create that within ourselves. Using an affirmation process where we empower ourselves and reprogram and retrain our brain to believe in ourself is the best offensive strategy. We can convince our inner curmudgeon with affirmations. That little nasty guy who lives inside of each one of us, who talks us out of things, is only doing it because he just wants the best for us; he's trying to protect us. We shouldn't blame him, we should just train him!

Wright

Now that we've identified these seven elements, what is the next step to implementing them?

Wagenhals

Now that we have boiled down each of the seven elements to what goes into the process of empowerment step by step, you can actually take and apply them in your own situation. Once you are able to identify what they are and how they relate to you individually, you can then work to employ them for yourself.

NLP is all about modeling excellence. It's about taking successful patterns that have been established for accomplishing desired results from others and incorporating those patterns in ourselves. By utilizing that NLP foundation, we are able to go from empowering others using these seven elements to empowering ourselves. It may seem like there are many different ways that we can do this process. One can have a multitude of tasks to accomplish just getting started, though I would say it's just like eating elephant—do it just one bite at a time.

One concern with taking on new goals and new challenges is that there is a suspected or imminent fear of failure. Internally we have this curmudgeon inside of us trying to keep us from pain. As a result, he talks us out of the very thing that is going to make us successful and give us our big success just because it feels risky to him. Our little curmudgeon has been damaging us for the longest time and keeping us from achieving our own self-actualization by this coping mechanism—his way of keeping us safe. We must overcome this by "Convincing the Curmudgeon™." We know what is best for us, not him, and we must turn him from curmudgeon to cheerleader.

Wright

So where do you think people go wrong?

Wagenhals

What a wonderful question. Most often, the time where people go wrong is right in the beginning. People go wrong when they try to shortcut or circumvent one of the elements thinking that they can still create self-empowerment without one of those elements.

We know we can miss the "belief and support of others" because we can do it "against all odds," though the other elements can't be usurped. If one doesn't have belief in oneself, it's not going to work. We must believe in ourselves. We could have other people believe in us but if we don't believe in ourselves, it's not going to work.

We can start without a plan and maybe have a mental assumption of what we need to do here and there. Without a formal plan, we are not going to be able to identify obstacles or overcome them because we don't have a system in place for managing things or a way to track and measure our results.

Without being flexible and open to new ideas we may not be able to accomplish what we set out to because the one thing that is going to take us over the edge and make us successful is the one thing that we refuse to accept or believe. So flexibility is the key.

Without the right attitude, we are filtering all the things that we are trying to avoid. If people say, "I just have bad luck," then every bad thing that ever happens, they are going to be looking for it. Every bad thing that happens, they are going to feel it has been done to them on purpose and they are filtering for negativity when it could just be the normal course of things. On the other hand, somebody who was filtering with the right attitude would think of those things as minor disturbances, "Oh well, things happen," and brush it off as coincidence at best. It is all in one's perspective. If we are filtering with the wrong attitude and we have several things go wrong during the day, we are going to feel that we are doomed and overwhelmed and think, "Why am I bothering to try?" On the flip side, the person with the right attitude would just say, "What doesn't kill me makes me stronger." That person would keep on going in spite of everything else. So attitude is everything.

Can people go forward with the wrong resources? Absolutely, they can; however, if they have the right resources they probably would be a whole lot more effective. People can play golf with a stick instead of a golf club, though they might hit the ball farther if they use a golf club.

We can't do without skills. When we don't have skills, one of two things happen: incorrect operation of machinery can damage or break it and harm others, or worse, without having skills it is necessary to rely on someone else. Having to rely on someone else could materially affect your performance or your outcome.

I don't believe that we could be empowered if one of those elements were missing or missing for very long. I believe it is a united front and it's part of an ongoing process that helps to uplift us.

I think there is also a level of commitment that hasn't been addressed internally and, rather than capability, it is willingness and ability to do this process, which goes back to belief. If people don't believe they are capable or they don't have the capacity or that in some way they're unwilling to put forth the necessary effort, that is where they will go wrong. Simply by working on their belief system and Convincing that Curmudgeon using an affirmation process can completely change their odds for success and actually give them more of a fighting chance, if they're able to get that part on track.

Wright

So how can people increase their odds of success?

Wagenhals

I have an affirmation process that I teach on my radio show when we do the first key in our "Keys to Riches Financial Freedom" series. The first key is Acceptance and Affirmation. Acceptance as a Key Statement is: "I may or may not know everything there is to know about money but what I do know is I cannot continue along this path any longer, I must change."

What I have discovered through the financial coaching and money management programs I teach is people don't change until the pain of change is less than the pain of staying the same. Only at that point will people accept that what they are currently doing isn't working and they have to change. Then the willingness to change will become easier.

Once that acceptance phase has been acknowledged and worked through, they are able to move forward. As Elizabeth Kübler Ross talks about in her book, *On Death and Dying,* grieving is a process. When catastrophic events happen to us or around us, we go into denial. For example, if you are told "you have cancer," you will go into denial first. Then you must work through the grieving process to accept it. Only at that point of acceptance are you able to move forward. Although now, because of everything that has gone on and you've been beaten down so hard, you have to build yourself back up in order to believe that you are actually capable of this change! You will finally accept that you must change, but you may not have the intestinal fortitude to make the change.

We use a process here at the Unlock Your Wealth Foundation that I have created called Six "P's" For Affirmation Success^{TM}. To begin, an affirmation is a statement of truth. Simply put, an affirmation is a truth or known piece of information about someone according to Webster's Dictionary. I think back to when I used to run around with some other professional speakers when I was in my twenties. One of my friends would always say to me, "I'm a millionaire; I'm just telling you the truth in advance!" That is what affirmations do for us—they allow us to tell the truth in advance because the brain always succeeds at whatever we "say" we want.

The brain is the greatest supercomputer in the entire universe. What we think about, we bring about. If we are highlighting negativity in our thoughts unintentionally through our words, we are going to get what we don't want. By not focusing directly on succeeding and focusing on trying to stay away from failing versus focusing solely on our success, then we're going to get exactly what we're thinking about.

For example, by saying, "I don't want to be poor," the brain omits the words "do not" and only hears "I want poverty." The brain will create that scenario in your life, keeping you right at the poverty line. To correct the negative aspect of that affirmation would be to swap out the word "poor" for a positive word like "wealth" or "health" or any other "move toward the positive" type of goal. It is very simple—the brain works just like a standard computer does. If you put garbage in, you're going to get garbage out, and if you put good stuff in, you'll get good stuff out.

The Six "P's" For Affirmation Success are:

- Personal
- Present Tense
- Positive
- Power
- Precise
- Practiced

Words mean things. The way our minds process these words have a direct effect on our success or failure. This is why word choice and sentence structure is so vital, not only in the affirmation process but in communication between individuals. Those who can master language and sentence structure will not only have control of their own lives, but will also be able to use that same process to influence the behavior of others. (Note that I used the word "influence" and not "control." There are only three things we can control: 1) our thoughts, 2) our feelings, and 3) our actions. Outside of that sphere, we only have influence.)

That leads us to the first "P" in our affirmation technique. What we know about the affirmation process is that first and foremost we can only make affirmations for us, so it must be "Personal." It must be in the first person. When we start our affirmation process we first have to use the word "I." I is the personal, first person portion of our affirmation. "My child gets good grades" won't cut it. We cannot affirm the success or failure of another because we do not control them. You can wish the best for your loved ones but you cannot make things happen for them. Knowing that we can only control our thoughts, feelings, and actions, our affirmations must begin with "I" or "my"—you own it, you do it, and you are it.

The second portion or the second "P" in the affirmation process is it must be "Present Tense." This doesn't mean it will happen in the future—"I will"—but it is already happening now. This starts transforming the way the brain is going to process the rest of the affirmation statement. It will say, "Oh, okay, it's happening now so I must address this now to prepare myself for the next new thing." You must act "as if" it is already occurring. So we're going to start with "I am" or "I have."

"Want" is a bad word. "Want" is to be without or be deficient in, so we don't "want"—want is something that is for others. We have and enjoy things in the present tense. Since our second "P" is "present tense," I am— Examples are: "I am happy," "I am healthy," "I have six months of emergency funds in the bank," etc.

The third "P" in the affirmation process is "Positive." If we're affirming something negative, remember that the brain always succeeds at what you put in it to do. If you think negatively, you're going to get negative results. We get what we "say" we want, not necessarily what we desire.

One of the interesting things about our supercomputer is our brain doesn't hear the words "no" or "not." We are a "can do" computer, so if the brain is not acknowledging the "no" or the "don't," you must watch how you construct an affirmation. For example, "I don't want to be poor," is constructed for failure. All the brain is going to hear is, "I want poor." It's not going to hear the "don't" because the brain only knows how to succeed, it will execute on creating poverty. We must make sure it's stated in the positive. Some examples are: "I am healthy," not "I am not sick." "I am healthy," "I am wealthy," and "I have a nice house." "I have—" (whatever particular material possession, item or intangible you're looking for). "I have a great attitude about my life." These are all great examples.

The fourth "P" is it must be within our "Power." I will not have a successful affirmation saying "I am a lottery winner" because I have no control of how those numbered balls blowing around that big bubble will come out. Since it is not in my power or my ability to control, an affirmation like that is useless. It must be within one's power in order to do an affirmation. An example is: "I am a great mother." I can mother children and do it in a way that I can have a positive influence on them—I control that ability. "I am a great wife." I can control how I respond to my spouse.

One of the things that will keep anybody in any goal-setting arena from being successful is lack of specificity. The fifth "P" in the affirmation process is that it must be "Precise." You must have a clear definition. For example, if wealth is your goal and you are going to affirm financial wealth, saying, "I am wealthy," sounds like a great affirmation, though wealth comes in many forms. Wealth can be personal happiness and satisfaction in one's life and one's career, but if you want something specific, something tangible, like financial wealth, you've got to assign a value to it, so it must be precise. It can be, "I have $1,000 in the bank collecting dust and interest." "I am wealthy" is vague because everybody has a different idea of what wealth is to them. Your idea of wealth is going to be different from mine, and different from the guy's down the street. We have to attach something precise so we know exactly what we're affirming. We can't act "as if" when there are different levels of wealth. I know that sounds silly but it is true—wealth is different for everyone. Most of the time people don't have a tangible definition of what they truly desire; we must make our affirmation precise.

The last "P" in our affirmation technique that makes an affirmation worthwhile is that it is "Practiced." You use it repeatedly whenever you encounter negativity to create consistent results. It will help you by repeated exposure. Beat down all of the garbage that the curmudgeon inside of you is throwing up and change his mantra. He is inside and should be saying the same thing that you're saying on the outside. Because we are so heavily invested in him, it's important that we get him on the same page as we are, which will increase our personal power and effectiveness by increasing our personal belief.

Wright

So how can Neurolinguistic Programming techniques play a factor in these elements?

Wagenhals

NLP techniques can play a major role in your formula for blending all of these elements together and specifically for your own self-empowerment success because Neurolinguistic Programming assumes success. How we model success and the aggregation and deployment of these seven elements work so well together. We're communicating mostly with ourselves in many of these elements before we reach out to others. The way the brain works and the way we language what we are attempting to accomplish must be done in an appropriate fashion because our words mean so much. We need to have what we are saying be congruent with what our thoughts and our actions are. If we are not languaging our thoughts and our actions in line with what our stated goals and desires are, we're going to be defeated before we get started.

Articulating our intent is important. And we must *correctly* articulate our intent using the same tools that we use for The Six "P's" For Affirmation Success. We must use language in a way that supports what we want to accomplish in a positive way. Whether or not we understand NLP, or we study the system of Neurolinguistic Programming, by leveraging The Six "P's" For Affirmation Success and languaging our stated goals correctly, in addition to actively responding versus reacting to stimulus is what's going to give us a leg up in our ability to move forward and accomplish what we're setting out to with this self-empowerment process.

Wright

So how does one get started in the process?

Wagenhals

I truly believe that if we have all seven of these elements and we began with planning, ultimately the process begins with belief in ourselves. As individuals, we must believe in our heart of hearts that our goals are worthy of investing personal time in them. We must make sure we employ Neurolinguistic Programming tools in the mix by acquiring specific knowledge and then applying that knowledge. We don't have to reinvent the wheel.

When people were saying, "knowledge is power" and "pay attention to your personal power," everyone became fixated on the word "power." Then it went from "power that I hold" to "empowerment of others." It is my opinion that something was left out. Knowledge is only so much of that power. Knowledge is superfluous without application. One must go forth and acquire the necessary skills to deploy any project effectively including self-empowerment. You must take action with that knowledge or else you will be among the ranks of destitute scholars who spent their lifetime learning, talking, and teaching with no execution. I believe if we lay the process out in this fashion and know that the core element in the self-empowerment process is personal belief, we will get that much further ahead when we work through each of the Seven Elements For Self-Empowerment.

Wright

Well, what a great conversation. This is an important chapter and I've learned a lot here today; I'm sure that our readers will as well. I really appreciate all the time you've taken with me today to answer these questions.

Wagenhals

Thank you for the opportunity to participate in one of the last original works by the late Jim Rohn. What is so important to remember about the self-empowerment process is first to believe in yourself and remember the answer to your destiny lies within, though you must look for it. If you are unsure, you just need to re-read the title of this book. Self-empowerment works if you invest in the process. Could you be successful with the self-empowerment process outlined here? By all means, Yes You Can!

Wright

Today we've been talking with Heather Wagenhals. She is a celebrated columnist and host of the *Unlock Your Wealth* radio show. She was named as one of the Top One hundred Financial Experts to Listen and Learn From by Accredited Colleges Online.

Heather, thank you so much for being with us today on *Yes You Can*.

Heather Wagenhals has been empowering others to achieve financial independence for the last twenty years. Heather's ability to take intimidating financial information and communicate it in easily digestible forms through all mediums, coupled with her personal mission to help others help themselves, make her one of the premiere personal finance experts today. Residing in Arizona with her husband, Fred, Heather is an internationally recognized writer, speaker, and broadcast professional carrying her message of financial literacy to the masses through The Unlock Your Wealth Foundation. Her favorite saying is, "Knowledge is superfluous without application."

Heather Wagenhals

The Unlock Your Wealth Foundation, LLC
6401 E Thomas Rd., #106
Scottsdale, AZ 85251
480-522-1066
me@heatherwagenhals.com
www.unlockyourwealth.com

CHAPTER FOURTEEN

The Leadership Role Model

by Pete Blank

David Wright (Wright)

Today we're talking with Pete Blank. Pete Blank is a former leadership consultant with The Walt Disney Company. At the Disney University in Florida, he designed and delivered leadership training classes to thousands of cast members each year. Today, he is President of ATLAS, which stands for Alabama Training, Leadership, and Strategy. In this role, Pete shares concepts of leadership with businesses all across the country and assists them in the development of their leadership teams. He is also the leadership trainer for the Personal Board of Jefferson County, where he is responsible for the leadership development of over nine thousand civil service employees working in Jefferson County, Alabama.

Pete, welcome to *Yes You Can!*

Pete, leadership is such a global term. Let me get your definition of leadership. I understand you believe that leadership begins by knowing your ROLE (an acronym I will explain later). What do you mean by that?

Pete Blank (Blank)

This book is all about reaching your potential, and I think people cannot reach their potential unless they are constantly looking to improve their leadership skills. When it comes to a leader knowing his or her ROLE, keep in mind that there are three definitions to the word "role:"

211

A role can be a part or a character played by an actor or an actress.

A role could be the proper or customary function such as the leader's role in society.

A role could be tied into the rights, the obligations, and the behavior patterns that are associated with a particular social status.

When we use the word "role" in the context of leadership, I believe that all three definitions help to define the true role of a leader.

We are all playing a part of a leader, just like an actor or an actress.

We have a customary function associated with being a leader.

There are definitely rights, obligations, and behavior patterns that are a part of leadership.

I worked at The Walt Disney Company for thirteen years. The Disney organization does a great job of making sure employees know their purpose and their role. As an employee (or "Cast Member" as we were called), we all had the same *purpose*, and that purpose to make sure that guests who visited the Walt Disney World Resort had the most fabulous time of their life. However, your *role* was your actual daily job. Even though our roles were very different (e.g., a housekeeper, an operator, a quick service food host, or an attractions hostess), our purpose was always the same.

One challenge was always trying to make sure that each of the more than fifty thousand Cast Members knew how their *roles* fit into the big picture. The example I always use is someone working in a fast food location, cooking a hamburger. The person's primary role is to cook the burgers and fries. These employees are in a backstage area with little to no guest contact. They may feel that they are constantly cooking the same burger and the same set of French fries day in and day out for thousands and thousands of people. What they have to understand is to see the big picture—there are people who come from all over the world who have saved money for many years to take their Disney dream vacation. They have chosen this particular fast food restaurant in Disney, and the employees should want to make sure that their meal is fantastic! The guests will then tell their kids and their friends back home that everything at Disney is marvelous. All of a sudden, the Cast Member who is cooking burgers and fries is not just cooking a hamburger anymore—he or she is creating an experience; it is not just quick service food.

Other examples are housekeeping hostesses rearranging the room towels to look like Donald Duck. It could be retail salespeople cleverly displaying the T-shirts in their merchandise location. Your role has to tie into your purpose, and you have to know how the two go together. That's why everybody at Disney is considered to be a leader.

Leadership at Disney has nothing to do with your title. It has nothing to do with what level you are or the color of your ID badge. There are plenty of frontline Cast Members who don't have any supervisory responsibilities but who are great leaders. Some of them may even be better than their supervisors. It is because they follow the concept of "knowing your role."

Part of a leader's job is to know the technical aspects of that job and managing the day-to-day operations, but they must also understand that with leadership there are certain rights, obligations, and behavior patterns that must be addressed. That is where the ROLE concept can assist them.

Wright

Let's break down the acronym, ROLE, one letter at a time. What does the R stand for?

Blank

The R stands for *Relationships,* and it's by far the most important part of the ROLE model. It's been said that it is not what you know, but who you know. In my opinion it's also who knows you, and it also matters if anybody *cares* that he or she knows you.

Social networking is very popular these days, and the current rage is to gain as many contacts/friends as you can on your Facebook, LinkedIn, or Twitter account. You may have two thousand friends on your Facebook or LinkedIn account, but only two hundred of those are based on quality relationships. The other eighteen hundred are not really "relationships." Relationships are based on time, attitudes, feelings, and behaviors. Nobody wants to have a relationship with someone who isn't putting in the time and effort.

Relationships are not just about one-on-one connections. In business, you need to make sure that people in certain departments have good working relationships with each other. An example would be public safety, where people in the dispatch department had better have a good relationship with the officers. Do the people in your accounting department have a good relationship with those in your operations department? You never know when they're going to need each other.

I was a front office manager at Disney's Port Orleans Resort for a couple of years. The front desk staff needed to have good relationships with the housekeeping staff. Check-in time was always three o'clock in the afternoon. To our guests, this meant that their room would be ready at three o'clock and not one second later. When rooms were not cleaned by three o'clock, the first reaction from some Cast Members was to find out who was to blame.

"I told housekeeping these people needed their room at three o'clock."

"What could they possibly be doing down there? They had all day to clean this room!"

"I'm sorry sir, but our housekeeping staff must be behind schedule today."

Playing the blame game doesn't do anything to help build relationships. The best thing for us to do in that case was to figure out how to solve the main issue, which was that rooms were not clean at three o'clock. We made sure that all of our front desk managers and our housekeeping managers were cross-utilized, shadowed each other's department, and did shifts in each other's departments. Once you work in a housekeeping location for a week, you come back with a whole different idea of why some rooms may not be ready at three o'clock. Relationships are less about the blame game and more about how to get people in your departments to work together. That's one of the key components.

The concept of relationships can take a turn for the worse if people try to use them to gain backdoor access or to circumvent the system. However, if done properly, they can add another valuable resource for you as a leader (especially if you build them across multiple layers). We get so bogged down in the business world today, separating ourselves by titles and levels and what our company ID says we are—hourly or salaried, exempt or non-exempt, blue or yellow ID color. The first thing you need to do is break down barriers and establish yourself as a leader who is going to work with anyone and everyone.

Relationships are now global! They are built via the computer and the Internet. The Web allows us to build relationships all around the world. As a business professional and current leader, you need to be Web 2.0 savvy. You do need accounts on Linkedin, Facebook, and Twitter. You need to have an electronic presence, as relationships are being built in a whole different realm than they used to be. There will always be power lunches, coffee breaks, and water cooler talk, but if you do not have an electronic presence in the world of relationship-building, you are going to fall behind.

Let me sum up the R for *Relationship* by sharing four action items for you.

1. Be sure to build your relationship both in person and over the Internet. Be very strategic in building your electronic reputation. While doing that, don't forget about professional organizations in your area as well.

2. Take on volunteer tasks in your organization. Many times, employees are sitting in a conference room and the leader of the meeting asks for a volunteer. Most people's eyes go down, their heads go down, and they start doodling. You need to be the person to raise your hand! Is it for the safety committee? Is it for the newsletter committee? Is it for a new project team? When you jump in and show that you're going to put yourself out there, you build relationships across the organization, and that's going to help you gain more success.

3. You need to be known as the person who has a fantastic and uplifting attitude. There is nothing wrong with having your personal brand as the person who is friendly and outgoing. The next time you are at work, make a concerted effort to say hello to people in your building. If you can brand yourself as an outgoing, extroverted, friendly, can-do person, you're going to build those relationships, which will build your leadership skills, which will help you be more successful.

4. Finally, don't forget to ask for assistance with a work project. When that project is complete, make sure you brag on that person and thank him or her. People love to hear how important they are. When you ask for help from a different department or from another person in the organization, write an e-mail to the person's boss and tell the boss what a great job the person did. All of a sudden, you're building relationships and gaining skills that are going to help you throughout your entire career.

Wright

So the R stands for relationships, and I can agree with how important that is in business. Let's move on to the letter O.

Blank

The O is for *Oversight,* and that may sound strange. When you think of bad leadership traits, one that comes to mind is usually micromanagement (i.e., "big brother is watching"). Another negative connotation of oversight appears when your area or department has not been performing up to the expected standards, therefore, someone has to come in and oversee your department. You hear about this in government all the time. Something bad has happened, so there will soon be a "government oversight task force." One final negative definition of oversight is "an unintentional mistake." For example, the fact that you forgot to pay one of your vendors was an oversight—it was an unintentional mistake. While these are the commonly thought of words and phrases associated with oversight, I want to introduce a new definition of the term "oversight" and show how it plays into our concept of great leadership.

My definition of "oversight" is "watchful care." That's a great definition for our purpose of creating great leaders. Both words are equally important, but the word "care" can be an essential component of leadership. It's been said a million times that people don't care how much you know until they know how much you care.

Remember that the R for *Relationships* helps us to build the people side of leadership. The O for *Oversight* ("watchful care") is going to help with the tangible or the hard side of business. What should you care about as a leader? A successful leader needs to have oversight of his or her physical environment. Employees will only follow a leader who shows that he or she cares about them and their work environment. Here are some things you can do:

- Pick up trash in the parking lot
- Listen to employees who complain that their cubicle or their office is too hot or too cold
- Allow them to turn their work space into a fun and friendly environment
- Drive a corporate culture where others would also have "watchful care" over the environment and each other

In my current office, there was a dead roach on the floor in a little used hallway. After not being picked up by the custodial team for three days, someone took the time to create a sticky note and placed it on the ground next to the dead roach. The words on the sticky note read, "I am dead. Please throw me away!" That roach stayed there for another couple of days before I saw it, whereby I promptly picked it up and threw it away. In a way, it was both funny and depressing at the same time. The first option of my teammates was to not pick up the roach; but instead, they let someone else (the custodial staff) know that they weren't doing their job properly.

Leaders who have mastered this concept of oversight would have picked up the roach right away! They do not say "it's not my job," "it's not my area," or any other non-involvement phrase. True leaders get involved and show oversight over their physical environment.

In addition to the oversight of your "physical environment," you also have to have oversight of your "corporate culture." One person can have a tremendous influence on a corporate culture. Corporate culture is often defined as "the way things are done around here." Great leaders adjust the corporate culture in good times and bad. If sales are up, turnover is low, employees are getting along, and people enjoy coming to work, it is your job as a leader to feed that positive culture. Conversely, if you work in a challenging culture with backstabbing, gossip, and micromanaging, it's your job as a leader to influence that culture for the better. You need to have a positive influence on the culture, and you can only do that by staying connected to your culture via oversight.

Another benefit of leading with oversight is that you move from a reactionary state to a preventative state. Disney Theme Parks are a great example. Before any new attraction opens, the company holds what they call a "test and adjust" period. During this time, they are going to work the ride, try new things, have soft openings, listen to feedback from the guests and the Cast Members, and then implement as many positive changes as they can before the attraction or the shop opens up to the general public. This "test and adjust" concept applies not just to attractions, but also to merchandise shops, food locations, and new entertainment venues. You can't have true oversight without open and honest feedback.

Back in the late 1980s, Universal Orlando (at the time it was Universal Studios Florida) and the Walt Disney World Resort were battling head to head to see which could open up their new movie studio theme park first. Along the way, there was some lack of oversight by leadership at Universal Orlando, and Universal opened its theme park on day one with many challenges. Many of their biggest attractions were not operational on opening day, and many guests left unhappy. The key lesson is to take the time to do it right.

Let me just sum up the O for *Oversight* by sharing four action items for you.

Pretend that you own the company. Treat the company as if it were your own. Keep your facilities clean, keep your employees happy, and keep the brand protected. Anyone who wants to be a leader in your organization can do those things—it does not matter what title he or she has.

Be a positive influence in your corporate culture by being a role model. Be open and honest. Share your truths with your employees as well as your struggles. Create that trust and respect that your employees are looking for, and shake-up the culture with your words and actions.

Remember that oversight means prevention! Look for ways to put out the best product the first time. Try to be more of a proactive leader in a proactive organization. Create some accountability groups for special projects.

The most important thing is to be a customer in your own organization! If you are in a managerial role, make sure you walk your area daily. Make a phone call to your organization, listen to people in your phone trees, and see how frustrating it can be. Try and see what your customers go through on a daily basis. Use the tools and resources that are at your fingertips to provide positive oversight for your organization and your employees.

Wright

If I were to guess, I would say the L in ROLE is for leading; is that correct?

Blank

Leading is the common thread that runs through the model, but the L actually stands for *Leverage*. Leverage has become a very "HR" term, but it fits well here as our third component of the ROLE model of leadership.

The concept of leverage is as simple as a see-saw. Have you ever seen anyone having fun on a see-saw alone? Probably not. The person just sits there until someone else comes along, and that is when the fun starts. This is what leverage is all about. A great definition of leverage is the power or the ability to act or to influence people, events, and decisions.

Let's begin with the very first word in this definition, which is power. Most people know there are many different types of power—position power, referent power, legitimate power, position power, and so on. While power can be used in a positive way, power can also corrupt. Similarly, the L for Leverage is the part of the model where most leaders can get tripped up. To return to the see-saw example, do you remember as a child when the person on the other side would jump off at the top, leaving you to crash down, bottom-first, onto the ground? That would be a harmful use of leverage. Leverage, used incorrectly, can cause undue harm to a leader.

There are multiple ways to apply leverage in an organization. But be careful! Look at big private companies like Enron and smaller government agencies across the United States, and you'll find someone in leadership was using leverage in a way that he or she shouldn't have. Beware of the power of leverage!

Leverage can also be used to influence people, events, and decisions. True leaders will use influence to gain the leverage they need. So many leaders, even today, still rely on what I call the old "demand and command" model of leadership instead of the "influence and inspire" model so prevalent today.

Back in the 1950s, Walt Disney was trying to get funding to build Disneyland, which was going to be the first ever "theme park." He wanted to build it in California. Getting that much funding back in those days was not an easy task, especially for such an unknown venture as a theme park. Walt got in touch with the ABC Television Network, and he and ABC actually used each other as leverage. Disney needed some funding for a theme park. ABC was a distant third in the ratings, and needed some top notch programming. In a visual sense, both of them were sitting on the see-saw alone. They were not having any fun until they got together, and that's when success started to happen.

What really happened with Disneyland and ABC could also be termed as "partnering." *Partnering is a huge part of leverage.* In the business world, success comes with having multiple partners who will work with you because you can't do it alone. So think about the ROLE model again:

- You can't start creating partnerships until you have *Relationships* (R) that will help you with the "who you need to know" component.
- You can't move forward until you have the *Oversight* (O) that helps determine the "what you need to know."
- Now you can use the *Leverage* (L), and the leverage is "how are you going to get it done."

There are many ways to apply leverage, especially if you focus on partnering. Partnering can and must be a two way street. If a partnership becomes one-sided, it is very likely to dissolve. If you want to fail as a leader, call somebody your "partner," ask him or her for assistance, and then don't reciprocate. That relationship is likely to fall apart. When you partner with somebody, it needs to always be two ways.

Let me just sum up the L for Leverage by sharing three action items with you.

1. Use your power wisely. Remember how it feels when you're on a see-saw with a friend and the person jumps off. It hurts, and that's what it will feel like if someone feels you're abusing your power as a leader and he or she jumps off. Make sure you keep your power in check.

2. Make sure you build your relationships first before you try to apply leverage. You can't apply leverage until you have built relationships.

3. Get involved in the concept of influence. There are plenty of great books, Web sites, and other resources out there on how to influence people. For many leaders, influence may be their only way to get work done. Perhaps you are an individual contributor or you don't have direct reports; your only way of getting your message through to people is via influence. Figure out how you can improve your influence skills, and then try to apply those practices in your work environment.

Wright

I'd like to buy a vowel, and I will buy an E, as the last letter in ROLE. How does the letter E tie into ROLE?

Blank

The E is for *Evolvement,* and this is a very simple one. A great definition for "evolvement" is "to develop gradually." Most importantly, evolvement ties the other three together.

- Not everybody is comfortable building *Relationships* (R), or some people may be introverts. In order to *evolve*, they need to work on this by improving their business communication skills.
- Some leaders may be unsure of their corporate culture. They may need to grow or they may be new in a leadership role. They need to *evolve* in their *Oversight* (O).

220

- When it comes to *Leverage* (L), a new employee or a new leader may have problems knowing where to start or who they can partner with. They're going to need to learn what and with whom to leverage so they too will need to *evolve* in this skill.

As you can see, when you "evolve" as a leader, the first three components continue to evolve as well.

One of the biggest stumbling blocks to evolvement is a leader's current leader. As an employee in local government, I teach basic supervisory skill sessions to city and county leaders. We spend time in these classes sharing ideas and best practices, but then the classes end. Although the knowledge and ideas gained should influence their behavior back in the workplace, sometimes it does not. I send changed leaders back to their unchanged environment, and you can figure out what happens. They get back to their working locations where their leaders are stagnant and unwilling to change. When these new, younger leaders attempt to evolve, they are reminded to keep their ideas to themselves and are told, *"We've always done it this way."* Sometimes it feels like that statement is the rallying cry of poor performing organizations.

But it doesn't have to be that way. There are hundreds and hundreds of great leaders in civil service who want to change and evolve. They want to change themselves, they want to change their culture, they want to become great leaders, and they want to leave a legacy for the future. But they hit the roadblock—their current leader—and that's a hard speed bump to overcome.

Most high performing employees constantly feel the need to evolve; they refuse to conform to the status quo. I began my career as a sportscaster. After two years, I decided I wanted to work at Disney, and I started in attractions. I never planned on staying in one area too long. I transferred to become a resort front desk/bell services host, then a front office manager, then an orientation consultant, then a college intern instructor, and then a leadership consultant, all because inside me I have this inner drive to evolve. That spirit still lives in me today.

The Disney theme parks are great examples of evolvement. When Walt Disney was creating Disneyland, the most exciting part of it to him was that it would never be completed. It could hold all of his dreams. He marveled that even the trees would continue to grow. All Disney theme parks continue to evolve today.

As attractions and entertainment options are replaced with others, they continue to evolve and get better, and so do the employees.

One of the funny nuances of working with Disney is the impression of staying in one work location for more than two years. I was a college intern instructor for about five years. I loved that role, but when I saw my peers out and about in the parks or resorts, the following dialogue would always occur:

"Hey, Pete, good to see you! Where are you working now?"

"I'm with the College Program as a college instructor."

"Still?"

That always stuck with me—*"Still?"* The word "still" comes across when people are staying in one job too long. Part of the Disney culture is that if you're not up and moving around, you're getting stagnant. If you're in one location for two, three, or four years, you are looked at as having little motivation, and that was not the case at all. People in that situation may just have found the perfect job for them. That may exist in other organizations as well. I get the image of a stagnant pond with stuff floating on top, and I think of evolvement as a fountain in the middle of the pond. It's constantly moving the waters—it's constantly churning the waters—it's making the pond better, and that's what happens when we can evolve as leaders.

Let me just sum up the E for Evolvement by sharing three action items for you.

1. Make sure you have goals—one-year, two-year, or three-year goals. What do you want to accomplish, and where do you want to go? You want to revise those goals once a year. On the first day of every January, go back and revisit your annual goals.

2. There was a slogan for Bud Dry (beer) years ago, and the slogan was, "Why ask why? Drink Bud Dry!" The slogan for evolvement should be, "Yes, ask why!" There is nothing wrong with asking "why" and questioning the way things are done. This will not only help you evolve, but it's going to assist your organization as well. Don't be afraid to push back and ask "why" as you're evolving.

3. Don't reward complacency, either in yourself or in people that you lead. Walt Disney once said, "I happen to be an inquisitive guy, and when I see things I don't like, I start thinking, 'Why do they have to be like this and

how can I improve them?'" If you follow this idea of not rewarding complacency and trying to evolve, you will continue to grow and develop as a successful leader and toward a successful career.

Wright

Between the four concepts of *Relationships, Oversight, Leverage,* and *Evolvement,* which one do you think is most difficult for leaders?

Blank

It all starts with relationships. You're not going to be able to do any of the others if you're not good at building relationships. Everyone is going to have different strengths, but I believe that the concept of leverage may be the most difficult for leaders to grasp.

If we go back to the see-saw analogy, finding leverage is a true balancing act. For example, if you have an adult on one side of the see-saw, and a small child on the other side, it will not be that much fun for either of them. Can they use the see-saw? Yes, but it's going to take a little more effort and skill. The child will have to hang on a little more than the adult. But when you have somebody on the other side of the see-saw who fills an exact need, it becomes easy—it then becomes fun to be on the seesaw. Successful leaders need to know who to invite to be with them on the see-saw to help create leverage. There may be plenty of good choices out there, but only one or two are going to be perfect fits.

If we take that analogy into the business world, you may need to leverage someone to help you complete a project. The easiest part is just to fill the void—take the first person who comes along or who is the next person in line. But part of leverage is strategy. Sometimes in business, strategy is pushed to the side for efficiency or convenience. Both power and influence, which are part of the leverage model, also can make or break a leader, so you want to be careful and use your leverage very wisely.

Wright

I like how this all fits together. Today there are so many acronyms, phrases, and catchy sayings surrounding leadership. As a leader, why should I follow this ROLE model concept?

Blank

As a facilitator, I'm constantly teaching and training adults on matters like conflict resolution, change management, giving and receiving feedback, and listening skills. The one thing that I've learned from them is that adult learners will forever be tied to the KISS concept: "Keep It Short and Simple" or "Keep It Simple Stupid."

I think that the ROLE acronym is a way of keeping it simple. It's one of the easiest ones to remember. First of all, you're already in a leadership "role," so it's easy to remember this concept of ROLE. Second, the concepts of *Relationships, Oversight, Leverage,* and *Evolvement* are a little different. Granted, "relationships" is a word we hear over and over in leadership training, but you rarely hear oversight or leverage as a positive element of leadership. I think that by using discerning words, the concept will stick with readers and cause them to pause and think and remember what the acronym stands for and how to apply it.

There are many leadership models out there for employees to follow. A Google search for leadership models will return about thirty-two million hits. Now there are thirty-two million and one. After studying and teaching leadership for fifteen years, I truly believe people will be able to improve their leadership skills and move toward success by this concept of knowing their ROLE.

Wright

It looks like you have experience working with leaders in both the private and public sectors. How does the ROLE of leadership differ between these two arenas?

Blank

They should not be that different, but I can tell you firsthand that there are quite a few differences in the way one would lead a private company versus a public one. Let's take the very first letter R for *relationships* and start there.

In the private sector, relationships are how work gets done. When I worked at Disney, there never seemed to be an ulterior motive when people were working together. In the public sector, and more specifically, in local government, leaders still need to use relationships but with a sense of carefulness. Private sector leaders can build relationships in their sleep, but public sector leaders need to sleep with one eye open at all times. When you add elected officials and appointed employees into the mix, it brings lots of questions as to one's main focus—am I leading my team, am I leading to achieve a team goal, or am I leading to achieve my goal?

Unfortunately, cronyism may still exist in some public arenas. Leaders need to make sure that they're making relationships with the right people. There is an old saying that you are known by the company that you keep. Great relationships are confirmed when you can say *"No!"* or *"I'm not going to do that."* or *"I think that's a bad idea."* Those phrases don't damage the relationship. If you're not able to make those comments and keep that relationship alive, it may not be the proper relationship for you to be in.

The other main difference in private and public sector leadership revolves around the E, or the *Evolvement* concept. Private companies are constantly looking to stay ahead of the curve or break new ground. But what I found in the public sector as the status quo is not only expected, but in some cases, it's rewarded. Longevity is rewarded, seniority is rewarded, and the system may not appreciate or reward those whose thinking patterns evolve. This may be a bit of a stereotype, but depending on where you work in the public sector, those whose thinking patterns evolve may be branded as troublemakers and rabble-rousers. *"How dare you try and think creatively and grow?"* some might say. There may be more willingness for leaders to evolve in the private sector as opposed to the public sector.

Wright

Well, the title of our book is *Yes You Can!* Do you think there are leaders out there who will ever say, "No, I can't" to the concept of knowing their ROLE?

Blank

Unfortunately, there are some things that are out of your control. Don't forget that leadership is not something assigned to you. You know you are a terrible leader when you turn around and see no one is following you. You have to earn the title of leader. There may be managers in your area, or in your business, who choose to reject the title of leader. Why? Because it's hard—leadership is hard! Everyone has the ability to be a great leader, but some choose not to, and I suspect those people are not reading this book or doing anything to evolve.

When I first came to work in the public sector, I saw lots of opportunities for growth. We did a lot of leadership training for frontline leaders and frontline managers, but not a lot for executives. Nothing was available for deputy directors, directors, appointing authorities, chiefs, captains, high ranking officials, etc. I brought that up to a couple of people on my local team after being here for six or eight months. The first things they said to me were phrases such as:

"That will never work."

"You'll never get them all in a room together."

"This is not where you used to work."

"This is someplace that is a little different, so don't even bother trying."

I wouldn't accept that. I asked my leader if I could push a little bit and see if I can make this happen, and he supported me. It took longer than it would in other organizations, but after pushing, using good communication—talking and sharing and e-mailing and getting out the information about our products—we got twenty-five high ranking government executives from the local community into one room to teach them about leadership. It got such a good review that we're now offering it twice a year. When something like this is successful, then word of mouth happens; this is how we end up changing a culture.

There may be times when you need to step back and know when to "give up the ghost," so to speak, but there are also times when it is acceptable and actually required for you to push and to think about this "Yes you Can!" concept. This whole concept that "one person can make a difference" is very important in leadership.

Wright

The subtitle of this book is *Reaching Your Potential while Achieving Greatness.* What advice can you share that will enable readers to "reach their potential" in their ROLE as a leader?

Blank

I think that part of the problem with leadership today is that business and society have become okay with mediocrity. "C's in schools are the new B's." I had a good friend in college who always said "Dare to be average!" That's all anybody cares about, and I think that some of this mentality may have taken over in business today.

Take a look at your local neighborhoods, and any of the local businesses that may have shut down recently. You can find any number of retail, food, or manufacturing locations that no longer exist. Some people blame it on the economy, and some blame it on bad luck, but at the end of the day, most failures are the direct result of poor leadership. Leaders in those businesses did not make the right *relationships*, they didn't have the proper *oversight* of their business, they didn't *leverage* the right people, and in the end, they failed to *evolve*. The reason those organizations did not reach their potential is because those organizations did not let their *leaders* reach their potential.

So what can we do about it? There are three main tasks I think that current and future leaders need to address in order to use this ROLE model to help them reach their potential.

1. The first is for leaders to use the ROLE model to be a "role model." In order to be a great leader you must "first, know thyself" (Socrates). The ROLE Model will do you no good if you don't know your values, if you don't know your core beliefs, and if you don't know what you stand for. That's the basis of great leadership. Most leaders fail because they come across a troubling assignment and have to make a tough decision, and they don't have any internal basis for their decisions. You have to make sure you have a core set of values you will not shy away from, no matter what the cost.

2. Try to focus on one letter at a time instead of the whole model. If you're good at *Relationships* (R), then go ahead and start with *Oversight* (O). Just make sure that you take time to become successful at one instead of just being just so-so at all four. True leaders understand this process of becoming a great leader as ongoing—you will never come to a time where you've got it all. I'm not a perfect leader, you're not a perfect leader, and there are no perfect leaders out there who have conquered all four. That's because the last one, which is *Evolvement* (E) means that your journey will never be complete. You're always going to need to continue to evolve as a leader to avoid failure.

3. Ask for help. I'm amazed at the number of people I have known over the years who were too proud to ask for assistance or to ask for feedback. We do not know everything, and there is nothing wrong with getting help. At Disney, you were taught the very first day, in your traditions orientation class, that when you put on the Disney name tag, and you walk on stage in one of our parks and resorts, you are now expected to know everything.

    Now that's not true, but that is what our guests perceive—once you have a Disney name tag, you now know everything! That's the image we wanted portrayed, but we know that's not possible. So we set up many methods to assist all the Cast Members—phone hotlines, company intranet, open forums, meetings, etc. All Disney Cast Members are trained to never say, "I don't know," but to instead say, "I don't know, but let's find out together." That's puts the onus on the Cast Member to help the guest get the correct answer. At the same time, the cast member is self-developing his or her own leadership skills. What a great model! As we're growing our potential, if we don't know something, let's find out together.

I know this chapter will continue to enhance your leadership skills, and I encourage you to use the ROLE model to reach your leadership potential!

With both public and private sector work experience, **Pete Blank** is uniquely qualified to share leadership techniques with your business. He partners with organizations across America to enhance their leadership teams. His sports broadcasting experience combines with his Disney leadership experience to provide you with a speaker who can deliver real behavioral changes in your employees. Pete has spoken to groups in fields such as health care, banking, marketing, and human resources. He is an active member of the National Speakers Association (NSA) and is President of the Greater Birmingham Chapter of the American Society for Training and Development (ASTD).

Pete Blank

Alabama Training, Leadership, And Strategy (ATLAS)
407-376-8384
peteblank@peteblank.com
www.peteblank.com

CHAPTER FIFTEEN

Reposition the Servant in You!

by Shannon Bettis

David Wright (Wright)

Today we are talking with Shannon Bettis. Shannon is a native Texan, from the Dallas area. After receiving her undergraduate degree from Mississippi State University in 1995, she returned to the Dallas Metroplex where she was trained in sales and finance. She is a career commercial banking professional, an inspirational public speaker, and founder of the faith-based outreach platform "Defined by The Storm." Wife and empty-nester, she is also the North Texas Director of Women's Business Initiatives for Sterling Bank, member of the National Speakers Association, and active in mentoring. Shannon is a sought-after, high-energy speaker who is focused on compelling others to exceed the limits of their experiences—professionally and personally.

Shannon, welcome to *Yes You Can!*

When you heard about the opportunity to participate in this series of interviews centered on reaching full potential, what captured your attention? More specifically, why is this subject material something you have such an obvious passion for?

Shannon Bettis (Bettis)

Clearly, my interest lies in inspiring others to be all they can be. It is not that I believe I have "arrived," but I recognize and am grateful for the efforts of individuals who took the time and continue to make a difference along my journey. For that reason

231

alone I consider it a privilege to have this opportunity to sow that same seed with a difference-making purpose in mind. My philosophy is that we are all fellow sojourners and it is our reasonable service to bring as many along with us as we can. I hear my pastor say periodically that "people don't care how much you know until they know how much you care," and I am a subscriber to that theory. That is why I aspire to be an exultant leader—one who takes ownership in investing in others.

Wright

When you think of the word "potential," what is the first description that comes to mind?

Bettis

Webster's dictionary sums it up nicely with "existing in possibility; capable of development into actuality." If I could apply that to an individual and elaborate on that, I would say it is a person who never allows his or her expectations to be limited by his or her experiences. Life has a way of slowing us down when we only do what we have done. But when we live in the freedom of knowing that every day is a new day given to us to make the most of, we are empowered to hone, in a practical way, effective use of our gifts and experiences more productively. That's when we show real potential—professionally and personally—forgetting those things that are behind, and pressing toward the mark of our high calling.

In the literal sense, our gifts and experiences were not ever intended to serve our individual purposes solely, but to benefit in a greater way, the people around us. That includes our employees, employers, clients we sell to, communities we serve in, and the homes we live and love in. You don't see many runners looking over their shoulders to see how far they've traveled. But any seasoned runner—like any good coach—will tell you what happened the time they did!

Wright

What have you found to be the common denominator in an individual that lines up with that description, both in and out of an office atmosphere?

Bettis

There are several key things I see recurring in these individuals, but the main ingredient seems to be a vital sense of integrity. You can't go wrong making right choices—in anything. I always say that every choice you make has a consequence directly related to it—a good one or a bad one—but with certainty you can count on one or the other!

With regard to management, they exemplify integrity by setting a precedence people can follow with dignity and confidence. You cannot lay a foundation for those under your direction on a platform you do not possess. In its absence, it is impossible to attract and retain key talent with the same mindset. Without exception, they lose respect for management, and passion for the service or product they purport to believe in dwindles.

That downward spiral of morale doesn't stop at the employee or the next layer of management, but extends to everyone in their concentric circle they communicate with and market to. Unfortunately, too many corporations today overlook that fact and stock their teams with leadership that operates under the philosophy of "what have you done for me lately?" While employees under this type of influence may produce short-term results that resemble "potential," as soon as they figure out how expendable they are, they will find another place to serve where their efforts are appreciated. If we could capture the profound effect of total corporate dollars—literal sunk costs in the form of human capital racing toward the door to a competitor—that approach would cost management a demotion.

I am convinced we need to have more companies instilling integrity from the highest levels of the organization. Recognizing that it does not come from a name brand university, the top-level producer or the one with the highest average of daily sales calls is step number one. Integrity comes from within—character. You can't hire it from a resume per se, but you can recognize it when you see it.

While I am not saying quantifiable attributes have no value or that goals within an organization are not important, I am saying all things are not created equal. Some of the most challenging managers are those who rise to leadership based upon those merits alone. A great salesperson does not automatically have what it takes to provide the type of servant leadership necessary to empower the workforce to take a company to the next level in the marketplace. In fact, I would argue that in many cases, the personality profiles and the things that drive them are as inherently different as night and day. Not all the time, but a good bit of it.

Wright

You have had the privilege of working in some of the largest financial institutions in our country and alongside some very accomplished executives at the same time. In your opinion, what works and what doesn't?

Bettis

I have been blessed with great examples, and that remains the case today. As with many industries, banking is a closely held community, and often paths cross inadvertently, time and time again, either directly or indirectly. By far, the individuals who stand out from their peers are those marked by servant leadership styles. Inside the company, they are not intimidated and will tell you what they know about the business, their good and bad experiences, how they learned it, and what they would do if they had the chance to do it again. Outside of the company, they are the sales force seeking a place to add value on behalf of the bank's banner. They do not compromise truth vertically or laterally, and are constantly thinking of a way to improve. These people have mastered the practice of making their "yes" mean yes, and their "no" mean no. They are trustworthy in all aspects of the word.

Over my fifteen years in banking, I have discovered that our industry within the middle market is best managed on a relational level, and those who are servant leaders are pros at it. They have earned the trust and respect of their colleagues and clients, and have not allowed the pursuit of transactions to reduce them to order-takers. They are excellent risk managers for the bank and its depositors, and they realize that the longevity of their career depends upon their innate ability to build a discerning platform of advocacy at every level.

People of this caliber treat their peers in the same manner, which results in a mutually beneficial atmosphere where employees are emotionally engaged in the welfare of the institution they serve.

Wright

Over the course of our conversation, it has occurred to me that there are not many female executives in your field of expertise—commercial banking at mid management levels and higher. What advice do you have for a young woman today considering taking that first step up that corporate ladder?

Bettis

I am a huge proponent of the practice of mentoring young professionals in a corporate environment. Given the fact that men and women are so different psychologically, it is imperative that a young woman seeks out the role model of a more seasoned female. This mid to high-level manager should be trustworthy, personify dignity, authority, and professionalism in all ways. She should be observed in the way she balances family responsibilities with the office, her attire, communication (written and verbal), and the manner in which she conducts herself in corporate settings, including dining and networking. She should be on the young professional's calendar at least once per month for coffee or lunch, and be willing to articulate successful ways to navigate job situations. She can be a tremendous resource of knowledge in an environment that can be otherwise lonely, hostile, and counterintuitive to a newcomer.

I had the privilege of walking alongside two such women over the first four years of my career and that experience gave me an effective set of professional skills as a young woman, which gave me a certain level of confidence that has remained with me to this day. The advice I received also directly contributed to the development of my core competencies.

Wright

I notice there are few instances you reference leadership without pairing it up with the word "servant." It is almost as if those words are inseparable in your mind. Talk about that.

Bettis

Servant leadership is the differentiating factor between those out to fulfill their own interest and those seeking the greater good of others. The very word has become a popular buzzword—a watered down version of its original founding definition. The Greenleaf Center for Servant Leadership, named after the late Robert K. Greenleaf, strives to keep the original meaning intact. While I am not attempting to outline their platform, let it suffice to say that these leaders rise each morning and live the day on purpose! They naturally expend their gift of serving. They are thoughtful, insightful, altruistic people with a bent toward making a difference. Too many people live life, run their businesses, manage their employees, and sell their products and services as if the potential for personal gain is the main goal. But a true leader in this context goes about living out his or her potential in the opposite manner. True leaders fully recognize that meeting the needs of others will naturally produce the fruit of the leader they aspire to be. How much more productive would corporate America be if we actually had that mindset and took the time to invest in others first?

It's very similar to the analogy I have heard that if a parent feels compelled to shout to the children, "I am boss in his house!" it likely means he or she is not. Effective servant leaders do not need to announce it. Instead of competing to lead the greatest empire, everyone surrounding them rises to the highest common denominator to be part of a rising empire! Zig Ziglar says it best: "You can have everything in life you want, if you will just help enough other people get what they want." Said another way, the fastest way to a blessing is to be one!

Wright

What are "difference-makers"?

Bettis

Difference-makers are servant leaders who lead a deliberate life of consistent influence. Ten notable characteristics include:

- They learn from mistakes and grow better (not bitter);
- They spend less time looking out of the rear view mirror and more time anticipating the view through the windshield;
- They are vibrant because their joy is not predicated upon happiness that depends entirely upon what happens each day;
- They are steadfast and passionate about the task at hand, and are not driven solely by the applause of the popular vote;
- They possess a strong conviction for right and wrong that is not based in the fickle values of society;
- They are willing to stand alone for a season if that level of conviction is necessary;
- They tell the truth on all occasions, whether the news is good or bad, and will deliver that message without concern about how it may be received or to whom it must be delivered;
- They practice humility diligently, particularly in the presence of those around them;
- They are quick to admit an error and to be accountable for it;
- They recognize that sometimes the most valuable accomplishment in any single day is to show personal interest in someone else. When they have a smile, they share it without prejudice.

Wright

If I were to ask you for three take-aways for an aspiring manager who wants to make a difference in the lives and careers of those around them, what would they be? What would your aspirations be?

Bettis

Begin every day in prayer and quiet time with the intent of being rooted and grounded in the only thing that will never change—God's love for you. Carry that truth mixed with a spirit of gratitude for all over which you have been given responsibility. Faithfulness over what you have is an indicator of that which is to come.

Enable others under your leadership to be more successful than they are presently— never willfully withhold what you can do this day to make their dream possible. Be an examiner and exhorter of the gifts of those around you and capitalize on them. Not only will they experience great satisfaction in their contribution, but you will build loyalty through that exercise and find yourself surrounded with the success of others. They may be the most inspired and ingenuitive thinkers you would ever hope to have on your team.

Instill! Don't sit still! Make it a practice to communicate openly with your team on the corporate direction delivered to you, specifically on how you perceive their gifts will make a contribution. State expectations clearly and provide resources necessary to attain them. Offer recognition for a job well done in a way that is meaningful. Be prompt to solicit and receive feedback on things that keep individuals from reaching their full potential. Be willing to carry the team message either direction on the corporate ladder, particularly when it is necessary to effect changes within the organization. If you don't get a desired result, try again.

Wright

In your opinion, what is the single greatest limitation to an individual's ability to reach his or her full potential?

Bettis

Failure to overcome and grow from a significant loss is the single most contributing factor to the paralysis of ambition (personally and professionally). A movie titled *The Mission* did a great job of depicting this with actor Robert De Niro as he attempted to drag a bag full of iron that he had tied around his waist up the face of a slippery mountain in the rain, without shoes or gear. That bag full of regrets nearly cost him his life because of his choice to drag it around, even though he had been given a new beginning. In an act of kindness, a native in the movie sliced the rope and set him free. That is what we need to do with the circumstances surrounding our setbacks, and if we are not strong enough to help ourselves, we need to find someone who is. Job eliminations, disappointments, mistakes, betrayal, and acts of desperation have no place in the presence of this day. A saint is a sinner who falls down, but gets back up!

Ever met those people living in the past, lamenting over the same insurmountable situation? These people are on a field trip to the desert. Though we all walk through dry times, if we are not careful, a trip that could have lasted eleven days, may take forty years. While some of us may be slower learners than others, we must be willing to move beyond that experience and, as one young minister says, "turn our messes into messages."

Wright

Have you ever been labeled a Type A personality, yet in a non-traditional sense? I ask that in light of the fact that your passion to influence others for a greater good seems to be the overwhelming message here. Not only are you obviously excited about that, you are compelling. Who inspired you?

Bettis

While I have always been the glass-half-full person, the real change for me occurred at the age of thirty-one when I surrendered my life to the Lord Jesus Christ. Until that day I was chasing treasures on a never-ending treadmill of the expectations of others. Each person had a different opinion and everything was subject to change. My identity was wrapped up in performance and I felt constantly at risk of being replaced. It drove me to sacrifice the most precious things in life, for which I received dreadful emptiness in return. While that 180-degree turn is another story, it changed my life in direct proportion to the degree of His love for me. So the direct answer to who inspired me is simply, Jesus. He repaired the ruins and restored the years I had wasted. He even saw to it that I prospered and lived a richer life than I ever dreamed possible.

Shortly thereafter, I made my way to church and the first Sunday school class I attended was led by none other than Mr. Zig Ziglar. Every Sunday we were ushered in to the "largest weekly sales meeting for Jesus in Dallas"! He and his wife, Jean, welcomed and inspired me and still do to this day. I only hope to have the same level of influence on just one individual by the end of my life as this couple has had on me and thousands of others.

Of course my response would be incomplete without my sincere expression of gratitude for my best friend and husband, Scott. He is my steadfast encourager, and generously loves and supports me in everything I do.

Wright

I can see that your faith is important to you and that you are not ashamed to share it. Why do you find that to be the case?

Bettis

My faith is my foundation and without it I am nothing. I have personal proof it is true and many have been witnesses to the difference it has made in me. After experiencing the authenticity of it, some made the same decision for themselves. We all are driven by the need to worship something; it is just that most (like me) try the created things before they meet the Creator.

It most certainly has not been the most popular message to share, and it is not always well received, for that matter. But the transformation it has provided and the unexplainable state of peace in very difficult situations have been more than enough sustenance for me. My desire is not to merely speak of things I have only read about, but to live in the light of that truth so that my "fruit" will be evidence enough. Then, when I am asked for a reason for this hope I have, my explanation will be more convincing. I aspire to live my life in such a way that if there were to be an investigation I would be on the Most Wanted list, and that would not be because I was wearing a t-shirt that said "I am a Christian." That might be cause for further investigation before conviction these days!

Just as if had I won ten million dollars and were featured on *The O'Riley Factor, Hannity,* and *Fox News*, this transformation is also too good to keep a secret. If you don't know this faith, I implore you to seek this relationship with all that you are, and you will find it.

Wright

We have traveled an abbreviated journey through this chapter, capturing in a limited amount of time the essence of your perspective on living out potential. I have the distinct impression there is more where this came from! Do you have any closing thoughts for our readers?

Bettis

That is a loaded question I will use to expound upon an illustrative analogy of the Master Gardener. The use of comparisons is intended to exemplify the characteristics of that of a servant leader at the office. It's a snapshot of a difference-maker in action who is busy crafting, investing in, and mentoring a team that personifies the virtues of maximum potential defined by excellence. Everything worth having is worth working for! With that in mind:

Don't let the fruits produced under your care die on the vine. Become a motivator and intentional gardener of your office! Start by planting the seeds that produce the fruits you desire. Since apples don't grow in lemon tree orchards and acorns don't fall from weeping willows, it all begins by choosing the right people for the job.

Fertilize the ground with nutrients specific to the needs of your field to prepare the soil for maximum productivity. Do your research on the composition of the soil in your area in order to understand what it needs to reach full production capacity, just as you would ascertain what it takes to meet or exceed the directive of corporate goals before issuing action items. Plant the seeds at the right depth and distance apart, and water at the prescribed intervals. Figure out which seed varieties grow well in close proximity, and layer different ones in for diversity purposes.

When timelines are tight and the corporate pressure for results is on full throttle, do not fall into the practice of digging up the seed to check for progress. Doing this only detracts from productivity because it shocks the seed in its regeneration process and interrupts the chemical changes occurring at the molecular level in the soil immediately surrounding the seed.

As it is in nature, so it is in life. Employees need supervision, not impatience. The greatest transformations take place in dark and moist surroundings, not on ominous mountaintops in broad view. Just because we can't see it, doesn't mean progress is not present. Growth and maturation takes time, patience, discipline, safety under cover, and adherence to the process.

Watch for weeds that threaten to choke the life from young saplings, and do so regularly. It's amazing how quickly unwanted weeds sprout up overnight, particularly in new gardens. In the same way, protect your employees from office politics and do not be found guilty of promoting divisiveness. At the same time, use caution in your efforts to exterminate such interference with the rapid fire of poison. If the wind carries the droplets, it could be harmful to the crop. Likewise, avoid haphazardly pulling a handful of weeds at one time, as you risk uprooting the sapling along with them. Even if you manage to leave the sapling undisturbed, you may break the roots of the weeds beneath the surface that are entangled with the roots of your crop. It's best to identify spoilers individually and remove them before corrosion sets in. Whatever you do, don't unscrupulously pull out the weed-eater at this stage. It's too dangerous to use that tool with precision around delicate growth. Be diligent and remove what you can on your hands and knees during this season, and soon you will be driving a riding lawnmower around mature crops.

Irritants and interruptions are inevitable in the work place and in the long run make us better stewards as we learn diligence in preventive maintenance. Remember, we are tested and held accountable by those watching our reaction to adversity, particularly in places of leadership.

Keep a close eye on the transformation of the buds as they turn into flowers and ultimately the fruit you have been anticipating. It will remind you of how rewarding all of your careful attention has been. When the time is just right, pick that fruit and place it in packaging for sale and delivery. In the process, you will thereby redirect nutrients to the other branches for additional production of healthy fruit.

Depending upon the type of fruit you planted, it may take as many as three seasons of fruit production to attain just the right flavor. So be willing to invest more time in training the branches to ensure the fruit is grown in full sunlight. If you pick it too soon it will be edible but not flavorful, but if you wait too long, it will be useless mush if the birds don't get it first. Management should practice the same observation regarding the condition of their team.

Finally, if it becomes apparent that the crop has fallen prey to an unscheduled fungus at any phase of the season, pull it up, cut off the impaired portion, rinse carefully, and repot it under different conditions. Whatever you do, don't choose to ignore it. Unchecked, it may infect the entire garden.

Mistakes breed success in production and that can be said about anything. Be first to admit it, then try to do something different. The definition of insanity is doing the same thing over again and expecting a different result.

Shannon R. Bettis is a native Texan, raised in the Dallas area. After receiving her undergraduate degree from Mississippi State University in 1995, she returned to the Dallas Metroplex where she was trained in sales and finance. She is a career commercial banking professional, an inspirational public speaker, and founder of the faith-based outreach platform "Defined by the Storm." Wife and empty-nester, she is also the North Texas Director of Women's Business Initiatives for Sterling Bank, member of the National Speakers Association, and active in mentoring. Shannon is a sought-after, high-energy speaker who is focused on compelling others to exceed the limits of their experiences—professionally and personally.

Shannon Bettis

P.O. Box 700922
Dallas, Texas 75370
214-212-0788 cell
sbbot@aol.com

CHAPTER SIXTEEN

The Critical Elements

by Steve Hasenmueller

David Wright (Wright)

Today we're talking to Steve Hasenmueller. Steve writes and speaks about what it takes for businesses and employees to thrive in the demanding and ever-changing marketplace. With over twenty-five years' experience of frontline selling, Steve travels over one hundred days each year working with companies in the United States and Europe. He has conducted seminars and keynotes in nine countries reaching over seven thousand people. His challenging and uplifting messages of personal responsibility, accountability, and faith, along with real-life solutions to improvement will resonate with people who are trying to improve their personal lives through their work.

Steve, welcome to *Yes You Can!*

Steve Hasenmueller (Hasenmueller)

Thank you very much.

Wright

Is there any one strategy for success?

Hasenmueller

You know, I wish there were because then we could all just do that one thing and we would be successful, but there isn't. There are many components to success; however, if there is one overriding or overreaching strategy at this point, I would say that it's to take a long view of life and your career and give yourself the freedom to fail.

What I see mostly in the seminars I conduct is that salespeople are struggling in sales, but at the same time a lot of their efforts are designed to not fail versus to succeed. By not failing you have gotten into a comfort zone of feeling good—"I feel good, I feel comfortable, I don't think I'll fail." But that's not going to stretch you and that's not going to get you where you need to be, especially now and especially not in the future. If there is one strategy for failure I know, it is to settle into that comfort zone and to stay there, but we've got to keep stretching, we've got to keep reaching.

They say these days the average worker is going to change jobs eight times in his or her career and the shelf life of a college degree is eighteen months due to the tremendous speed of change. So my advice is, don't get too comfortable because it's going to change.

Back to the freedom to fail—understand that not everything works out just because you try hard and it doesn't mean you're always going to win. You know, David, failure is an event, it's not a person, and when you can truly internalize this concept, it gives you the freedom to be more creative and bold in your efforts. Napoleon Hill says that the most important moment in your life is when you recognize that you have met with defeat. This means that you get to figure out that you've got self-resilience, you're going to push on, or you are going to give up, one or the other. Also, figuring out what doesn't work is just as important as figuring out what does, and what worked last year might not work this year or ever again.

Another important thing to remember is that anything that has meaning in life and anything that has value will have a fear component attached to it.

Wright

So your background is in sales. What do you see as the critical elements of successful selling?

Hasenmueller

Well, it's a couple of things: first and foremost, it is to really become a student of what successful selling entails. Selling is a lot more than product knowledge and just showing up, although these are a couple of skills that are needed and can carry you a long way. Woody Allen said, "90 percent of success is just showing up," and though he's a humorist, he's right—showing up is a big component of it. But professional selling is a lot more, including continuing to learn and relearn, how to ask questions, how to really listen, and how to figure out who is standing in front of you. That's really been my latest, advice to salespeople—figure out who is standing in front of you. In the past we would have the boilerplate sales training about the masses basically saying, "Hey, do this and you will sell almost everyone," but that's just not the case anymore. I think that the boilerplate technique or mentality is now a great source of frustration for salespeople and customers.

Another key element is never to confuse effort with outcome; outcomes are all that matters in the sales world. This may rub salespeople the wrong way more than anything else I say, but you can do your best, you can be a great person, you can volunteer at your church and local humane shelter, but if you aren't hitting or exceeding your quota, if you aren't building your client base and establishing a reputation as an asset to your customers, if you aren't successfully selling, when that's your job, if the outcome of your efforts is lacking, you've got to change. So as salespeople, we've got to get clear on that distinction—the difference between effort and outcome, and outcome in sales is all that really matters.

In training seminars, I used to show a clip from the film *Glengarry Glen Ross* and I eventually had to stop because of the language (some people were offended) though I believe every salesperson in the world should see that movie. The meeting room scene where Jack tells the salesman, who is getting a cup of coffee, to put the cup of coffee down; the coffee is for closers. And then, he starts really ripping into these guys, telling them they're no good, and if they can't sell, they're nobodies; he says, "If you want to be a good dad, go home and play with your kids," and I would show that very, very harsh scene, and then I'd ask the question: "What's the difference between these sales guys and us, what's the difference between their job as salespeople and ours?" There are two correct answers, one of the correct answers is "nothing," and the other is "presentation." We don't have people speaking to us like that (hopefully), we don't have people beating us over our head and telling us we're no good and to go home if we want to be a good husband, but there really is no difference, the baseline is outcome, we've got to deliver the goods and that's what we get paid to do.

One more key I would add is to develop the ability to handle rejection. The best salespeople in the world have 60 or 70 percent closing ratios, meaning they're rejected

30 or 40 percent of the time. When you really understand this—that nobody gets them all—and you figure out it's a numbers game, then that helps get it out of the personal and into the professional. You know rejection isn't personal for the most part—your prospects are rejecting your business proposal or rejecting your sales presentation—they're rejecting what you're offering, but they're not necessarily rejecting you. When you can figure this out, it goes a long way in helping you focus on becoming a student who is continually learning and adjusting to the selling environment.

In summary, I'd say, become a student of sales, focus on outcome, and learn how to handle rejection. These are the critical elements of successful selling.

Wright

So what would be next?

Hasenmueller

Something very simple—work hard. These days I think this can become your biggest single competitive advantage. Do your best, whatever job you have.

I always ask audiences during the seminars I do, "Who here could do better at your job? Seriously, you are a group of high achievers, who could do better in your job?" Everyone raises his or her hand. It's almost 100 percent everywhere I go, because we all know there is always room for improvement. Improvement, however, takes work and the reason most people don't work hard is that somehow it's gotten into the America psyche that our jobs, or life, should be easy. We spend an incredible amount of time and energy trying to make life easy, which only makes life harder. I've always said, "Hey, if you want life to be easy, you've got to be hard on yourself. If you want life to be hard, then don't worry about it and take it easy on yourself."

Recent research on the human brain has revealed that thinking actually burns calories. Thinking burns three hundred more calories than watching television or listening to music. To the body and to the brain, thinking is hard work so it's easier to watch television than to think or to read.

Watching television is also a very unpopular subject that I talk about. Several years ago (and I think the numbers have increased), *USA Today* reported that the average American watches 4.3 hours of television a day. Based on sixteen-hour days, that's three months a year—three months a year watching television! I've got to tell you, David, that's not working hard. Wouldn't it be easier to get up tomorrow and decide,

"Okay, I'm going to do my best. I'm going to work as hard as I can in my job." That would be easy; but here is the kicker: it would be just as easy not to.

Our lives are filled with temptations—the temptation to watch television versus reading or working out, the temptation to eat or drink too much, to take it easy in our jobs, relax our morals or our values. The news is filled daily with reports of people who have given in to temptation with disastrous results.

Here's the thing to remember: any temptation that we give in to, from minor to major, is a lesson we don't get to learn or to get an outcome we can't possibly enjoy. What we remember the most is the times we gave our best. So work hard on your job and work hard on your personal development.

Wright

Personal development is a broad subject; what specifically can a person do to succceed in this area?

Hasenmueller

Jim Rohn says you've got to work harder on yourself than you do on your job. That statement has stuck with me since the first time I read it more than eight years ago. So if working hard on my job is the key to my financial future, and I have to work harder on myself than I do my job, wow, I'd better get busy. Personal development is self-development, self-development is self-discipline.

The word "discipline" scares most people. Discipline has several definitions listed in the dictionary. One definition is "to punish or correct," but another is "training and studying to learn a subject." So self-discipline is really self-study and self-study is the only way we can get better—we don't have to be sick to get better. Your level of personal development is going to set the tone for all your relationships. Whatever aspect of your life that you aren't happy with, personally or professionally, the answer won't be found in other people—the answer is in yourself. If you want to see the biggest obstacle holding you back from achieving everything that you've ever dreamed of, go look in the mirror. And conversely, if you want to see the greatest asset and opportunity to achieve those things, go look in that same mirror. It all comes down to you—that's our burden and our blessing.

Wright

In your upcoming book and speeches, you use the metaphor of the Triple Jump, a little-known track-and-field event. How does this apply to success in life?

Hasenmueller

The triple jump is considered the most demanding event in track and field. My son is a middle-distance runner. I asked his coach one time why didn't they include the triple jump event. The coach replied, "Because it's hard." I remember I thought geometry was hard, but I didn't see it being dropped from the curriculum, and this is an Olympic event. So I started thinking again about this whole "easy" disease and the reality that life is hard. There is no doubt about it, there are high points and there are low points and they are ever-changing, so the triple jump, the most demanding event in track and field, seemed like a good metaphor. A life well-lived is the most demanding challenge any of us will ever face.

The triple jump is actually three distinct phases: 1) the Hop phase is where you run down the track and leap off of one foot as far as possible, landing on that same foot. 2) The Step phase is when you reach out and stride with your other foot, and 3) the Jump phase is when you plant that foot and leap as far as you can.

These are the three steps to the triple jump and I think they can define three critical components for a successful life. The first thing we have to do is to define success and here is the best definition that I've come across so far: *do the best you can, with what you have, where you are*. I always have to say though, do not let the simplicity of that fool you—*do the best you can* means work hard, and doesn't mean the same thing for you today as it meant one year ago, five years ago, ten years ago, or when you first started out. It means something different constantly, or at least it should. With *what you have* means who are you—who are you today? The skills you possess today don't define who you were one year ago, five years ago, ten years ago, and shouldn't define who you will be five years from now. Your skills should be constantly changing. *Where you are* then, is a result of those first two, and where you are today is not going to be where you will be in the future. So you want to make sure you keep moving forward.

Success is *doing the best you can* with *what you have, where you are* during the three key phases of life.

The Hop phase (the first step in the triple jump), is doing the *best you can*, which means developing your skills. It also means work hard. We touched on this earlier, but working hard is the true catalyst for anything that we hope to accomplish. Whatever the job is, work hard, and if you're likely to change jobs eight times anyway, you should work hard and keep on moving, for that is truly the key.

The Step phase, is working with *what you have*, which is the person you are. This is the personal development part because the person you are and your development are intertwined. You can work hard and be great at your job, but if you don't develop yourself, there will be a serious price to pay.

In my seminars, I use the example of Mike Tyson, but there are hundreds you could substitute for him such as Steve McNair, recently. Though both are great at their sport, they fell short in their personal development and things didn't turn out very well for them. Just being good at your work isn't enough, but paired with personal development, it's definitely going to be important in getting you anywhere you want to go. Start working hard, then begin to understand what personal development and self-development are and how they can help you to get where you want to be.

The last step then is the Jump phase and that is *where you are*, which means develop a vision of where you are and where you want to go. Have a vision of the future you want. The only way to get that vision of the future is to develop a vision of yourself as the leader of your life, then to act accordingly.

We all think of leaders as presidents of companies, or managers, but in reality we are all the leaders of our own lives. Just because we might not acknowledge or accept that responsibility doesn't mean the responsibility has shifted. In movies there is always a lead character, usually a star we know, and then they hire all the extras. The extras are the people sitting in restaurants, in the big crowd scenes. They are hired to be in scenes alongside the leaders.

I actually had a friend who was an extra in the movie *Evan Almighty* because it was being filmed near his home. Though the extras show up and they leave, when they go home, are they extras now? When my friend went home at night, was he an extra? Of course not—he's the lead character in his own life. We are the leading characters and the stars of our own lives and we've got to understand that and make being a leader part of our vision. There are six billion people in the world, and there are no extras—everyone is a leader in his or her own life.

So the Triple Jump for Life is:

Hop—Do the best you can, develop your skills
Step—With what you have, develop yourself

Jump—Develop your vision as a leader in your own life and identify where you want to land—where you want to end up.

Wright

Will you elaborate on the third component, leadership?

Hasenmueller

Yes. This is important because many people don't think of themselves as leaders. Also, this is a big one to understand. When you read or study experts on leadership what you soon figure out is that leadership is a set of characteristics that can be developed by anyone. A Harvard study cited that the top two characteristics people were looking for in leaders were honesty and someone who is forward-looking. Both of these characteristics are within anyone's grasp.

There are three components of leadership. The first one is awareness of the role, which is an important component. Develop a vision of yourself as a leader in your own life. Be aware that you are the leader, whether you want to be or not. Leadership is a gift we all have for our own lives and you can't give that gift to someone else. If you wanted to give that gift away to your wife, your brother, your boss, or anyone else, they can't accept it because it not theirs—it's yours. This is the definition of the awareness of leadership—you've got it and you're the only person who can have it.

The next component is to recognize you have the ability to be an effective leader. If the top two characteristics people are looking for in a leader are being honest and forward-looking, we can develop those characteristics as well as many others. John Maxwell uses these words to describe a leader: a leader is competent, influential, trustworthy, disciplined, loyal, vision-oriented, and dedicated. But notice this: where is he citing college degrees or doctorates or levels of learning? Nowhere. They are not there because these are characteristics we can all develop without degrees.

The third component of leadership is commitment—commitment to being absolutely dedicated to your goals. Awareness, Ability, and Commitment are the vital components that make up leadership.

Wright

If I understand the metaphor of the Hop, Step, and Jump, what then?

Hasenmueller

Then we go to work. Don't delay one second; make a list of improvements that you can make in your work and life. If everyone knows they can do better, the next question is how can we do better? Put it down on paper. Make a list of improvements you want to see in your life—personally, physically, spiritually. Write them down and see where you can go.

Create a vision of where you want to be in one year, five years, and ten years. Where do you see your life going? There is a fourth phase to the triple jump—the landing. Where are you going to land in one month or one year from now? Developing your skills will mean something different than it does today. Developing yourself will mean something different than it does today. Your vision of yourself and your future will change as those components also change. We keep working until we die, until we can see exactly how far we go and how far we can land. I heard someone say once that if we knew what we were actually capable of, we would literally astound ourselves.

Wright

You refer to yourself as the CEO—the Chief Encouragement Officer. Why did you choose that title?

Hasenmueller

There are a couple of reasons. One reason is that traditional titles don't mean much to me. I'm more interested in what people really do. But primarily, I believe the most important role that you can play, or skill you can develop, is as an encourager of people around you. I believe that more today than when I first began speaking eight years ago. You never know what that one word of encouragement is going to mean to another person—telling someone to hang in there, telling someone how much you appreciate him or her, telling someone not to give up. You just never fully realize the power of encouragement, not only to your coworkers, but to your spouse, your children, and for all the people around you. The big key—the secret—is that you become the one who is most encouraged when you encourage others. Encouraging others can become your competitive advantage and it can literally change lives.

I write a Monday message of encouragement called TGIM, an acronym for Thank God It's Monday. It goes out to about a thousand salespeople. There are many times when I don't feel like writing, but I have to. The thing is that it ends up encouraging me—it changes me. That's the point—even though it's going to a thousand people, I'm the one who is most encouraged. Encouraging others helps us to not get too caught up in ourselves, which is never a good place to be. The title Chief Encouragement Officer reminds me of my true job, as well as what it does for me.

Wright

So who has encouraged or influenced you?

Hasenmueller

I think this is a great question that we all need to ask ourselves because no one gets anywhere by themselves. There are literally hundreds of people who have influenced me and encouraged me over the years. There are four people who stand out and the funny thing is, I don't think any of them fully realized the influence they had on my life.

First of all is Jim Mayfield, the father of my best friend when I was growing up. Jim and his wife, Lyda, loved and cared about me, which was a very powerful influence on my life. During this time I didn't fully appreciate them or even know what their love and caring meant. But by example, they planted seeds of integrity, kindness, and character that finally blossomed in me after many years. Jim was also the greatest example of a Christian man I'd ever met. So early on in my life, during my teen years when so many things made such a profound impression on me, these people were caring about me.

Another man who was significant in my young life was Leland Smith, a high school coach who touched many hundreds of young men's lives. He taught me hard work and determination. He taught me that doing things that others are unprepared to do is a major key to winning. Another thing he taught me was to not be a "dumb jock"—not to be a cliché—but to be smart and take learning and school seriously, which I didn't do at the time but which I did eventually.

Kevin Wright was the first employer I had who demanded more of me than I thought I had to give. He was a very knowledgeable and successful businessman who did me the biggest favor of my life. When I first started working for him, I used to go to him with every question I didn't have an answer for; he was very well informed and he'd tell me the answer. One day he got tired of my questions or I irritated him with the question I asked. He turned to me in front of other people and said, "Don't come to me with every question; go figure it out yourself." Even though I was embarrassed at that moment, it was a turning point in my life. From that point on it clicked for me—I understood that "just go figure it out" meant that you don't have to ask anybody everything because you can take the initiative and, more often than not, figure out the answer. That was the beginning of developing the initiatives within my career.

Kevin and I didn't agree on everything—not by a long shot. We had some major arguments, but that's a big part of the learning process too—you don't always agree with people. I took the things I learned in five years with Kevin and built a career. He and I have been in business deals together over the years and we're still involved in a project today.

Rik Tally was the first professional salesman I ever met. I was twenty-one or twenty-two. Though you usually think of the top sales guys as being sharks or totally aggressive, he actually was the nicest guy. He was totally competent; he was a great encourager and still is today. He encouraged me early, taught me some sales techniques, and showed me that you can be a nice guy, a good husband, and father, and still be an extremely successful salesperson. These terms are not mutually exclusive.

All of these people took an interest in me and influenced my life dramatically. These people are examples of why we don't want to get caught up in ourselves—we might miss out on making a difference in another person's life. I read something about children recently. The biggest difference in any child's life is one adult taking an interest in him or her. So even if it's a child, a young adult, young people in their careers, that word of encouragement, that word of help, and taking an interest in someone is very, very powerful.

One reason why I like to recall those people who encouraged me (and the reason you should do this too), is because you need to have a chance to thank them. I didn't get a chance to thank Leland before he passed away, but luckily Jim and I remained in contact over the years and I was able to tell him how much he had meant to me before he passed away. And now, here it is in the book for Kevin and Rik. So figure out the people who have helped you and give them a call.

Wright

What do you see as the biggest obstacle for putting these ideas into practice?

Hasenmueller

In a word: procrastination. If you do these things today, the results are not immediate, but you need to start. Being successful and a leader both take time; they are the cumulative effort of all our actions.

There is a book published by the Harvard Business Review called *The Knowing-Doing Gap*. The basic premise is that most people know what to do but they just don't do it. The gap between knowing and doing is more critical than the gap between ignorance and knowledge. That's an amazing concept. We put things off or we take it easy or someone else's expectations are so low that we aren't pushed. We procrastinate usually until tragedy strikes, either physically or professionally, and then we try to correct years of neglect in a very short time, which is hard if not impossible. A better way to think about this, then, is in making progress, not perfection, but continual improvement. Make a little progress in your job, in your personal development, in your vision, or even as a leader. Just make a little bit of progress constantly. Don't concentrate on perfection because no one is perfect, but taking small steps will change your life. Don't spend three months a year in front of the television; don't let yourself fall apart physically or mentally, just keep making progress.

The only difference between doing something and not doing it is actually doing it. The only difference between writing a book, giving a speech, running a marathon, encouraging your family, and so on is simply doing it. Nike was really on to something with the "Just Do It" campaign because that's all it takes—just doing it. This is simple but unfortunately, not easy. There is magic in beginnings, so you've just got to get started on anything in your life to improve. One of my favorite quotes is an old Chinese saying: "The best time to plant a tree is twenty years ago. The second best time is now."

Wright

Well, what a great conversation, Steve. I really appreciate all this time you've taken with me to answer these questions. I have been taking notes furiously here as you talked and I've learned quite a bit. Usually, when I ask people about those who have influenced them, they mention well-known authors and speakers, but Jim Mayfield, Leland Smith, Rik Tally, and Kevin Wright can be proud can't they?

Hasenmueller

They sure can.

Wright

I know that our readers are going to get a lot out of this chapter.

254

Hasenmueller

Alright, David, I appreciate it.

Wright

Today we've been talking with Steve Hasenmueller. Steve helps individuals and organizations learn how to thrive in the demanding and ever-changing marketplace. His challenging and uplifting messages will resonate with anyone trying to improve his or her personal life through work, as we have found out here today.

Steve, thank you so much for being with us today on *Yes You Can!*

Hasenmueller

Thank you very much.

Steve Hasenmueller writes and speaks about what it takes for businesses and employees to thrive in the demanding and ever-changing marketplace. With over twenty-five years' experience of frontline selling, Steve travels over one hundred days each year working with companies in the United States and Europe. He has conducted seminars and keynotes in nine countries reaching over seven thousand people. His challenging and uplifting messages of personal responsibility, accountability, and faith, along with real-life solutions to improvement will resonate with people trying to improve their personal lives through their work.

Steve Hasenmueller

P.O. Box 770762
Memphis, TN 38177-0762
901-761-6945
steve@leadmotivate.com

CHAPTER SEVENTEEN

How Badly Do You Want It?

by Thomas Riche

David Wright (Wright)

Today we're talking with Thomas Riche, a leader, administrator, and motivator. From leading a team of ten-year-olds selling pies door-to-door when he was only ten himself to completing a successful twenty-eight-year career in the United States Air Force as a Field Grade officer, Thomas has been a leader most of his life. Since retiring from the Air Force, he has held senior leadership positions with federal and state departments. He holds a bachelor's degree in Sociology, a Master of Arts degree in Human Resource Management and an MBA. He is a Personal Development Coach, a certified seminar leader, and a motivational speaker. He is a past president of the Tennessee Music City Toastmasters, a member of the National Speakers Association of Tennessee, American Seminar Leaders Association, American Society for Training and Development, and Middle Tennessee Society for Human Resource Management. He is a certified facilitator, coach, and facilitates the "48 Days to the Work You Love" workshop. He is also certified to present the DiSC and Platinum Rule behavioral Assessment tools. As of this interview, he is planning to launch SlightEdge Training and Coaching, a company that will specialize in showing people how doing the little extra things on a consistent basis over a period of time, can make the difference between success and failure.

Thomas, welcome to *Yes You Can!*

Thomas Riche (Riche)

Thank you, David. I'm glad to be here and appreciate the opportunity to speak to your audience.

Wright

Well, we're glad to have you. You call yourself a "slight edge coach," and I've recently heard you say that in order to get ahead in life, one must apply the slight edge theory. Tell our readers what you mean by the "slight edge."

Riche

The term "slight edge" simply means doing the things that are necessary to get ahead. In order to get ahead in anything you do, you must do just a slight bit more on a consistent basis.

Using the slight edge theory doesn't just allow you to get ahead in the workplace but also in life in general. Successful people do what unsuccessful people are unwilling to do. Very successful athletes, for example, stay on the practice field long after everyone else has called it a day. Tiger Woods and other great golfers use professional golf coaches, which gives them a slight edge over those who don't. I once read that Michael Jordan shot hoops until late into the night long after regular practice was over. During meetings I often ask my managers to stand and raise their hand as high as they can. Then I ask them to raise it just a tad higher. Just doing that little extra is what gives you the slight edge.

It doesn't matter whether you're competing in sports, academics, or any other area of life, if you want to win you have to do what losers won't do. Successful people set goals in every area of their life, not just one area, but every area—health, spiritual, family, educational, social, financial, and career. They know exactly where they are every step of the way and make minor adjustments along the way. Their goals are *specific, measurable, attainable, realistic,* and *timely.*

One of my favorite quotes by the late Paul J. Meyer says that if you are not making the progress you would like to make and are capable of making it's simply because your goals are not clearly defined. I believe that to be true. In order to be successful and get a slight edge above everyone else, you've got to set clear goals.

Wright

So how would you define success and what does it mean to you?

Riche

The best definition I've found for success comes from a book I read by Paul J. Meyer, and he defines success as, "the progressive realization of worthwhile, predetermined, personal goals." He says that "success does not come by accident; you can't buy it, inherit it, or even marry into it; success depends on following a lifelong process of goal-setting and achievement." Another way to define success is to go from failure to failure without losing enthusiasm.

I recently spoke to a group of young high school students who were attending a workshop hosted by my fraternity. I asked them to define success and several of them raised their hands. Although the responses varied from being an astronaut to having a nice home, family, and money, most of the responses centered around sports and music. I told them that based on my research, approximately one of every sixteen thousand high school athletes go into professional sports. I don't know about you, but I don't like those odds, and you'd better believe the ones who do make it into professional sports worked very hard every single day and shed a lot of blood, sweat, and tears along the way. They were laser focused and they never quit, even though the odds were against them. That's the kind of commitment it takes to be successful at anything.

So often we talk about the things that we want to be, do, and have, but we have no plan to get those things. I'm not trying to discourage aspiring athletes or rappers when I asked them how they plan to get these things; but rather, I want them to realize they must have a plan—success requires action.

Most people would probably agree that Michael Jordan is arguably one of the best, if not the best athlete who ever played the game of basketball, but it took work—hard work. What people don't tend to realize is that he had a plan of action—he had to work hard at it every day, he practiced when practice was over. He didn't start out being the greatest; in fact, I read somewhere he didn't even make his high school basketball team because he was not good enough. Successful people in any endeavor are willing to do whatever it takes to get what they want.

So to sum up the definition of success, it is simply setting goals and doing what is necessary to reach those goals. I love what Brian Tracy says. He puts it this way: "Success is goals and all else is commentary." He says, your life only begins to become a great life when you clearly identify what it is that you want, make a plan to achieve it, and then work on that plan every day. Success is not quitting, it is a combination of all the things that I just talked about. It's having a desire, being laser focused on what you want, being persistent, and having a plan of action.

Wright

What do you think are the biggest obstacles people face in the pursuit of their goals?

Riche

Not having the confidence and faith to keep pursuing their goals. Simply giving up too quickly. The biggest reason people give up is because they try things and when it doesn't work they feel like a failure. The fact is, you only fail when you give up. As somebody once said, you will miss 100 percent of the shots you don't take.

It's like the story *Acres of Diamonds*. The African farmer dug for diamonds most of his life and after years of not striking it rich, he finally gave up and killed himself. The new owner noticed a peculiar looking rock on the land, picked it up, and placed it on his mantle. A visitor noticed this egg-shaped rock and immediately identified it as a diamond. The land was covered with these strange looking rocks, but the farmer just didn't know what to look for; he gave up just short of reaching his mark—he gave up too soon.

I recently finished reading a book titled, *Three Feet From Gold*. The main theme of the book is that most people give up when they're on the brink of succeeding.

Another obstacle is fear—fear of failure and in some cases fear of success. I love what Nelson Mandela said when he quoted from Marianne Williamson's book, *A Return to Love:*

"Our deepest fear is not that we are inadequate. Our deepest fear is that we are powerful beyond measure. It is our light, not our darkness that most frightens us. We ask ourselves who am I to be brilliant, gorgeous, talented, fabulous? Actually who are you not to be? You are a child of God. You're playing small does not serve the world. There is nothing enlightened about shrinking so that other people won't feel insecure around you. We're all meant to shine as children do. We were born to make manifest the glory of God that is within us. It's not just in some of us; it's in everyone. And as we let our own light shine we unconsciously give other people permission to do the same. As we are liberated from our own fear, our presence automatically liberates us."

Wright

Thomas, you are a retired Air Force officer and have held numerous leadership positions after leaving service, and now you're launching a training and coaching business. What motivates you? Why training and coaching?

Riche

My last military assignment was at Tennessee State University as an AF ROTC instructor where I taught Leadership and Management to young aspiring Air Force officers. I was also the commandant of cadets and responsible for the health, morale, and welfare of all the cadets in the program. I had many opportunities to sit down and talk to these cadets about the Air Force, and find out why they chose this path. I shared my experiences with them and learned a little bit about how they wound up in this program. Some, of course, were there because of the scholarship, but many were there because they wanted to serve their country in some capacity. Most of the freshman, however, had no idea why they were there other than to satisfy an elective.

I spent most of my time with those who knew why they were in the ROTC program and had a fairly good idea about what they wanted to do once they were commissioned. As with most young officers, most of them wanted to become pilots. At that time it had been several years since anybody from TSU was selected for pilot training. This career field was extremely competitive and ROTC units were only given so many slots. My goal became to use every slot we were given and not only did we reach that goal, but many of those not selected for pilot training went on to become navigators. It was during this assignment when I realized how much I enjoyed encouraging, motivating, and coaching people toward reaching their goals.

I also enjoy working with and coaching those who have completed a career in the military and are looking for their next career move in the civilian world. Most come out without the slightest idea what they want to do next. Some naturally enter a career area similar to the one they left only to find out they don't want to do that anymore. Others have no idea how to find meaningful work, write a resume, dress for the interview, or how much pay they should request. This is where my work with the "48 Days to the Work you Love" workshop is helpful.

Based on personal experience and my work in the military, I know firsthand that it's very easy to make bad career decisions. It's even easier to reach forty-five or fifty years old to realize that you're not happy with what you've accomplished in your life. So I guess I'm driven by seeing others succeed. I think it was John Maxwell who said that "where there is hope in the future, there is power in the present." If I can help just one person realize that there is hope, maybe he or she will believe me and set goals and pursue those dreams.

Wright

Thomas, you are a student of Tony Alessandra and are certified to deliver the Platinum Rule workshop and assessment. What exactly is the Platinum Rule?

Riche

The Platinum Rule suggests that you should "do unto others as they'd like done unto them." This is obviously a spin on the "Golden Rule." Most of us learned the Golden Rule at a very young age and have carried that belief in our hearts our entire life. And, as you know, the Golden Rule simply states: "Do unto others as you would have them do unto you." I believe the true spirit and meaning of the Golden Rule is to treat people the way they prefer to be treated. In other words, once we realize that people communicate differently, have different fears, goals, motives, and overall behavioral styles, we can establish better personal and professional relationships.

The Platinum Rule suggests that people fall primarily into one of four behavioral styles: Dominate Director, Interacting, Socializer, Steady Relater, or Cautious Thinker. Each of these styles is based on certain behavior preferences.

For example, if a person is a *Dominant Director,* he or she is likely to be more direct, quick-paced, task-oriented, decisive, assertive, and want results now. Dominant Directors are sometimes perceived as poor listeners and very impatient with others. They're extremely competitive and winning is the only possible result. You might see Directors in higher level leadership positions, such as high ranking military officers, political leaders, and police officers.

Interacting Socializers have similar characteristics; however, they are more people-oriented than task-oriented. They are quick-paced, but love to have fun. When someone calls a meeting, the person who brings the goodies is probably the Socializer. They love visibility, recognition, and excitement and talk a lot about themselves. They are generally positive, always seeing the glass as half full. Unlike Chicken Little, they seldom see the sky falling. You often find the Socializer in occupations such as speakers and trainers, entertainers, and hosts.

Steady Relaters are motivated by positive relationships, compliance, harmony, team-building, and diplomacy. They are slower to make decisions and don't like to be pushed. They are great listeners and usually the ones people go to when they want a kind word or someone just to listen to them. People often take advantage of their kindness. Relaters despise conflict and sudden change, which may be viewed as a weakness considering the world around them. They are very sensitive and easy to get their feelings hurt. They usually don't speak up when you say or do something that bothers them, but they don't forget either.

And finally, the *Cautious Thinkers* are slower paced and motivated by accuracy and precision. They are logical thinkers and usually base decisions on data. They have a need to be right and want others to notice their accuracy.

Wright

How does a clear understanding of the Platinum Rule benefit productivity in the workplace?

Riche

Productivity is increased because, as a true student of The Platinum Rule, you are much better able to communicate with people at all levels. It gives you the advantage of knowing how people prefer to be treated. For example, if you work closely with a Director and you are a Socializer, your natural tendency might be to greet your co-worker first thing in the morning and start a conversation over a cup of coffee about your weekend activities. The Director may cut you off to talk about the work task at hand. If you don't know that most Directors are extremely task-oriented and their behavior is guarded—they usually don't share personal stories in the workplace—then you might think he or she is being rude.

A clear understanding of the Platinum Rule benefits productivity in three ways: 1) employees get a better understanding of themselves and their own strengths and where they can improve, 2) employees begin to identify and recognize the style of others, and 3) employees learn to adjust their styles to better communicate with their co-workers.

Wright

That is great, but how is it possible to read people so quickly that you can determine what style they are?

Riche

That's a great question and that's one that I'm always asked. You simply have to know what to look for. Through observation of a person's verbal, vocal, and visual behaviors you can determine if a person is direct or indirect and whether they exhibit open or guarded behaviors. Once you make those determinations, you can figure out whether they are a Director, Socializer, Relater, or Thinker. Directors tend to be Direct and Guarded. In other words, they are focused on the task (direct) and don't often share a lot about their personal life (guarded). The Socializer is direct, but more open (talks a lot about personal issues). The Relater is Indirect, but open, while the Thinker is indirect and guarded.

Wright

You facilitate a workshop titled, "Working Well Together in the Workplace," Why would people want to take that workshop?

Riche

Working Well is simply a take on the popular seminar and book titled *Dealing with Difficult People*. There is a very high demand for that workshop because managers tell us that one of the biggest problems in the workplace is getting people to work together as a team. People just don't work well together all the time. In this workshop I help people understand why they work better with some people than they do with others. I discuss how each person contributes to the team and how to value each other's contribution. We look at differences in people but we also look at similarities.

To help people understand their differences, I use the DiSC or the Platinum Rule model to expose the different behavioral preferences. And just so I don't confuse readers of this chapter, the DiSC correlates with and is used very similar to the Platinum Rule. We do an exercise using an imaginary person named Pat. Now, Pat could be a man or a woman, but Pat is normally that difficult person in the office and everybody has one. I'll ask them to tell me a little bit about this person, then we determine Pat's DiSC Style. I go through each style and pick out what might be perceived as a negative behavior and together we explore people in general with the same behavior pattern and try to determine why they are perceived as difficult. Once that is determined, we look at ways to best work with Pat.

After the workshop, participants leave with a better understanding of why they work better with some people than they do with others; but more importantly, they walk away

264

with a solid plan on how to understand and work better with problem employees. What's most intriguing is sometimes they realize that they are the problem employee. It's just that everybody doesn't want to be treated the way we want to be treated—they want to be treated the way *they* want to be treated.

Wright

I also noticed in your biography that you have worked with Dan Miller, author of *48 Days to the Work You Love* and *No More Mondays*. You facilitate some of his workshops. Tell us how that is going for you.

Riche

As a retired Air Force officer, I can tell you firsthand that it isn't easy to transition back into the "real" world and find suitable employment in the civilian community. I heard about Dan and the work he's doing to help people transition into the workforce. I read both his books and I was intrigued by this concept. Dan shows you how to dig deep within yourself and find a passion for the work you love.

Since I had already gone through this process and know how difficult it is to transition back into society, I wanted to help others make that same smooth transition through personal coaching and seminars. So as part of my work I now offer a workshop with optional coaching for military retired officers. There is a huge need today for people to find and have options. The economy is not good, and unemployment is at an all time high, as you know. So overall, this workshop is doing extremely well to help people find the work that they love to do.

Wright

What obstacles have you overcome and to what do you attribute some of your accomplishments?

Riche

I had to overcome my lack of faith and confidence in myself. I procrastinated a lot and just didn't follow through with the things I needed to do. I recall an experience in the Air Force that almost cost me my career. I wanted more than anything to become a commissioned officer and fly fighter jets, but it was only a dream. I never really believed that was possible for me. I casually mentioned this dream to my Officer in Charge and he obviously saw something in me that I didn't see in myself. He encouraged me to apply for a program that would allow me to complete my degree and immediately go into Officer Training School and later Pilot training. Of course, this would require an initial test to determine suitability.

As soon as I saw the portion of the test that would allow me to go into pilot training, I knew I was doomed. Anyway, to satisfy my captain, I took the test and, as I had already convinced myself, I failed miserably. It was a self-fulfilling prophecy. It would be another three years before I would reapply. Only this time, I had already completed my bachelor's degree, which was a requirement to get into OTS; the only thing left to do was to apply.

To my surprise, I was accepted into OTS only to later be denied because of a medical problem. Needless to say, I was crushed and it would be another three years before I reapplied for a third time. The big difference this time was that I was not going to let anything stop me from reaching my dream. I decided to give it one more try, but this time I was armed and prepared with all the things I needed to succeed. I had completed both my bachelor's and master's degrees but most importantly, I was in the right frame of mind. I knew that if it was to be it was up to me. There was no way I was going to give up. I continued to fight until I was finally admitted into OTS. Unfortunately, I had passed the age limit to enter pilot training, which was twenty-seven, but if not for that, I probably wouldn't be doing the work I'm doing today in the training and coaching field, which I love equally as much. From that day forward, anytime I think about giving up on something I really want, I read the poem that has hung above my desk for the last twenty years:

Don't Quit
Author Unknown

When things go wrong, as they sometimes will,
When the road you're trudging seems all uphill,
When the funds are low and the debts are high,
And you want to smile, but you have to sigh,
When care is pressing you down a bit,
Rest, if you must, but don't you quit.

Life is queer with its twists and turns,
As every one of us sometimes learns,

And many a failure turns about,
When he might have won had he stuck it out;
Don't give up though the pace seems slow,
You may succeed with another blow.

Often the goal is nearer than,
It seems to a faint and faltering man,
Often the struggler has given up,
When he might have captured the victor's cup,
And he learned too late when the night slipped down,
How close he was to the golden crown.

Success is failure turned inside out
The silver tint of the clouds of doubt,
And you never can tell how close you are,
It may be near when it seems so far,
So stick to the fight when you're hardest hit,
It's when things seem worst
that you must not quit.

Wright

What is the message you want people to hear so that they can learn from your experiences?

Riche

I once clipped an article from an Ann Landers newspaper column and I'd like to share it with others. She wrote, "Expect trouble as an inevitable part of life and when it comes, hold your head high, look it squarely in the eye, and say, 'I will be bigger than you. You cannot defeat me.' "

When I was ten years old I sold pies door-to-door. I charged ten cents for a small one and twenty-five cents for a large one. My aunt would bake them on Saturday mornings and my team of employees (the neighborhood kids) and I would head out in the late morning. I did this for several months and at that young age I realized I wanted to own my own business. I didn't know what it meant at the time, but I was an entrepreneur. That was my dream until one day a new customer asked me if I had any samples. I said no, but tried to guarantee her that she would be satisfied. She then asked me if I had a license to sell pies. I said, "No ma'am I don't think so."

"Well," she said, "you'd better stop selling those pies or I will call the police and have you arrested!"

For a young black kid from the South in the 1960s, to just hear the mention of "police" would send chills up my spine. So, I talked to my aunt and we decided to close shop because we didn't think we could get a license to sell.

I tell this story because I don't want anybody to ever let somebody steal their dream like my aunt and I did. Our dream was to eventually own a bakery and sell pies, but because of one negative remark from someone who was upset because I refused to give her a free pie, we let our dream die. There are a lot of negative forces out there that would like nothing more than to see you fail. They might be your friend or they might even be a family member. But, because they neither have the ambition or confidence to follow their dreams, they are afraid to death that you will succeed and leave them.

And, always remember what Les Brown tells us:

> *"If you want a thing bad enough go out and fight for it,*
> *to work day and night for it,*
> *to give up your time, your peace, and your sleep for it,*
>
> *if all that you dream and scheme is about it,*
> *and life seems useless and worthless without it,*
>
> *if you gladly sweat for it and fret for it, and plan for it,*
> *and lose all of your terror of the opposition for it,*
> *if you simply go after that thing that you want*
> *with all your capacity, strength, and sagacity, faith, hope,*
> *and confidence, and stern pertinacity,*
>
> *if neither cold, poverty, famine, or gout,*
> *sickness nor pain of body and brain can keep you away*
> *from the thing that you want,*
>
> *if dogged and grim you beseech and beset it,*
> *with the help of God you will get it."*

Wright

Amazing. Tell us how faith has played a role in your life and your successes.

Riche

I couldn't have done anything without a strong faith in God and my ability to do what He has told me to do. All that I am and all that I will ever be I owe to Him. He has put opportunities before me throughout my entire life. I haven't always seen them but He has never given up on me. The obstacles He placed before me only made me stronger and more determined. This was all necessary for my own growth. As I grow older I grow wiser, and I'm beginning to see those opportunities that have been presented to me in a new light. One of the things I am supposed to do is help other people see that same light in themselves.

As a young boy, **Thomas Riche** often dreamed of doing more, being more, and having more than what life offered most African American kids growing up in the South during the mid-sixties. After leaving college at nineteen to join the Air Force, he quickly realized he enjoyed the traveling, meeting new people, and, to an extent, the discipline. His first goal was to complete his college degree and apply to become a commissioned officer—a challenge he had almost given up on but persevered despite numerous setbacks. Although he was unable to fulfill his biggest dream to fly fighter jets, he learned a great lesson about not quitting. Whether he is doing a personal development, a career training, or delivering a motivational speech, his message is clear: never give up on yourself and live your dreams.

Thomas H. Riche

Founder and CEO
Slight Edge Training and Coaching
www.slightedgebiz.com

CHAPTER EIGHTEEN

Who do you think you are . . . and why does it matter?

by Scott V. Black

David Wright (Wright)

Today we're talking with Scott V. Black. Mr. Black is a passion generator and his mission is getting people emotionally involved with their cause, helping individuals and organizations reach their potential. He is an inspirational leader committed to passionately challenging leaders to be under construction. He is the author of *Becoming Your Dreams: Want it. Create it. Live it* and he **co-authored** *Discover Your Inner Strength* **with Ken Blanchard, Brian Tracy, and Stephen Covey.** His company, Empower U International, offers the most powerful leadership training available today. Empower U's Transformational Leadership Training catapults individuals and corporations to raise the bar and become the best of the best. Clients include MillerCoors, TPI Composites, Kraft, and hundreds of other national and international companies.

Scott welcome to *Yes You Can!*

Scott V. Black (Black)

Thanks David; I'm glad to be here.

Wright

From what I understand, you are a master of motivation. I've heard and read incredible things about what you help successful people accomplish through your trainings. What do you believe separates you from other people who profess to do what you do?

Black

David, I see dead people! I say that for two reasons, David. First, I don't know if you remember the movie *The Sixth Sense,* but the little boy is walking around saying, "I see dead people." He saw things that other people couldn't or wouldn't see. I, too, see things that people don't usually see—I see patterns that are all around us. We all have patterns that get us the results we receive in our lives. David, everybody is working perfectly. I didn't say we were perfect—I believe there was only one perfect Person to walk this planet, and it is not me. These patterns we have give us the results we get in life. The second reason why I say that is because of the lack of passion in people's lives. Dead people have no passion! I see so many successful people going through life and just getting through things. Passion is the fuel that propels us to greatness, to a life worth living.

Everybody is working perfectly. David, I did not say that we are perfect. I believe you and I can agree that there is no perfect person out there, but people are getting exactly the results that they have programmed themselves to get. These patterns, or programming, produce our results, yet they are not seen and they are not understood by most people. Most of the time, they don't even know these patterns exist. So part of what I do is help people identify these patterns in their lives and then basically ask the simple question, "Is this getting you what you want?"

One of the biggest patterns in our lives is our system of beliefs. Everything we do, or do not do, is driven by what we believe. Yet most people are not aware of the basic beliefs that drive their lives. I help successful people delve into the unchartered waters of the structure of their beliefs. In essence, I am dealing with leaders at the structural level. For that reason, I am able to help successful people "Raise the Bar" in their personal and professional lives. When I can get people working at that level, real and lasting change can take place. When I can get successful people to identify their patterns, to understand the structure of their belief systems, and get them in synchronicity, a fire is ignited internally. That is why I like to say, "I bring fire!"

Wright

From what I've heard and seen, you have a good understanding of what makes people tick and what makes people do what they do. Would you tell our readers what that is?

Black

As I said, everything we do, or do not do, is driven by a belief system. The structure of our beliefs creates the foundation upon which we build our lives. If you look throughout history you will see that man is constantly looking for meaning—why am I here, what is our purpose, is there a God, what happens after this thing called life, how should we treat each other? These are questions that successful men and women have been asking for centuries, for millennia. People are looking for meaning and looking to reinforce or build a powerful structure of beliefs.

As a matter of fact, when Mortimer Adler was asked why the God section was the largest in the *Great Books of the Western World* series, he observed that it's because more implications flow from the subject of God than from any other subject. Indeed, the five most consequential, important questions in life come from this:

Our origin—where do we come from?
Our identity—who are we?
The meaning of our lives—why are we here?
Morality—how should we live, what do we want, what will it take to get there?
Our destiny—where are we going?

If you think about all those questions, David, it really gets down to the structure of our belief systems. These core questions create a structure of a belief system that has eternal implications. From these beliefs come a mission for one's life. When we have a mission that is driving our life, then we have a purpose and life has meaning. My motto for my life and my family's is, *"When you live your life like it matters, it does."* That structured belief is a cornerstone for a life "well lived."

Wright

Will you tell our readers why knowing what one believes is important?

Black

I have a four-year-old son, Major, and he is in that stage where he is constantly asking "why." That inquisitive nature he has gives him a desire to know . . . why. He is a little sponge taking in everything. The Bible tells us we are to have a reason for what we believe. We need to be like little kids and know the reasons why we do things. That is important for many reasons, one being, if we don't like the results, we can change the approach. I always like to have a reason for everything I do and it is driven by what I believe. I don't believe in the "because" philosophy. In other words, I don't do things "just because—" and neither do you. We do things based on what we believe, and yet most people are not aware of their own deep-seated beliefs.

Blaine Pascal said, "People almost invariably arrive at their beliefs not on the basis of proof, but on the basis of what they find attractive." Most people don't know, at the core, what they believe. It sometimes takes stirring them up and throwing some beliefs out there that are not PC (politically correct) to get them to take a look at what they believe. Phillip E. Johnson said, "One who claims to be a skeptic of one set of beliefs is actually a true believer in another set of beliefs." So I will throw out my strong beliefs so that people know what I believe. It will give them something to use as an example of what they do or do not believe.

David, I am blessed; I get to be a part of successful people's lives and their families. I get to walk with people in their deep, dark places. I know thousands of people (I have met presidents) and I get to build intimate relationships with very successful people. With all that said, I'm a single father of three kids and, next to my relationship with Jesus Christ, the most important thing in my life is those kids. I get to be a role model for Faith, Christian, and Major. I get to help them structure a belief system that will be the foundation for everything they do, and do not do, for the rest of their lives. When framed that way, that is an awesome responsibility and an honor!

Being a father and a leader of leaders, I always want to give a reason for what I am doing and why I'm doing something. Not that they should question me, but for my own benefit I always want to be able to explain it to them. One of the greatest things I get to do is to help create a powerful belief system in my kids and in my clients that will propel them to greatness.

My background includes Neuro-Linguistic Programming (NLP), and I've studied the work that Dr. Robert Dilts has done with change. Dr. Dilts created what's called the Neurological Levels of Change:

- Spirit
- Identity
- Belief Systems
- Capabilities
- Behavior
- Environment

There are six different levels: the lowest level is environment, and above that is behavior. Above those are capabilities, and higher up is belief systems. Above that is identity, and at the top is spirit. By spirit, I mean your bigger connection to this universe. For some of us, that is God; however, some in the field of NLP have a tough time with God since He can't be quantified. So instead of God, Dilts used Spirit.

What Dr. Dilts realized was that change takes place from the top down. The example I give people is that you can take alcoholics out of their environment—take them out of the bar—but they're still alcoholics. To really change, they need to change at a higher level. Within each of these levels we have belief systems associated with that level: Is there a God? Who am I? Why was I given the gift of life? What can I accomplish on this planet? How should I act? What types of places should I be?

Einstein told us that the definition of insanity is doing the same thing repeatedly and expecting different results. Einstein also said, "You can never solve a problem at the same level it was created." I never really understood what that meant until I learned about neurological levels. If I want to change my environment, I must deal with the behavior that keeps taking me back to the environment. If I want to change the way I perceive myself and my identity, then I need to look at the bigger meaning of life and my connection to this thing called life. That is to be dealt with in the God/Spirit realm.

Change takes place from the top down. In other words, if you change someone's capability then you change his or her behavior and this can change the person's environment. But the great thing about the Neurological Levels of Change is that belief systems are right smack in the middle. I believe that when you can affect someone's belief system, you can effect change going both ways. By changing your beliefs you change what you think you're capable of. That changes your behavior and changes where you hang out—your environment. But it also changes your identity—who you believe you are. It also changes your bigger picture of the universe and your place in it. That's why it's so critical to understand, and sometimes to question, what you truly believe. If you want to change your life, change your thinking. Our thoughts come from the overflow of our B.S.—our belief systems.

Wright

So how does this information fit into the field of leadership or personal development?

Black

That is a great question, David. My question to you is, "How does this *not* apply to leadership development?" This is the foundation of true leadership. We are dealing with the drivers, the structure of what makes leaders, and the fuel source that drives leaders to do what they do. A leader's Belief System is what makes him or her do what he or she does. It actually becomes the "Operating System" that is the main driver for what leaders do.

What I have found in my years of studying people and myself is that many of these beliefs are based on erroneous concepts, not the truth. Some of our deepest beliefs are built on lies. Big chunks of most people's belief systems are at the unconscious level; we are not even aware of what they are. Most of our belief systems are in place by the time we become young adults. Some have been imprinted through tragic events; some are put there by others. What we see, hear, and experience creates our "map of reality." This set consists of all our belief systems and experiences. The key is to understand how these belief systems affect everything we do. It is also important to understand what these beliefs are and make sure they are founded in truth and reality. So many beliefs are put in place without out our even knowing they are there. I have learned throughout the years that many are based on information that is not correct.

That is why as leaders we need to constantly be growing and learning. As a leader, I believe that our sign should be "Under Construction"—we are a little bit better today than yesterday and a little bit better tomorrow than today. As we expand our learning and seek the truth, then we can start restructuring our beliefs. As we gain knowledge, wisdom, and experience, what we used to believe is replaced with a truer, more powerful driver and a more accurate belief system to get us what we want.

Let me give you an example.

There is a famous book that causes a lot of us to do and not do certain things. It's called *On the Origin of Species by Means of Natural Selection* by Charles Darwin. We accept this book and this belief system (the theory of evolution) as science—as fact. Most have never read the book, never spent time researching the theory of evolution versus the biblical account of creation. Yet, based on Mortimer Adler's "five most consequential [important] questions in life," this one belief affects at least three, if not all five questions. As important as this is, most people have had this belief implanted in them. It reminds me of the quote by Winston Churchill, "Men stumble over the truth from time to time, but most pick themselves up and hurry off as if nothing happened." That could be a statement for how most have stumbled along as their belief systems have been structured in the deep recesses of their being.

The ongoing act of learning and growing allows us to clean up and restructure belief systems that serve us better. This will allow us to function at an optimal level. Let me give you a couple of reasons why the *theory* of evolution is flawed. The belief system that all life came from some primordial ooze is a poor belief system that is rooted in something other than the truth. If you read Darwin's work, he said that if the nucleus of a cell of an amoeba —a single cell organism—is more than a simple organism, then his entire theory is invalid. Based on his own statement, his theory is invalid. In the 1950s, with Watson and Francis Crick, the discovery of DNA, and with increasingly powerful microscopes, we have enough information now to refute Darwin's theory based on his own stated belief system. Today, we know that if you take a single cell amoeba, the nucleus of that cell has enough genetic information to fill thirty books—one set of the Encyclopedia Britannica. The entire cell has enough genetic material to fill up a thousand complete sets!

The sad part is that most people don't know the difference between reality and something that is just made up. The reason why this is so important is because a lot of our belief systems stem from other things that we buy into that may or may not be correct. If everything we do or do not do is driven by belief systems, then some of us are doing things based on concepts that are based on lies. One thing I have learned throughout the years studying the human mind is that the mind reacts to what we put in it. Whether it is true or not, the mind does not know the difference between, for example, Hollywood and reality.

Wright

If I might be so bold as to make a statement in a question, you seem to be going pretty deeply. You don't dwell on the surface much, do you? We've been talking just few minutes and you're already into God and evolution—you don't do that "politically correct thing" well, do you?

Black

Not well at all. I think we're surface dwellers—we dwell too much on surface issues. Life is too short to do that. I never know if this is the one chance I have to affect someone's life. I want my life to matter! I want to bring as many people across the finish line of life as possible. A party of one is not much of a party. David, I live my life with a sense of urgency as though it matters. I like to say, "Planes crash and people die; it is a fact of life!" I don't know how much time I have on this planet, so there is no time like the *present!* The time is Now. It is like that saying:

One Minute to Destiny

It's 11:59 on the clock of Destiny
And you've only got a minute,
Only 60 seconds in it.
Forced upon you—can't refuse it;
Didn't seek it; didn't choose it,
But it's up to you to use it.
You'll suffer if you lose it;
Give account if you abuse it.
It's only a minute,
But eternity is in it!

In my years of working with people, I have learned that there are too many people just existing through life, David. I have seen too many people getting through another day, another pay period, another anniversary, another tragedy, with no real purpose in their life. That is why I am so driven to help people put in a structure of beliefs that drive them to live their life with some purpose. Dr. Benjamin Elijah Mayes put it this way:

"It must be borne in mind that the tragedy of life doesn't lie in not reaching your goal; the tragedy in life is in having no goal to reach. It isn't calamity to die with dreams unfulfilled but it's a calamity not to dream. It's not a disaster to be unable to capture your ideal, but it's disaster to have no ideal to capture. It's not a disgrace not to reach the stars, but it's a disgrace to have no stars to reach for. Not failure, but low aim is sin."

To me, too many people are dwelling on the surface; they're just existing, they're just getting by. Life is too short, life is meant to be delicious, it's intoxicating. Life is meant to be lived, and yet so many people are just getting through it. They're getting through the next pay period, they're getting through the next book, they're getting through the next anniversary. I am driven by my mission of getting people emotionally involved with their lives. The biggest gap for most people is the distance from their head to their hearts. I bring *fire!* Passion is a fuel source that is best ignited from the sparks of a great belief system!

Wright

Can you give me an example of how our belief system affects the majority of what someone does?

Black

All you have to do is watch the news or read the newspapers; it is all around us. I have heard different psychologists say that a child's map of reality—the basic structure of their belief system—is in place by the time he or she is six to eight years old. If you want to know why our kids are struggling today, look at the pervasive beliefs in our society. Kids are growing up with implanted beliefs that mock the Judeo-Christian values that this country was founded upon. They now consider activities and values that thirty years ago were discouraged and frowned upon. Now, those activities and values are considered normal and just "choices." Their beliefs about God, about the value of life, about why they are here on this planet, about what happens when this is all over, about what they are supposed to do while they are on this planet, and about their value and the value of others. All these beliefs show up in their actions. Look at how our country is changing drastically in front of us. The structure of our constitution was founded on three words "We The People." It is written larger than anything else in the constitution. The belief system has changed from "we the people" to "we the government." If anybody wants to know why our country is falling so fast, just go back to the twenty-eight principles (which, by the way, is another way to say belief system) that our founding fathers used to create this great country. If you don't know what they are I would recommend the book, *The Five Thousand Year Leap; 28 great ideas that changed the world,* by W. Cleon Skousen.

Two years ago, when I was doing a class in Iowa, I remember hearing about a teenage boy who walked into a mall at Christmastime, killed eight people, and then took his own life. I was watching the news about this event and I remember the interview that the media did with the woman this boy had been living with. They asked this woman what was wrong with the boy—what caused him to do what he did. Her answer was powerful, "He was the puppy dog that nobody wanted." Consider how a person with a belief system like that would act. Feeling of helpless and hopeless is a pandemic disease in America today. When people feel like the puppy dog that nobody wanted, they take their "pound of flesh" before they take their own life. Hurting people hurt people! That is why I am so stirred up to change this world one person at a time.

Those who know me know that I take my role as a parent very seriously. The role of a parent is one of the greatest leadership roles we can have because we get to instill B.S. into our kids (B.S. means Belief System, not the stuff you step in while walking the plains of Texas). As parents we get to program our kids. I know that sounds weird, but it is one of our greatest roles and if we're not doing it, then MTV, the school system, or somebody else is.

I am very aware of the structure of beliefs I am creating in my kids. I know that structure will be the foundation they build the next eighty years of their life on. We have the same opportunity as leaders, but with kids it is a clearer, purer path than with an adult whom we are mentoring or guiding. I have spent years of conscious activity and discussion knowing that they are creating their B.S. based on my actions and interaction with them and those around them.

As I have so proudly stated before, I am a single father of three kids. My son Major is four years old, Christian is ten, and my daughter, Faith, is fourteen. If you were to ask Faith or Christian what the Black family motto is, they will tell you: "When you live your life like it matters it does." They have a relationship with Jesus Christ. They know that everything we have is God's. They know the best way to get to Carnegie Hall is to practice, practice, practice. I even use my mistakes in life to help teach them about how to overcome mistakes that all people make.

Think about the belief system, "When you live your life like it matters, it does." If one adopts that B.S. for his or her life, what type of activity do you think will come from that? Conversely, if your belief system is, "Life is a 'beach,' then you die" (yes, I changed the word to "beach" for PG purposes), what type of activity do you believe comes from that? If a child grows up believing that no matter what he or she does, "The Man" is going to keep him or her down, that child grows up as a victim. If one grows up believing he or she is stupid and a waste of life, what type of activity does that person generate? Would you die for a lie? Most people won't die for the truth. We can become self-fulfilling prophesies. Energy follows thought. What is thought? It is talking to ourselves. Our internal dialog stems from the structure of our beliefs.

For me, Empower U is my baby. Think about that, David. What would you do for your baby? You'd do anything, right? You'd sacrifice, you'd give up everything—you'd do whatever it took. Here it is twenty years later, and Empower U is still going strong. We don't have a sales team, and face it, there are a lot of people out there smarter than I am and more well known, but yet we are still doing what we're doing twenty years later. We're still changing people's lives based on a simple belief system that when you live your life like it matters, it does.

I've been all over this world, David, and everywhere truth is truth. In China, two plus two equals four. In Russia, two plus two equals four. I've trained classes in Mexico through the Maquilas. In Mexico, two plus two equals four. I've been to the Gaza Strip and I've been through Israel and on the border within three hours of three warring countries. And in both Israel and the Gaza Strip, two plus two equals four. Just like that is true, no matter what country, no matter what language, so is this powerful belief system—when you live your life like it matters, it does.

Wright

So you are saying that our belief system—the structure of our beliefs—affect everything we do. You are saying it's the primary motivator?

Black

Absolutely, without a doubt it is the primary motivator. Everything we do, or do not do, is driven by our belief system. It goes back to those core questions. There are certain core questions that are foundational for creating a belief system that ignites powerful action. That is why movements can be so powerful. Once you can get people to buy in at that "core" level, there is power there. In my training, I pose questions that cause people to take a look at the structure of their beliefs. So many people are unaware of the structure of their beliefs.

In our trainings we ask a lot of questions. I want to help people get emotionally involved with their lives and to create an internal fire that will help them live their life with passion and purpose. We ask people those life-altering questions that define our existence: Who are you? What do you want? Why are you here? If today were your last day on this planet, did it matter one bit? If you were to live your life the way you were supposed to, what would people remember about you when all was said and done?

Famous author George Bernard Shaw was once asked by a reporter, "If you could go back in time and you could live your life all over again, and you could be anybody you wanted to be, who would you be?" He thought about it for a moment and he said, "If I could be anybody I wanted to be, I would be the George Bernard Shaw that I could have been." What he was talking about, David, was living to his full potential, without all the walls, without the fears, without the limiting belief systems.

Things like that stir me up and they stir others up, as well. Most have never really considered those questions and what I have found throughout the years is that there are some belief systems that are built on false premises. There are some major beliefs that have been constructed based on lies that were implanted by others or by bad experiences. Some people have logically sound belief systems, but they are based on a false belief system.

Let me give you an example of a logically sound belief system that is based on a false premise. There is a transitive principle that most people learn in Algebra. If A=B and B=C, then A=C. Nobody can argue with that logic. So based on that logic, let me give you a belief system that some women might agree with. All men are four-legged creatures. Bob is a man. Therefore Bob is a four-legged creature. That is a logically sound argument; however, it is based on a false premise that *"all* men are four-legged creatures."

So I question people and I question myself a lot. Am I the father I want to be? Am I the man that God put me here to be? Am I using my gifts and talents and resources? True leaders know the basic structure of their belief systems. Men and women of vision who make a lasting impact are driven by strong, structured belief systems. They know who they are, they know why they are here, and they know what they want. They come to my classes to dig deeper, to go higher!

Let me give you an example of a belief system that I had to investigate in relation to my training. A few years back, when my mission was clearly changing, I had to ask myself this question: "Is my outcome for my training to make everybody who goes through my training happy?" It might surprise you, David, to know that my answer was,

"No." You see, the reason I get results that others can't get is because I'm pushing the envelope—I'm not politically correct and I'm getting people out of their comfort zone. If my belief system were that every single person coming out of my training should be happy, then that belief system would create activity that would cause me to "tone it down," to "fall in line," to not push the envelope. As I tell people, "I love the impossible because I get to experience it every weekend in my training." If my B.S. were that my outcome was to make everybody happy, then I could not experience the impossible on a regular basis.

Those are just a few examples of being aware of what I believe. I'm aware of who I am and I'm aware of what I want. That doesn't mean I'm perfect and it doesn't mean I don't struggle. It doesn't mean I don't have moments where I hit my head against the wall. But I really want to be an example for other people that when you truly get in touch with and understand your belief system, you will understand what the foundation for your motivation is.

Wright

So if I understand you correctly, what you do in your training is that you get people to look at their belief systems and challenge them during your intense training. You actually help people question themselves at the deep core level.

What are some of the belief systems that you challenge them on?

Black

That's a great question and much of that challenging process begins with the environment we create in our trainings. We create an environment where they can take a 100 percent honest look at themselves so they can ask and answer those life-altering questions.

One thing I have learned throughout the years is that we all have stuff. Psychologists tell us that we live up to 10 percent of our potential. Just like the George Bernard Shaw story, we are doing "goodnuff." It might be better than most, but is it all you have? A lot of people are just getting by, doing better than some or most, but there is so much more!

One of my favorite quotes is by Bob Moawad. He says, "You can't leave footprints in the sands of time if you're sitting on your butt, and who wants to leave butt prints in the sands of time?"

Think about this, David: how do you get successful people—people who are already doing better than most people—to say that doing merely good enough is not acceptable? So I've got to stir them up a little bit and I've got to challenge them. Sometimes I've got to hit them "upside the head" a little bit, figuratively speaking. I've got to shake them out of their comfort zone because they think that what they're doing on the outside already is pretty impressive. I challenge them by asking if what they are doing good is enough—are they really living their potential? I challenge them to take a look at themselves and stop comparing themselves to others. I challenge them to compare themselves to the people they could have been. That is a major challenge—to take leaders/people who are doing better than most and tell them it is *not good enough!*

I work with successful executives, pastors, NFL football players, and some very successful companies. For a company that no one has ever heard of, led by a man most people may never have heard of, we have a pretty impressive client list.

One of the things that we do is challenge people—successful people—to "Raise the Bar." We have them consider that maybe they are not the husbands or wives that they want to be or the parents that they want to be—maybe there is still room for improvement. I challenge them to dig deep and find that there's always room for improvement and to find that next level.

As I said before, psychologists tell us that we live to 10 percent of our potential and that we use 3 to 5 percent of our brain. So I don't care who you are—I don't care if you're Tiger Woods, I don't care if you're Barack Obama, I don't care if you're LeBronne James—we all have stuff and we are all living to a fraction of our potential. We all have the same disease—we are human beings, and we are flawed. Some of those flaws come from belief systems that are not serving us well.

One of the biggest belief systems that I challenge people on is the idea of settling for "good enough." People don't realize they're just doing good enough. People think they're giving 100 percent and I challenge them on that. I hear it all the time, David, "Oh, I give a 110 percent," "I give 120 percent," and I've got to bite my tongue to keep from calling them on it. Forget 110 percent; most people have no concept of what 100 percent is. There are a select few who can get pretty close to 100 percent on the field or in the classroom or on the battlefield, but they don't know how to bring it to the home or to the school or to their spouse or kids.

One of the things I do is to help people redefine what 100 percent is. When I can get them to understand the flaw in this belief system, then I have their respect to look at other flaws. I ask, "Are you *really* giving 100 percent?" Then I define it for them. I say,

"Let me redefine 100 percent, that way you're not a liar, you just misspoke." One hundred percent is giving everything—heart, body, and soul. And I'll prove my point because, as I told you earlier, I don't believe in the "because" philosophy. Here is why giving everything heart, body, and soul is 100 percent: If I take away your heart, and I take away your body, and I take away your soul, what's left? Nothing!

Wright

In your years of working with leaders from the total spectrum of society, do you believe that most people know what they believe?

Black

It's strange—I believe that they have a basic understanding of some of their core beliefs, and again, it all depends on what they've been through, but no, most people don't know what their core beliefs are. But believe it or not, a lot of people are more knowledgeable about what they *don't* believe. The irony is that people almost invariably arrive at their beliefs, not on the basis of proof but on the basis of what they find attractive. I quoted Blaine Pascal earlier. He said that most people have never questioned what they believe or have looked at their belief structure. In other words, they really don't know what they believe

There are some core things most people believe: they believe they are good people and some people believe that they're here for a purpose. Phillip Johnson (I love his stuff) says that anyone who claims to be a skeptic of one set of beliefs is actually a true believer in another set of beliefs. People don't understand it's all about what you believe.

You're right—I truly think that most people don't know what they believe. In fact, some of the things they believe are just wrong. There is a lot of hurt in our world. There are many kids who are growing up in less than ideal situations. There are a lot of hurting people out there and remember, hurting people hurt people. The Bible says the sins of the father go three and four generations (Exodus 20:5 and Deuteronomy 5:9). I believe that this is not a curse, it is a sad reality. Alcoholics beget alcoholics, molesters beget molesters. We not only pass on our "stuff" but more importantly, we pass on our B.S.

Think about our country and our society's changing belief systems. Think about these belief systems that we adopt as a society and the effects, both positive and negative, that they have. For a long time people believed that the world was flat, that you couldn't run a four-minute mile, that the Bible was the foundation for all great

285

learning, that having a child out of wedlock was not a good thing, that life begins at conception, that the United States is a Christian nation, that adultery is a bad thing, that the option to fail was part of what makes success possible. From these beliefs come activities that define us.

Wright

You talk about how many people have bought into lies. Will you give me an example of one of these lies that people have bought into?

Black

One of the biggest lies that most have bought into is the "Easy Button." I always joke that we should file a class action lawsuit against Staples—the office supply company—because Staples is out there selling us on the Easy Button. So many people want the easy way out, hoping they get the easy button. I'm going to tell you that this is a big lie—you don't want the easy button. I don't know a man who wants to marry an easy woman. And most people don't really want the easy button—it will not get us what we want. What we really want is the "Go Button." Most people learned a long time ago that when something was really easy, then everybody would be doing it and it's probably not worthwhile.

Remember when we were little kids, or maybe when you had your kids when they were younger. We got those little slot racecar tracks. We'd put them together and they'd have the slot that went all the way around the track. Then we had these little cards with a metal stud sticking out of the bottom. We would take the metal stud and we would place that in the slot on the track. Then there was a wired hand-held controller that had a single button on it. It was either a thumb button, or a trigger button. When we pressed that button, the car moved. The button made the car go wherever the track was laid out.

The car had no steering wheel, you didn't need to figure out where it was going to go; you didn't need to think about it, and you didn't need to philosophize or theorize or analyze. All you needed to do was bring some juice to it. And the way you brought some juice or "fire," was by pressing the go button. That button created action—it made things happen.

That's the button we're looking for. Read any good book based in truth; it'll tell you two things: life isn't fair and life is tough. So I tell people to put their "big boy pants on." Let's expect that and just push the go button. The go button brings fire, it brings juice, and it creates action. We don't want to leave butt prints in the sands of time, we want to make things happen. I want to inspire people to live their lives in such a way that in hundred years from now people are still talking about the impact that they made when they were out there living their life like it mattered.

There is a great book out there called *Telling Yourself the Truth* by Dr. William Backus. It is a simple concept—identify the lie and replace it with the truth. Too many people are functioning using belief systems that are built on lies.

Richard Rohr has written extensively about the five essential truths people must awaken to grow into the people they are to be. As you will see, these "truths" are belief systems. Notice how this structured belief system will pave the way to a life well lived. They create a sense of urgency, they create a servant mentality, they allow one to elevate others above themselves, and they negate a "victim mentality." Those five truths are:

- Life is hard.
- You are not that important.
- Your life is not about you.
- You are not in control.
- You are going to die.

Wright

Would you give our readers another lie or leadership fallacy that you believe people have bought into?

Black

Another one of my favorite ones is that we love to place blame; we have become a victim society. It is everybody else's fault. We love to blame everybody else. We love to blame our parents, we love to blame society, the evil banks and mortgage companies, our ex-spouses, and one of the most powerful people to ever walk the planet, George W. Bush. It seems that people think he is responsible for everything bad that has ever happened in this world.

People like to blame. Life isn't fair, it's too hard. People complain and say, "I've got this monkey on my back," and it is a big lie. "It's everybody else's fault, I had no role in my own misery." It's not the monkey on your back it's the coconut on your hand.

In certain parts of the world, when they want to pay tribute to someone, they will have a meal in the person's honor. At that meal they will usually have some special delicacy that they serve in honor of the guest. One of the most famous is monkey brains.

They have an interesting way they catch these monkeys to get the delicacy. (It is also a great understanding of the human experience.) What they do is take coconuts and the bore out all the meat from inside them. They then fill them with raw rice. Then they place the coconuts along the floor of the jungle and wait.

When monkeys come by along the tree line, they see there is something on the ground. Monkeys are inquisitive creatures. They make sure the enemy, man, isn't around, they come down from the tree, and pick up the coconut. They then notice there is something inside. They reach inside the coconut and grab a handful of the rice inside. Of course, raw rice has no value at all to them, yet they grab a handful anyway. When they attempt to pull their hand out, they can't because it's stuck—they have a fist full of rice. It's stuck because their hand, in the form of a fist, is much larger than their hand is when it's relaxed.

So they keep attempting to pull out their hand but they can't and they start to panic. In a state of panic they run to climb a tree and escape. Have you ever tried to climb a tree with a coconut on your hand? It's difficult. So instead of just letting go of the rice and fleeing, the monkey takes the coconut stuck on his hand with a handful of uncooked rice, and beats the coconut against the tree. Right next to that tree is a big bush and in that big bush is a young man with a sharp machete in his hand. The banging on the tree initiates a simple, swift move that leaves a monkey's head in the young man's hand.

What a stupid creature, again, no ancestor of mine! If that stupid monkey had let go of the rice, it could have lived a much fuller, longer life. Before you go passing judgment on this little creature, you might want to consider the following question that I ask people in my classes: "What are you holding on to?" Just like the uncooked rice had no value to the monkey, neither does some of the garbage that we carry around with us throughout our life. What if you would just let it go? Would letting go free you to live a far better life? Truth be told, we carry around a lot of stuff from our past that is not serving us well. Yes, people might have "done us wrong." Maybe we didn't have the best childhood and maybe that person did treat us poorly, but to just sit around and blame everybody else for problems in our lives is useless.

At some point, no matter how bad somebody has wronged us, we have to pick ourselves up, dust ourselves off, and live the life that we were given. When it comes down to the very end, it's going to come down to this: did you live your life like it mattered? Did you take this gift called life and live it abundantly?

One of the reasons I want to get people stirred up is because there is this gap between their head and their heart. It is a great chasm in most people's lives. They shut off their heart, but it is the power source. Passion comes from the heart; that passion is the rocket fuel. Far too many people are going through life tired and worn out. They just don't have what it takes because they've turned off their passion. I stir people up because once I can have them engaged with their heart—with their passion—then all of a sudden they realize that it is the rocket fuel. They realize their heart is the source that will move them through the ups and downs of life. It is the Go Button—the power source!

Wright

As a developer of people and a coach to leaders, is there any other pressing fallacy or issue that you feel is imperative for people to hear so they can to go to the next level?

Black

I read a lot and like to study leadership books. What I believe is one of the greatest books on leadership, believe it or not, is the Bible. The Bible says very clearly that you can tell where a person's heart is by where he or she spends time and money. The two great commodities of life are time and money.

I always joke with people that before my daughter gets in a serious relationship, I'm going to have her get the guy's checkbook and day-timer. I don't want these items to see how much money he has in his bank, but to see where he has spent his money during the last six months to a year. I also want to know where he has spent his time during the last six months to a year. People can express what they find important and what really matters to them, but what they are doing speaks so loudly that I can't hear what they are saying. What truly matters to people is illustrated by where they spend their time and their money.

I love sayings and I love words because the right word at the right time can change someone's life. Words put together in a powerful way can move people. We know this from Dr. King's "I have a dream" speech; it moves people. These sayings or quotes become the "Belief Systems" by which people live their life. I know that when I die I will have influenced many people's lives in a positive way. I will help people move toward some things or move away from some things. One of my goals in life is to bring more people closer to God than I scare away from God. I know time is short and that God already knows my last day.

I shared with you earlier one of my favorite sayings titled "One Minute to Destiny." Remember, It says, "It's 11:59 on the clock of destiny, and you've only got a minute, only 60 seconds in it, forced upon you, can't refuse it, didn't seek it, didn't choose it, but it's up to you to use it, you'll suffer if you lose it, give account if you abuse it, it's only a minute but eternity is in it."

From that we understand that the *time is now!* It creates a sense of urgency in our lives. Planes crash and people die, it's a fact of life. That stirs me up so I want people to grasp that the time is now. Life is short and can be unpredictable. One of the things I challenge people about is that we think we're going to live forever; we think we're immortal, but sometimes "stuff happens."

When I moved to Dallas-Fort Worth, one day I was stuck on the freeway and traffic wasn't moving. I was there for an hour. When I went home that night, I watched the news and found out what had caused the traffic congestion. A guy who had a local radio show got off work at noon. After work he was driving home and called his wife to tell her he was on his way home. On the freeway, he was driving two cars behind a flatbed truck. On the truck was a forklift that wasn't tied down properly. It was also sitting too high. The semi-truck was going down the freeway at seventy or eighty miles an hour when it hit an overpass and catapulted the forklift into the air. The forklift crushed the driver who was two cars behind the truck. This is a true story and I want you to think about it. I know it sounds funny, but how many people do you know who have been killed by a flying forklift?

Wright

None.

Black

That's my point, and here is the sad part: the man died, but what I don't know is how he lived his life. I always question people and ask them that when it comes time and all is said and done and you're going six feet under, are you going to be remembered by how you lived or are you going to be more remembered by how you died? This is why I say that when you live your life like it matters, it does. I've just got one question for our readers: what do you want?

Wright

Well, what a great conversation, Scott. I always enjoy talking with you; you always make me think.

Black

I appreciate it, David.

Wright

And you always challenge me to be better than I am, and that's a good thing.

I really appreciate all the time you've taken with me today to answer these questions. I've learned a lot and I'm sure our readers will, too.

Black

You are very welcome, David, and I look forward to our future conversations.

Wright

Today we've been talking with Scott V. Black, speaker, trainer, and author. As you can tell, he brings fire! He is an inspirational leader committed to challenging leaders to be "Under Construction." His company, Empower U International, offers the most powerful leadership training available today. If you want to "Raise the Bar" in your personal or professional live you can contact him at **www.empoweru.net**. I can't wait for his new book, *What Do You Believe and Why Does It matter?* to come out.

Scott, thank you so much for being with us today on *Yes You Can!*

Black

You're welcome. Have a great day, David.

Scott V. Black is CEO and founder of Empower U International. He has been described as one of today's greatest inspirational influencers for those in search of their optimum self. As a certified behavior specialist, Black has the ability to get straight to the inner core by reawakening others, helping them identify what's really important. His methodologies for helping identify one's true passion are powerful and proven, and often separate him from other life coaches and masters of NLP. Scott has the dual gift of energy and experience, which empowers him to elevate others to excellence. His invigorating and move-to-action spirit is commonly evidenced at his trainings and with the corporate speeches he is hired to deliver. He brings fire! *If you want to "Raise the Bar" in your personal or professional life you can contact him at* www.empoweru.net.

Scott V. Black

P.O. Box 430
Kennedale, Texas 76060
MrBlack@empoweru.net
www.empoweru.net

CHAPTER NINETEEN

The Intersection of Intentional Resilience and Leadership

by Redia Anderson

David Wright (Wright)

Today we're talking with Redia Anderson. Nationally recognized in the field of diversity and inclusion, Redia is an executive coach and diversity strategist with more than twenty-five years' experience in human resources and change management. As a former Chief Diversity Officer, Redia has successfully engaged and led enterprise-wide change efforts in industry-leading organizations such as Deloitte & Touché, Equiva Services (joint venture between Shell, Texaco, and Saudi Aramco), Sears, Roebuck and Company, and Abbott Laboratories. She has engaged highly talented leaders in positive behavioral shifts that tightly align their performance and business results in today's complex, global business environments.

A popular speaker, Redia has spoken at national gatherings of such organizations as The Society for Human Resource Management (SHRM), The Conference Board, Diversity Best Practices, and Working Mother Media. Redia received her graduate degree in Clinical Psychology.

Redia, welcome to *Yes You Can!*

Redia Anderson (Anderson)

Thank you, David, I'm delighted to be here with you.

Wright

So what were some of your pivotal learning experiences that told you "yes you can" as you were growing up?

Anderson

The driving philosophy behind many of my professional and personal experiences is this concept of Intentional Resilience. In response to your question, several incidents come to mind about the power of intentional resilience and leadership, but I'd like to share one or two personal stories to begin with that involve my family.

My father grew up in a relatively poor, rural part of Mississippi, a town just outside of Meridian. His mother died of cancer at the age of thirty-three when he was only eight years young. She left behind six small children, of which my dad was one. They were raised by his maternal grandmother.

My father, the second oldest, tells many stories of wanting to live a better life as he daily faced the hard life of working in the fields as a child in order to earn and save money with which to help his grandmother.

What he learned from his grandmother was an unconditional love, a strong belief in family unity and God, and a sense that with hard work he could become a man who represented something far greater than the life he was born into. He learned that he could make change happen.

So he worked hard and developed a clear plan for his life that he methodically implemented. You see, my father has always been a very thoughtful and proactive man—a man of incredible vision, energy, and actions. His plan involved a clear vision of a better and more financially secure future life. My dad was determined and intentional in how he went about structuring his life and career. He advanced to the highest level he could achieve without a four-year college degree as a noncommissioned officer in the U.S. Air Force and became a decorated and highly respected Chief Master Sergeant.

His responsibility in material supply was the warehousing and storage of millions and millions of dollars of supplies and equipment and oversight of hundreds of men and women in support of procurement and distribution. As a young woman, I recall visiting my father at the massive warehouses that were the size of several airplane hangars strung together. I always left feeling proud and in awe of this man I called Dad. I was struck by how well regarded he was and how people admiringly spoke of him—

unsolicited—and regardless of what level they were or their backgrounds. They had great respect for his performance, his development of his people, and his sense of fairness. He distinguished himself in his specialty, the need for which caused him to return to Vietnam on five separate occasions during the Vietnam War.

What I learned as a young woman from watching my father was that a good leader always has a vision—a personal and a professional vision—and a plan that is fully aligned with what he or she believes in and a willingness to embrace and influence change. When the leader's values and beliefs are aligned with that vision, progress will be made. You need only to do certain things: use your smarts, have a plan, remain focused on outcomes, and surround yourself with good, smart people who aren't afraid to differ and speak up. If you as the leader have the motivation and managerial courage, others will want to follow you. Influencing, collaborating, and working through others are the ways leaders make a substantial contribution—a tangible difference for the greater good. Leading with intentional resilience—something my dad embodied—is a demonstration of effective leadership.

Here's another personal example and a true story. On a more personal side, in addition to Dad the military leader, there was Dad, the leader of our family. My younger sister was born with cerebral palsy. As you know, middle school marks a change of schools for most children and it was at this time that my sister was incorrectly labeled by a psychologist and was admitted to a school for disabled children who had severe mental and physical disabilities. Many of the young students were unstable, uncontrollable, and incapable of learning the state curriculum for middle schoolers.

My father recognized the disparity between what my sister already knew, what she was being taught, and that she tested well above average intelligence. He began a campaign to correct an egregious wrong that would affect her life negatively on many levels if not corrected. What bothered him most were the insensitivity and the tacit messages by this particular school and school district to "not rock the boat." To many people this would seem a daunting task, as essentially it was. It was my parents' word, her physician, and their collective knowledge of my sister against that of a trained school psychologist for the school district. That didn't matter to my parents. My father saw a different future for his youngest daughter. He had a vision that his youngest would not be saddled with an incorrect label that would negatively affect her for the rest of her life. It wasn't so much that the label was negative, because surely there are those who do fit into the category of mentally challenged, it was the fact that, in my sister's case, it was undoubtedly and clearly wrong. All one had to do was spend five minutes with her.

My point is this: in personal circumstances and clearly in professional settings, I have repeatedly witnessed intentionally resilient leaders who are absolutely grounded with an internal, visionary compass of fortitude and courage to persevere for what they believe—a better future state. Their compass drives them to actions that benefit key stakeholders and/or the organization for the greater good. These are the leaders who are willing to stand alone, perhaps endure relentless criticism and resistance to their ideas. They are leaders who are courageous in the face of the nearly impossible—leaders who have enough ego strength to encircle themselves with others who will offer thoughtful and diverse perspectives. And finally, these are leaders who are willing and who want to be challenged and will then make better decisions because of the challenges. These are the leaders who demonstrate intentional resilience.

Warren Bennis is credited with saying, "The most dangerous leadership myth is that leaders are born—that there is a genetic factor to leadership. This myth asserts that people simply either have certain charismatic qualities or not. That's nonsense; in fact, the opposite is true. Leaders are made rather than born." I, for one, strongly believe Bennis is right.

I learned very early on that when leaders have determined, substantiated, and communicated the facts, and have strong beliefs regarding the effectiveness of their actions, these leaders are compelled to put in motion those actions that will end in a positive result for the organization. I believe that when leaders truly believe and are passionate and committed, the drive for accelerated change results.

I believe in the power of intentional resilience. I've witnessed leaders and their teams navigate organizations through very difficult times through clarity of vision, transparent communications, and commitment to a better future for the organization. I have seen ordinary people achieve extraordinary results when they are fully aligned, engaged, and committed to their values and intent.

Wright

You've mentioned this concept a few times today. What is "intentional resilience"?

Anderson

I have indeed been speaking quite a bit about intentional resilience. I define the concept as being fully aligned, being on track and on purpose with what you want professionally and personally for your life. It means that you're able to weather organizational and personal ups and downs with overt clarity and intent for a better future as your anchor and North Star. So think of it this way: intentional resilience is a deliberate, thoughtful approach to reflect, refocus, re-energize and proactively re-engage in overcoming barriers in order to achieve the best possible outcomes. Think about a ship that has no anchor and it's in turbulent waters and high winds. Under those circumstances, it's going to go wherever the wind blows, literally. But a ship—a person in this case—who has an anchor and who is very focused and practiced at using the sails and a compass (read this as vision, communication and influence skills, emotional intelligence, and courage), will still move about, but in the end will stay on course and achieve the objective. This is what is meant by intentional resiliency. Outcomes happen on purpose—not by accident, and not by happenstance. Outcomes are achieved as a result of proactive, focused commitment to a plan that yields future results, though difficult to achieve, that are far better than the status quo.

Wright

How is this different from just being resourceful?

Anderson

Intentionally resilient leaders are future focused. They are intentional, and proactive in terms of the challenges they strive to overcome both professionally and personally. For instance, you can be resourceful but often that may be in response to something that has already been set into play, so now you are trying to adjust and adapt. When leaders are intentionally resilient, they anticipate, collaborate, look out into the future, attempt to see around corners, and initiate, engage, and put proactive and deliberate milestones and measurements in place to achieve defined results. These leaders are literally laying down the tracks they'll travel over as they position their organizations to achieve the expected outcomes.

Being intentionally resilient actually accelerates outcomes. The leaders' sights and energy go toward the work and the people who deliver the results. The leaders are fully cognizant of their core beliefs and values and commit themselves to what matters most, and plan and practice for organizational change constantly. Anticipating, planning, and practicing for future change, and driving for the necessary results are the key actions that make intentionally resilient leaders different.

Wright

Would you talk about the intersection of intentional resilience in leadership? How is this a key element—a crucible—for effective leaders?

Anderson

I'll start with another Bennis quote: "Leadership is a function of knowing yourself; it's having a vision that is well communicated, it's building trust among colleagues, and taking effective action to realize your own leadership potential."

In one of his earlier books, he goes on to talk about something called "crucibles." Some of the most effective leaders I've known have gone through crucibles—gone through the fire, if you will—in order to be the leaders they became. Crucibles are about being tested. Literally it means enduring intense heat in order to fortify and change elements into something that becomes a different, stronger, more durable, forged, substance. It becomes a substance that is better than what it might have otherwise been had it not been tested with intense stress.

Many of the great leaders have been tested. The leaders who I believe have shown intentional resilience are those who have owned and accepted responsibility for driving difficult but necessary changes. They have used setbacks to create different and better future outcomes that might not have otherwise occurred but for the fact that they had a vision and communicated what and how things could be better.

When you talk about intentionally resilient leadership, some of the better known leaders have each gone through their own crucibles. They have each forged a future outcome that has made them, other people, and/or their organizations stronger and better as well. In fact, some have changed the world. I would submit that each has been intentionally resilient.

While there are numerous examples (too many to list here), think of Benazir Bhutto, Dr. Martin Luther King, Jr., Jesus, Gloria Steinem, Mahatma Gandhi, Muriel Siebert, Martha Stewart, Tiger Woods, Nelson Mandela, Steve Jobs, and Oprah Winfrey. They each encountered extreme and defining circumstances along the way. In almost every case, they surrounded themselves with an inner circle of confidants with diverse perspectives and in the end had the courage to act in the face of the nearly impossible, guided by their personal compass and fortitude to move toward their compelling vision of the future.

When you think about leadership and you think about how that all intersects, those leaders who have the greatest amount of self-awareness, who have learned that they, themselves, are instruments of change, are intentionally resilient.

In an article, The Harvard Business Review reminded readers that "Executives who fail to develop self-awareness risk falling into an emotionally deadening routine that threatens their true selves. Indeed, a reluctance to explore your inner landscape not only weakens your own motivation but can also corrode your ability to inspire others."

Highly focused, reflective, motivated, and engaged leaders strongly believe they can make a difference in achieving different results. These are the leaders people want to follow. Peter Drucker stated that the real test and definition of a leader is whether others will voluntarily follow. I believe this is the true litmus test of intentional resilience in leadership as well.

Wright

So how has intentional resilience influenced you and who you are today?

Anderson

We've talked about being intentionally resilient from a leadership perspective. I believe many of us can look back over our careers and recount a difficult leadership circumstance or two where we've had to make lemonade out of lemons—where we've created a better outcome as a result of our compelling vision for a different and better future. I know I certainly have done that. I believe being intentionally resilient has informed people about how I've been able to implement many change management strategies in past organizations. Today, I use the concept to help leaders and executives I coach realize another tool they have access to that can help them achieve personal or professional results they are trying to achieve. I help them recognize and name their strengths so that they can deliberately call upon these strengths to achieve specific outcomes needed to advance their careers.

A personal story might be the best example I can share with you at this time about how intentional resilience can have a big impact. There was a time fifteen years ago when a corporate professional and a young single mother with two very young kids wasn't so sure that she had what it took to be intentionally resilient and turn things around to create a better future. She discovered that her husband had a greater love for drugs than he did for his family. She was devastated. It was so very shocking for her, never having been around that kind of circumstance before or known anyone who was involved with or addicted to drugs. She initially found it unfathomable and incomprehensible. It was inconceivable that she could find herself in those circumstances with all the challenges—emotional, financial, and work related—that came along with it. She didn't come from an environment like that. Neither did she know anyone with drug addiction in her community. Her family and the people she knew seemed to be wholesome, goal-oriented people who worked hard to make things better for themselves and their families. Until that time, her ex-husband himself had seemed to be very focused on achieving the American dream—a high paying corporate position, a wife, two kids, a house in the suburbs, a dog, and a nice car. Isn't that what many people strive for?

Somewhere along the way things changed and became very difficult and unwieldy for her and her young family.

There came a point in time when it was very clear to her that something was deeply, irreparably wrong and had to change. The only way that things were going to change was if she made the change. She realized this and learned that you can't change anyone but yourself. It was a very scary time for her and she wasn't sure she could do what was necessary in order to literally save the lives of her kids from the effects of addiction.

After much praying and soul-searching to determine if she had done everything she could, there was no looking back, only forward, as she envisioned a compelling and better future for her small family. She became intentionally resilient and willing to stand alone. Having the strong belief that one person could make a difference and having an unparalleled belief and vision that a better life was forthcoming when circumstances changed, she literally removed the negative source of impact from her family.

She earned a promotion to gain more income. She simultaneously became more focused on her career and the financial well-being and future of her family. She wore three hats—corporate executive, Mommy, and head of household. Having enough humility to know that she could not do this by herself, she sought the counsel of others. She saw that "yes" she could make a difference. She recognized there would be resistance from many fronts to seeking a divorce with such young children. She prayed a lot, and began to surround herself with key individuals who had experiences similar to her own. Counselors, financial advisors, her pastor; and she talked with marriage counselors, and addiction counselors. In a situation like hers, she realized that people do a lot of things that they never had to do before—things they didn't know they had the strength to do.

Through it all, she always believed that she could change her family's circumstances. In fact, she knew that she was the only one who could change their circumstances. She was willing to be challenged and listened to other perspectives. In the end, it would be her own internal vision, compass of fortitude, and courage that were going to help move her small family forward. I was unequivocally, intentionally resilient.

So when I think of the concept of this book, *Yes You Can!,* I absolutely believe that anyone can become intentionally resilient and change his or her circumstances for the better.

As a leader and Chief Diversity Officer for major organizations, I've often felt that my role was akin to being the conscience of the organization in terms of positioning it to anticipate and prepare for future challenges as they relate to human capital trends. In this capacity, I've felt that I had sensitivity, a responsibility, and an obligation on behalf of the organization toward all, but especially toward those people who might not otherwise have access to a scat at the table. I've been privileged to work in great organizations and with great people. I've partnered with organizations to make positive shifts in programs, policies, and practices to make them more inclusive. In this way, we've fostered professional growth and development of all people. I continue to do this work today through my own organization, Anderson People Strategies.

So having experienced and witnessed the things I went through, I believe I was primed to make a difference in my role as corporate leader and partner and impart those lessons to and through others to shape a better workplace culture and a better tomorrow for many.

This is probably a very long-winded way of saying that many of my early influences, as well as personal and professional life experiences, have helped me as I share my philosophy of intentional resilience.

Wright

Is this something that everyone has already or can it be developed? How can we become intentionally resilient?

Anderson

I believe that everyone has the capacity to be intentionally resilient. But first, there are a couple of things to consider. Before people can really own that aspect of themselves, they must become extremely self-aware. By this I mean that they have to think about and be very clear about the question and the outcome expected: "what is your intent?" and "what outcome do you desire?" and "when is it needed?"

At the beginning of our conversation I talked a bit about intent, meaning being consciously, purposely, and proactively on track with what you want to achieve. In order to do that, you must have a high degree of self-awareness. Many individuals achieve a greater level of self-awareness than others and this requires work. Executive coaching is one proven method for helping individuals do just that and grow professionally. A great coach will help clients maintain focus on their strengths and provide clarity on opportunities to plan and practice for change regarding what they need to do differently. Think differently to behave differently.

There are five things that must be done to achieve higher levels of self-awareness:

1. Have a clear vision of *your* success—envision success the same way top athletes use this visioning technique. See your success, feel what it feels like when you achieve success.
2. Seek others' input and perspectives to strengthen *your* vision.
3. Prepare to be FREE: Focused, Reflective, Energized, and Engaged.
4. Practice *your* intent. In the middle of the word prACTice is the word "act"— behave your way into the behaviors you most need to demonstrate; just do it.
5. Tell your story to others who support you; they will become your network of accountability partners for feedback on the results you desire.
6. Act like you can't fail!

You'll know when you're Intentionally Resilient because to not *act on your objective will cause you considerable stress!*

I believe all people have the capacity to be intentionally resilient when they have a heightened degree of self-awareness and are committed to driving new, sustainable change.

One word of caution: Watch out for the R word—Resistance. Resistance can show up in a number of forms such as procrastination. Or it can turn up as denial, not wanting to believe the reality and the facts around you. It can show up as generalized FEAR

302

(False Evidence that Appears Real), or fear of STUFF (Scientific Term for Unidentified Foreign Feelings) and a desire to protect oneself from the unknown. Sometimes people will hold onto past practices and patterns of behavior just because they are familiar and comfortable, even if they are no longer effective and useful for them. Release them!

As we've discussed, being intentionally resilient is to be results and future focused. To move forward, you must release any fear of the future and go through the crucible. You must be able to envision, engage, and embrace what a new future will mean as you strive to meet your objectives. So if you've got a great imagination and you can imagine what it would be like if certain circumstances were different professionally or personally, then you already have the fuel to become intentionally resilient. Everybody has the capacity to dream a different world.

Wright

So are there steps associated with becoming intentionally resilient and if so what are they?

Anderson

There are Seven Steps for Intentional Resilience:

1. An unparalleled vision for a better future for your organization, yourself and others.
2. Clear, fact-based approach. Having done the research, know your supporting facts.
3. A compelling passion for driving future results. What happens if you don't change?
4. Strong belief and ability to communicate vision, and results, particularly in the context of equity and fairness to the stakeholders.
5. Compelling obligation to drive change and be a steward of that change. That old saying of "If not now, when? If not me, who?" resonates very strongly with those who are intentionally resilient.
6. Be FREE:

   Focused
   Reflective
   Energized
   Engaged

7.   Act with humility; lead without following your own ego.

I believe having intentional resilience is to lead from these seven essential steps. Anyone who is operating from a standpoint of intentional resilience is calling on these traits in one way or another, separately or together, as they influence and effect change. When you're operating from a standpoint of intentional resilience, the response is always, "Yes, you can!"

Wright

You were talking about resistance a while ago. What do you think are the biggest obstacles to people becoming intentionally resilient?

Anderson

The biggest obstacle is fear. Many fear the change more than the status quo—fear of the unknown, fear of the future, fear of letting go, fear of exchanging what's certainly comfortable although it's not working for you, in exchange for the uncertainty of what might work and be uncomfortable. Having fear is not necessarily a negative thing because if, in taking that time to acknowledge fear, you become highly uncomfortable, then the sparks of change are ignited. At some point, people begin to realize that the status quo is simply not sufficient; settling for something less than what you really want or deserve is uninspiring and not enough. When this cognitive dissonance causes enough psychological discomfort or pain, the phrase "when is now a good time?" takes meaning and fuels the desire to change. Only when people arrive at that point are they ready for real sustainable change and not a moment before. Again, this is where the concept of the crucible begins to come into play as new thoughts, beliefs, attitudes, and the desire for different future possibilities emerge, energize, and provide profound motivation and excitement. This is when one has forged enough courage to be able to move forward, however tentatively, but move forward nevertheless.

Wright

I think a lot of us have experienced the refiner's fire.

Anderson

That's exactly right; the refiner's fire helps create an entirely new substance than it was previously. You become a stronger, different, and, in many cases, a much better person than you were before.

Wright

Let's say I've got this thing down—being intentionally resilient— and I know it. What are the most important things I could do with this knowledge?

Anderson

The most important thing to realize is that life is full of peaks and valleys, ups and downs. Remember to call on the knowledge you've gained from working through past circumstances and apply what you know to future scenarios, confident that you'll succeed because you've done so before. Remember that you are already intentionally resilient the next time you come against an obstacle that seems larger than you. Know that you can and will overcome it. Become more self-aware and remember the Seven Steps and get to it!

Secondly, this may seem a bit counterintuitive if you're working to achieve intentional resilience, however, I'd recommend that while you're working on your own issues, hit the pause button. There's nothing like *perspective* to make one take stock and realize that despite our own challenges, others often have challenges that seem even more daunting and difficult than your own.

Take a few hours out of your time and volunteer in a homeless shelter, a children's cancer treatment center, a women's shelter, a halfway house or a food kitchen. If these individuals can strive for a different and better tomorrow, surely you will make it. While you're working on becoming more intentionally resilient, share your time, expertise, and skills with an organization that aligns with your values and devote some of your time and energy to supporting other people who are trying to do more with their life, just like you.

I believe knowledge and wisdom are meant to be shared. Think about where you need to make changes in your life and in your roles in life. Envision what it will be like when the difficult changes are made. Be a believer in you and the power of one to make a difference. Get to it! Yes you can!

Wright

What an interesting conversation. I have really learned a lot and you've given me a lot to think about. I really appreciate all this time you've taken to answer these questions. I'm sure our readers are really going to be enlightened by your comments today.

Anderson

Thank you. It was my pleasure to speak with you.

Wright

Today we've been talking with Redia Anderson. Redia is an executive coach and diversity strategist with more than twenty-five years' experience in human resources, diversity, and change management. She engages talented leaders in positive behavioral shifts that align their strengths, performance, and business results.

Redia, thank you so much for being with us today on *Yes You Can!*

Anderson

Thank you.

ABOUT THE AUTHOR

Redia Anderson is Founder and Managing Partner of Anderson People Strategies, LLC, a Human Resources management consulting and executive coaching firm committed to talent optimization and leadership excellence.

Nationally recognized as a leader in the field of diversity and inclusion, Redia is a senior executive with more than twenty-five years' experience in Human Resources and Diversity management. Redia is a former Chief Diversity Officer across industry leading organizations recognized for their management depth and leadership strength. Her work experiences include: Deloitte & Touché USA LLP, Equiva Services (joint venture between Shell, Texaco, and Saudi Aramco), Sears, Roebuck and & Co., and Abbott Laboratories. Redia has successfully engaged and lead organizations in enterprise-wide change efforts focused on the advancement and retention of top performing women and people of color and enhancing a more inclusive work environment and culture for all. She has coached and engaged highly talented leaders and executives in positive behavioral shifts that tightly align their performance and business results. Redia's work as an Executive Coach has helped leaders leverage and gain greater insight into their leadership strengths, learning edges, and interpersonal skills, as each area affects their ability to succeed in driving business results in today's complex, global business environments. Redia has worked closely with executives at Shell, the University of Houston, ExxonMobil, Sunoco, and PricewaterhouseCoopers to name a few.

Redia brings a unique style and approach for driving tangible, comprehensive, practical business results for accelerated leadership development and organizational change in an inclusive environment. She is a Certified Hudson Institute Coach and a member of The International Coach Federation, the American Society of Training and Development, National Speakers Association, Six Seconds Emotional Intelligence Network, and Society for Human Resource Management.

Redia received her undergraduate degree in psychology from Incarnate Word University and her graduate degree in clinical psychology from Trinity University, both in San Antonio, Texas. Redia consults and holds certifications in Six Seconds

Emotional Intelligence, Myers-Briggs, The Birkman Method, Leadership Effectiveness Analysis and several other leadership assessment instruments. She has served on numerous boards focused on health and children's and women's issues.

Redia lives in Houston with her young adult children, Jarred and Taylor, and a Samoyed dog named Tundra. She is co-author of the book soon to be published by John Wiley & Sons Publishing titled *Trailblazers: How Top Business Leaders Are Accelerating Results through Inclusion and Diversity,* due out August 2010.

Redia Anderson

5826 New Territory Boulevard, Suite 110
Sugar Land, Texas 77479
713-906-2866
redia@andersonpeoplestrategies.com
www.andersonpeoplestrategies.com

CHAPTER TWENTY

Being a Modern Manager: What Does it Take to Become One?

by Dr. George Kastner & Brenda Erickson

David Wright (Wright)

Today we're talking with Brenda Erickson and Dr. George Kastner of Reditus International.

Dr. George Kastner is a distinguished international professor, business scholar, CEO, consultant and coach with experience advising companies throughout North and South America. His commitment to merging academic excellence with practical application has resulted in increased efficiencies and higher profits in his client companies.

A proven leadership professional, Brenda Erickson has led teams in sales, marketing, development, and customer service to success by articulating a challenging vision and mobilizing talent around it. She is an experienced management consultant, business leader, and an accomplished executive coach.

Brenda Erickson, George Kastner, welcome to *Yes, You Can!*

Brenda Erickson (Erickson)

Thank you very much, David.

George Kaster (Kaster)

Hi, David; it's a pleasure to be here. Thank you.

Wright

So what makes a manager modern? Has the manager role changed over the past ten years?

Kastner

The role of the manager has changed dramatically over the last decade. The role of the manager was changing—evolving—even before that time. Actually, if we look at some statistics from the top corporations in the world, in the top 200 of the Fortune 500 companies, most often, today's CEOs are liberal arts graduates. That has not always been the case. In earlier years, the CEO position in a company was filled by individuals with an engineering degree or another exact science background close to the field of work of the company. This change suggests that the human element—what we tend to call the "soft side of management" —has increased in importance and has added a new and different dimension to corporate management demands and needs.

Management today must focus on capturing and mobilizing talent. They mobilize their top talent energy toward a unified vision—a drive towards supporting the objectives of the corporation. So managers have become in many aspects the internal culture drivers, rather than just unit chiefs in terms of hierarchical structure and revenue or share value aspects, and that is a very important change. In addition, a greater focus on excellence in execution has taken precedence over quality of planning. Simply stated, planning is the promise and execution is the delivery. No longer does the market celebrate quality promises; rather, it supports exceptional execution.

In summary, modern managers have a more balanced outlook on their role as great communicators and motivators—as the ones who shape corporate culture, talent, and become people coaches as well as financial caretakers, technology pushers, and marketing thought leaders. Moreover, a new breed of modern managers base their decision-making in what I call "Values Based Management" (VBM), reflecting the values they cherish and live by and want to protect and emphasize, in their efforts toward modeling behavior and motivating in the workplace. When combined with quality delivery, values shape the new top management role.

Erickson

That's right. Managers must pay attention to creating the business environment that will attract, engage and keep talented individuals who can work together towards a vision of excellence. The management element in leadership is critical to maintaining the competitive edge. Managers direct, implement, facilitate, coach and identify training areas. They must effectively communicate the vision of the organization and demonstrate the corporate values on a daily basis.

At this time, we are experiencing of rapid change on multiple dimensions. In the command-and-control "organization man" era, conformity and obedience were key corporate values. Managers concentrated on measuring results. Today, managers must become more adept at the soft skills like coaching, mentoring, working as the leader as well as a participant on the team to create an environment that supports knowledge worker engagement. The demands of leadership are dynamic and intense. No matter what industry you are in, the leader must now provide leadership that is clear, yet flexible punctuated by frequent information and motivational communication— interactive when possible—to allow for questions and input. This demand really tests all the things that make an executive a good executive: self-knowledge, confidence, trust, loyalty, integrity, managerial capabilities, values, and decision-making.

Wright

So where do we consider how leadership fits with management? What is the role of values in a leader?

Erickson

Values are fundamental to executive leadership. Values are the foundation for the governing principles that drive the company and set the cultural tone that the leader brings to the organization. The values practiced at the top of the organization permeate throughout. That's why leadership behavior and communication must steadfastly and consistently reflect values that are worthy as the foundation for future growth.

Leaders model the behavior they want their followers to demonstrate. When you are at the top you are being watched. You cannot afford to be false in your communications and that is not difficult when you are self aware and lead consciously and conscientiously. Roy Disney said it best when he said, "It is not hard to make decisions when you know what your values are."

Kastner

As I mentioned earlier we should push the ideas behind Values Based management, or VBM.

We have seen over the last decade several companies that were praised as models of excellence and innovation, models that other companies should emulate.
We even used their stories as case studies in management training programs. Then, this model fell apart like a tower of cards. The reason? Leaders forgot their values, and by forgetting the clear values within the organization and their commitment to the values, they confused their objectives, so much so that they sacrificed everything for a quick, personal gain.

Managers are visible and when they accept leadership roles they should reflect on how their personal values and objectives align with the corporate goals. This reflection brings clarity to their commitment and to their values and helps define corporate objectives.

Our society has become a society where we judge people by what they have rather than by who they are. It is an empty success to only have material things. Particularly in places like the United States, which leads the world in new ideas, we need to return to what the Founding Fathers of this nation intended to achieve via the core values of society. Then we need to put our values into action day in and day out. Values need to be alive and in action within the corporation in the daily life of the managers and leaders. If we fail to incorporate values into the daily life of the manager, there is a risk that we lose the ability to sustain a consistent culture that continues to develop and positively evolve. The Strategic Planning Unit of a major oil corporation engaged in a study that addressed the question, "What makes corporations last?" Their study found that most corporations disappear after forty or fifty years of activity. Most corporations disappear after forty or fifty years of activity. As an example, think about which companies on the NYSE today existed fifty years ago; you will identify a very small proportion of companies. After a careful examination of the results, the company analysts concluded that those corporations that survive were able to readily adapt their business models, products, and services to new market trends, while sustaining and protecting their core values. These companies lasted longer than corporations that subordinated their values whimsically to changing business values and practices.

Wright

So what promotes the ability to deal with adversity and the speed of change, and how does a leader develop the resilience to lead through adversity?

Kastner

We have accepted the fast pace of an interconnected world—the Internet, new communication networks, the constant contact of cellular phones and other communication devices, and everything else that is available to us 24/7. We are bombarded by messages, by our bosses all the time, every hour of the day, in every place. Combined with issues like traffic and appointments, security and safety issues, environmental issues, and other elements that very quickly change our pace of life and scope of privacy pose an exponentially growing environment of daily adversity on every company and every individual in the company, as well as on every individual in society. The more resilient leaders look at adversity as an opportunity to practice the concept of possibility and creative thinking as described in *The Art of Possibility*, by Rosamund Stone Zander and Benjamin Zander. If we can find the strength to see the positive aspects of a seemingly negative situation, we can change adversity to a valuable more positive outcome. We need to know when to change the prism and then, how to communicate that reframing to followers. That decision creates better responses to all the growing adversity that surrounds us. That is what drives resilience.

Soon after Nelson Mandela was freed after spending twenty-seven years in jail during apartheid in South Africa, he was asked in an interview how he survived the horrors of that experience. His immediate response was that he wasn't surviving—he was preparing to be the President of South Africa. This is the resilience that leaders of corporations need if they want to leave their mark on the future, build positive legacies in society, and make their collaborators and corporations equally resilient.

Erickson

Developing resilience requires practice and feedback. When leaders reflect on their actions and modify their actions as the situation demands change, then they are strengthening their resilience muscle. Resilient leaders do not stick to a losing strategy; they have developed the ability to change when necessary. Research in resilience and success are providing more insight into this important executive and personal skill. In *Creating Your Best Life*, by Caroline Adams Miller, MAPP and Dr. Michael B. Firsch, researchers have identified elements that help individuals build resilience; such as,

313

celebrating little victories, using humor to cushion falls and reframe disappointing events, and reaching out to others for help. The importance of this skill for success in leadership should not be overlooked.

Wright

To paraphrase a famous quotation: "A manager is a manager is a manager." What's that about?

Kastner

When we study managers at different organizational levels and responsibilities across business areas, countries, and cultures, we find that there are many more people who "do the manager" role rather than people who *embody* management. Too many individuals look at their own business card and since it says "manager," they feel hyped up—all powerful. Some even declare that they are the "almighty manager." The cliché became "once a manager always a manager." This leaves us with the question: are these individuals really meeting the demanding requirements of their manager's role or do they represent the cliché?

On the other hand, we find people who understand that being a manager requires the exercise of a delicate balance between modeling behavior and level of knowledge. Leaders who model behavior by their actions and deeds are more successful in stabilizing business performance than those who seek knowledge superiority over their team members. Leaders build lasting business value by modeling behavioral values, attitudes and commitment. There is always someone who knows more. Knowledge is seasonal, like the changing leaves of a tree, but the core behavioral values of an individual are solid. Implementing core values in the organization establishes roots that keep the tree strong even in adverse weather. So "a manager is a manger is a manager" is a nice saying, but there is more to being a manager than just having the title.

Wright

So how does one achieve a balance between modeling expected behavior and demonstrating knowledge? As you climb the management ladder, which is the more important—knowledge or modeling behavior?

Kastner

Basically, from a graphical representation perspective, we look at two dimensions, one axis to measure level of knowledge on a continuum from low to high, and another axis to measure the intensity of modeling behavior which can also run from low to high. This axis represents a dynamic scale and at any given moment we may find ourselves at the Low-Low position. To achieve the management leadership position to which managers should aspire, they will have to scale from the Low-Low position to the High-High position. That is the high intensity of modeling behavior and a high level of knowledge position. Schematically, they can evolve from the low-low position to the high-high position by 1) increasing their knowledge level and then starting to model behavior or 2) by first increasing the intensity of modeling behavior and then acquiring high levels of knowledge or 3) by trying to change both simultaneously—changing and moving along both dimensions simultaneously. The third option is a challenging and difficult task and there are very few Leonardo da Vinci's around—people who can use their left brain and right brain simultaneously. Thus, this option is not a commonly viable option.

Most of us tend to choose either climbing the knowledge axis or enhancing the intensity of modeling behavior axis. In fact, the majority of managers choose the easier way by going through the knowledge axis, but by the time they start to model behavior, company members may have acquired contrary or inadequate habits and behaviors. On the other hand, when a manager chooses the intensity of modeling behavior axis, he or she immediately creates the desired values and behaviors on which the organization will grow and expand. During the early stages, if specific knowledge is needed it can always be acquired. Behavior cannot be acquired as easily. You can always acquire knowledge (buy it or hire it); but the manager must model behavior even while maintaining authority and leadership. It is almost impossible to delegate the task of leading by example. Behavior, especially effective behavior and actions, cannot be acquired easily. It must be practiced, and developed in a reflective and evaluative manner.

Thus, once the balance between modeling behavior and acquiring knowledge has been achieved, managers reach leadership positions.

Knowledge	High Knowledge Low Modeling Behavior	High Knowledge High Modeling Behavior
	Low Knowledge Low Modeling Behavior	Low Knowledge High Modeling Behavior

Modeling Behavior Effectively

Erickson

That's true. One key challenge for new leaders, especially as they are rising through the ranks into their first top managerial jobs, is that transition into their first leadership role. Former peers now look to them for cues about effective behavior, to understand how to treat their co-workers, and to learn how to evaluate the factors that go into making difficult decisions. Even a casual comment may gain more significance than was intended. So leaders have to understand that they are always being watched—all of their behaviors are being watched—and consciously or unconsciously, managers and leaders are always creating the type of followers that they deserve. Sometimes they will create unintended consequences. Working with an executive coach during these transitions can provide leaders with the support and feedback required to grow during this critical transition period.

Wright

So what leadership traits are key to leading change?

Erickson

Well, different leadership traits are important at different times. Many speak about situational leadership, suggesting that the situation makes the leader. At the same time, the situation also dictates the traits and skills that must be utilized. Key examples of effective leadership skills include adaptability, emotional maturity, knowledge, capacity for change, capacity to lead change, willingness to take charge and make decisions, willingness to accept responsibility for the course of the organization, and anticipation. It takes a whole individual—one who is willing to continue to grow and develop to be an effective leader. The Greek philosophers were right when they said, "Know thyself."

Kastner

One thing I want to add to Brenda's statement is that the ability to anticipate, to respond quickly, and to change whatever traits are necessary as times and business environments are changing becomes key at the managerial level. Not many of us can easily anticipate change and much less easily adjust to it. We are often slaves to inertia; we feel comfortable with what we have been doing and we believe we know and understand our business surroundings. This complacency is the reason why we don't adjust our leadership traits and style to changing times. That obviously creates a gap between what's needed and what's offered at a given point in time.

Erickson

This is an important point. As we mentioned earlier in this conversation, things have changed radically and dramatically in the past ten years. We have so many aspects of our lives and certainly corporate environment that are different, yet we still have some leaders who have only been managing during times when things were expanding, things were good, everything was going up, profits, staff, everything. Now I see leaders forced to dig deep into some of the foundation training that they had as new managers. If they were good managers as they were coming up through the ranks, as they were learning, then they're finally going back to applying some fundamentals that need to be in place to steer the ship safely through these adverse times. Change in complex organizations must be nurtured and well considered. There must be leadership but also the capacity for individuals to change and lead at their own pace and in their own individual ways in support of the organizational context.

Kastner

Recently, I was speaking at a conference in South America to a group of C level individuals. I asked them, "How many of you have had any kind of formal training in the last four years?" Less than 5 percent of the audience raised their hands. Somehow, once individuals have achieved their authority (or C-level) position, which they mistakenly automatically equate to leadership expertise. They behave as if they have all the tools—all the behavioral tools, all the knowledge tools—therefore, all the answers. This happens to many managers. That leads them to assume that no new development is needed in approaches to understanding and interpreting changing business situations. Yet if we look around the world at what has happened in the social world and in the corporate world in the last four years, we find that the world is not at all similar to what we have experienced just a few years ago. We can apply old knowledge in new ways; but we also need new knowledge and skills and fresh approaches that current circumstances and issues require. So it's quite evident that new traits or skills and anticipative capacity to manage the change still to come are necessary.

Wright

So can a leader lead independently of environmental conditions?

Erickson

In a word no! Leadership in a vacuum is called acting. People do it on stage all the time, and we do sometimes see some of that in the leadership arena. I think that a successful leader has the most interdependent tasks. They have perhaps one of the most important tasks in the world because they're entrusted with a sacred trust to grow corporate assets for shareholders, and at the same time, create the environment for maximizing the best performance from the individual human capital that is invested in the corporation. To lead with honesty, confidence, and vision based on values demonstrates the kind of consistent but flexible leadership that this competitive world demands. You must know who you are as a person to be an effective leader.

By 2025, one in five workers will be over age fifty-five. The slowing of influx into the workforce translates to an estimated shortfall of twenty million workers over the next twenty years in the United States alone. And this is also happening in India and other developing nations. The economic conditions are radically changing—global communication is instantaneous. The challenges we face are immense. We must all become expert in quickly reading situations and being attuned to the environment.

Kastner

I think that the simple answer is no! Why is that? People who try to lead independently of environmental conditions position themselves in a cocoon, oblivious to whatever is happening around them. What are the major conditions that our corporations have to face? It's not only economic, it's social, it's environmental, it's unprecedented changes in purchase power, and changing technologies and communication tools. Growing numbers of clients and increased types of diverse client needs create a demand that leaders become more flexible with the responses to the internal and external operating environment of the corporations.

So as a leader facing a corporate determination to respond to society's needs, the leader must not only drive the organization to produce services, to produce a product and deliver it to the market, but to do all of that in a new way that reflects the changing market requirements and environment with a capital "E.." Environment is the economic environment, the lifestyle environment, the future needs environment, the ecological environment, and the regulatory environment. We need leaders with the ability to deal with more sustainable energy sources and new energy sources, and to provide people cleaner life style opportunities. We need leaders responding to all the changing environment kindly and with courage. We need brave leaders for this brave new world.

Without leaders who can lead with courage, creativity and confidence, companies will just repeat what they have done in the past. We have seen that the status quo does not solve even current challenges and may even have a negative influence on the changing business and physical environment. This new breed of leaders must respond by building new business practices, building the future much more than sustaining and protecting the past. This requires an increasing level of environmental sensitivity and openness.

Wright

Good leaders need good followers. Can leaders be made or can they be chosen?

Kastner

I believe that you both choose followers and then develop them into "sub-leaders;" as you lead, you create more followers. We must choose followers because we need a team to help us jump-start the changes we want to achieve and champion the cause for which we assumed the responsibility and burden of leadership. Others will follow as leadership provides responses to the expectations of their audiences.

The immediate team around the leader becomes a leadership team. And many of the team members assume supporting leadership positions. They become sub-leaders, in a way. The team then is open to include in this immediate circle additional individuals after the initial picks have been made. If we do not have initial followers from the ranks of those we have chosen, a lot of energy may be wasted as we work to convince the audience about our new direction. That energy does not build value; it does build a form of consensus, but it may not necessarily generate the initial acceleration value needed to create big changes. To the extent that we can effectively choose the initial group of followers, then with them we can build on the momentum as we accelerate the drive toward our new organizational goals. Leading rather than constant convincing is more efficient as a model for change, but requires energy, communication, and excellent listening skills.

Erickson

Right; I agree and that's talking about having a foundation from which you can launch initiatives and lead. That's extremely important in terms of getting things started and getting things started quickly. It's very, very important and critical too, however, that the leadership team not be closed; it must be dynamic and they must communicate. They cannot be closed and exclusive or they run the risk of becoming a club and not a leadership team. There are too many clubs in today's organizations and not enough committed leaders. Leaders need to create an environment where it is acceptable to speak truth to power for effective change.

Wright

When people are tense they're afraid because they lack clarity of vision and direction when situations are tough. How can the management or leadership role be adjusted during tough times?

Kastner

When times become more difficult, how leaders communicate and what they communicate about becomes a very clear element of balancing the tensions within the corporation and how the corporation is positioned within the business world or society. During more difficult times when tensions are higher and the doubts among people are growing, reaffirming what the company or the management is trying to achieve. Reaffirming the value of their commitment to society and to the company, and rebuilding internal trust becomes very important tools of communication to calm the spirits of fear and doubt. Managers who are leaders will spend substantial time and will not waste any effort to provide many simultaneous positive internal messages for people to understand where the company is and where it is heading, where this element of society is driving toward, and what it tries to achieve. All these communications have to be fact-based, simple, truthful, and have a sense of future. These efforts will give members of the organization a sense of destination and of having a future they can identify with, and thus fear and doubt are significantly diminished.

For example, if in regular times, or in very calm times, management is committed to such communication efforts once a month, then in tough times where there are doubts and difficulties, management should intensify its communication efforts and probably communicate twice a week in many different forms and in many different venues. If people do not concentrate on their mission, if they're not concentrated on building the future that they want to achieve, they just spend a lot of energy doubting and not moving toward the objective that has been set. As they are calmed down by positive communication, building strengths from the content which is a manifestation of commitment to an acceptable shared vision, they, the members of the organization, are ready to move mountains.

Erickson

Yes. In summary, just communication, visibility, and transparency will move companies toward their goals. I can't say it enough—this is the right time to be communicating more, not less. And it is equally important for leaders to be listening actively to internal and external knowledge.

Wright

The ability to anticipate and the ability to adapt are key to any leader. Are these skills learned, developed, or taught?

Erickson

All of the above. The adaptability, I think, comes with practice—applying the leadership skills that they are learning every day at the workplace or in formal learning situations. I mentioned that leadership is a practice and George mentioned that it takes knowledge as well as the foundation of integrity and values, and continuous application and evaluation of the results of actions to learn from mistakes. Reflection and evaluation bring skills knowledge to a conscious level so that the skills can be effectively applied at the right time.

Leadership is a social activity. Fundamental to the successful leader is an understanding of the human element in the corporation. The effective application of human talent in the organization to the best and highest use will differentiate the talented leaders from the mediocre ones. It is this element that should drive a lot of what leaders do. Without it, we destroy value rather than enhance it.

Kastner

I've worked with some mid-level management in corporations throughout the United States and South America. I find that when they get together in informal settings, they tend to talk openly and frequently about anticipating the situation that is forthcoming and they talk a lot about what they could do to face such changes. Yet, when they are back in the more formal and structured corporate environment, they freeze, they do not decide and they do not act upon solutions. It seems as if there is some internal barrier either within the corporation that limits their ability to act towards the anticipated change, or within their managerial DNA that drives management to behave within the domain of proven formulae of action even when rationally they all admit and recognize that the existing plan of action is not suitable to the demands of the changed environment and conditions.

Working as a coach with many managers, I often challenge them by asking "What would you or could you have done differently if you had listened to your inner voice about the changes needed? And how would you have better anticipated the situation?" I have learned that by examining the truthful response to this question and internalizing the meaning of the response, over time they start acting differently, using new behaviors to face the changes they anticipate.

The barriers to action based on anticipation and gut instinct are often based on the way performance is being measured and evaluated. If managers anticipate, and act on it, it may move them away from their objectives. There is no easy way within the corporation to get "brownie points" if you move away from the declared corporate objectives by anticipating a situation even if it favors the company. By not achieving the objectives, the decision-making capacity is hindered due to compensation and evaluation schemes. So managers need support and coaching to help build the courage and confidence to do the right thing. That is the way to learn and develop needed skills and traits to anticipating and facing change.

Erickson

That reminds me of an article I read recently about organizations that have gone wild with performance measures. It's true that goals are needed—goals are necessary in an organization. In coaching, sometimes you work with folks on their performance goals, but equally important is the ability to understand when it's important to move the organization forward even when it's not on that performance measurement sheet. It may require more skill in selling your idea up the chain or to the Board of Directors, but it's very important to know when you need to move forward, otherwise you're always dealing with the prescriptive performance. That's really not where you want to be if you want to grow as an organization.

Leaders today need to find ways to unleash creativity, passion, commitment, and capacity in their talent. The new generation will require different management than we have seen in the past forty years.

Wright

Leaders who are successful in calm waters often fail in tough times, so the question would be "Why?" What are the adjustments that management must make to always be successful? Can they be found in one person?

Kastner

Well, yes they can be found in one person. Leaders who fall into the habit of perpetuating the past tend to fall into mediocre performance and run into difficulties. The reason is mostly because they allow the inertia of habit to impair objectivity in their judgment and thus they cannot effectively take into account the changes around them and do not anticipate the driving forces of their businesses.

The ability to be a step ahead of the driving forces that shape the business and the ability to react quickly to unexpected changes are very important in terms of being "always successful." The people who can independently read and "interpret the tea leaves" of the market situation have a great advantage. The leader or the person in the top managerial position of a company must invite other team members to share their interpretation of the driving forces that surround them so more qualified decision-making takes place. However, if they do not initiate that activity and do not demonstrate their courage and willingness to step into the unknown, the rest of the team usually does not follow.

Erickson

Adaptability and a continuous learning mindset support the ability to develop knowledge and resilience in leadership. Too many leaders and organizations do not continue education and executive development. When the economic time is stressed, training and development are the first areas to be cost restricted. Corporations need to be constantly training, educating, managing succession plans, and developing their organizational talent. You cannot just enter a crisis and run to find a "just in time" training on "how-to." Education in management skills, self-mastery, leadership skills, and emotional maturity should be continuous and ongoing to support not only what is known but to ensure preparedness for the unknown and unknowable situations that happen.

I would add that no one gets it right all the time and mistakes can be expected. Mistakes happen in the course of daily decision. Practice, practice, practice; evaluate, learn, and move on. Leaders who are successful are learning—they are learning all the time.

Wright

Does the intensity of leadership vary depending on the talent? Is leadership better when leaders are talented in terms of the attitude that they have to master?

Erickson

The best leaders develop their teams through strategic directions that support and enable creative contribution. It's great to set performance goals, but leaders, by definition, means that they move things beyond where they need to be. Not all initiatives are carried out by just strictly issuing commands. When forming a new leadership team, some directive behavior may be necessary to get the team on the same page. But as they move forward they need to be using their own creative capabilities, their own intensity, and their own values within the context of the corporation to move things forward. Leaders who have taken the time to develop their emotional maturity and to understand their strengths and weaknesses, to the point that they get to know themselves have the attitude that "we can do it, yes, we can." These leaders use their intensity to move the team forward positively toward their overarching goals.

Kastner

Earlier we talked about followers and how leaders may select or develop followers. Those followers are the core of the talent that surrounds leaders. For this talent to become more effective within the domain of daily activities and yet participate in building the future, leaders have to learn to be passionate and histrionic and to convert their passion into a contagious "virus" throughout the organization. It can be achieved only with strong values like integrity, as Brenda mentioned. Speaking the truth, even when it is painful, is key for building long-term trust and support within the team. When that trusting environment happens, talented people surround leaders. They want to come closer and work with them because the leaders have created an environment where talented people can flourish by being themselves. At the end of the day, these talented people develop themselves and evolve to become leaders because of the environment created by the leaders. Then, they can help build the value of the corporation and build the value of the company to shareholders.

Wright

Is it strategy or execution or both that make management successful?

Kastner

It is really both that make them successful but the question really is, "Is there a priority?" As we look around and we see success stories from which to learn, we find out that "execution is king."

Strategies and plans are amorphous, moving targets because of changing environmental conditions reflected in the availability of credit, development of technologies at very high speed, changing legal requirements, and so on. So you never, ever have a single strategy that is really the single one silver bullet shot. This means that adjustments are required with some regularity as market conditions and competitive response change. In that respect it's not the best or the worst, or the successful or the unsuccessful, or the good or the bad strategy—it's the management of the strategic process of a company that may make the difference.

Execution, on the other hand, is of a pass/fail nature. Once the strategy is set into play, you don't have a second chance. Over recent years, nearly 40 percent of the Fortune 500 companies fired their CEOs, because of poor execution. In that respect, both execution and strategizing are important but "execution is king."

Wright

Reading the market is a key executive skill. Can it be learned?

Erickson

Well, if you look at some of the things that have been written about the topic in a recent book titled, *Blink,* by Malcolm Gladwell, you can see that "reading the market" is that ability to rapidly use all of your knowledge and experience to quickly identify a pattern and respond. It goes back to management as a practice. Caution must also be paid though because reinforcement of this type of skill can also lead an executive to become rigid in thought and behavior and that can be a hindrance. When you build that management team and you build that leadership team out, you need team members who are strong enough and respectful enough to question decisions within the context of making sure you're moving toward that vision and you are demonstrating by your actions the character of the organization. Reflection and examination of these decisions, along with discussions and seeking counsel from trusted associates or with coaches or other executives, ensure that you as a leader stay on track with the communication and articulation regarding the direction of the company.

Kastner

Let me add a couple of things to that. Reading the market is a process of interpreting a whole lot of data and a whole lot of information. Larger corporations are broad based and attend to multiple clients with multiple services and products. There is no one single read of what the company does, so it really requires a team effort to try and correctly read the market and pull together all learning to one single interpretation that everybody accepts. That can be learned through in-house development or it can be bought. Those who cling to a single vision of the market and impose that single vision on everybody around them by pulling rank, limiting the scope of activity of their company and of their colleagues. That doesn't last very long. We see this in companies where there is high turnover in the top leadership positions and/or when multiple changes are made to the business model.

Now, some managers who became very skillful in understanding the scope of their business and the scope of the market within which they operate can very quickly surround themselves with the necessary technical skill to carry out the interpretation of the marketplace. They become successful, they turn companies around, and they can position them better within the reality of the market. They can meet goals and meet budgets year after year. Those who try to force their interpretation top down, who are not as skillful, who do not buy the required skill or knowledge, and who do not involve other team members in the interpretation effort, tend to repeatedly miss the target. That's where high turnover occurs.

Wright

Well, what an enlightening conversation. I could talk with you two all day long. I think our readers are going to get a lot out of this chapter. I want you to know how much I appreciate all this time you've spent with me answering these questions.

Erickson

Thank you again for speaking with us today.

Kastner

Let me just add that the readers, as they read through this chapter, may want to question themselves as far as their own managerial behavior is concerned. Soul searching about how one meets the role of a manager is a very helpful exercise.

Thank you very much for talking with us. We look forward to hearing from you soon.

Wright

Today we have been talking with Brenda Erickson and Dr. George Kastner. Both are proven leadership professionals. They have mentored and coached numerous executives as they adjust to the demands of the changing economic and professional landscape.

Brenda, George, thank you so much for being with us today on *Yes, You Can!*

Erickson

You're welcome.

Kastner

Thank you very much. We're looking forward to working with you again in the near future.

BRENDA ERICKSON is a proven leadership professional who has experience in leading teams to success in sales, marketing, development, and customer service by articulating a challenging vision and mobilizing talent around it. She is an experienced management consultant, business leader, and an accomplished executive coach. Working with new managers to develop their confidence, business acumen, general management skills, and sales strategy, these qualities contributed to her successful leadership as President and  General Manager of SAS Canada, a subsidiary of SAS Institute, the largest privately-held software company in the world, and her recognition as a leader in the information technology industry. As a member of the Executive Board of the Information Technology Association, Ms. Erickson represented technology leadership nationally by speaking about the vision and enabling power of technology. Her recent activities include management consulting, Business Development with ITpreneurs, and work with Keller Williams Real Estate and a continued interest the principles of Positive Psychology, which she studies, practices, and uses in her daily life. Her passion is making organizations more effective and successful environments by creating the right environment for leadership and participation, maximizing involvement and talent in organizations. A dedicated professional, she has mentored and coached executives as they adjust to the demands of the changing economic landscape and coached individuals as they weather changes. Her professional practice includes coaching managers, consulting in business on sales process and sales management development, and providing insight through observation in organizational environments. She is an excellent motivational speaker drawing on experiences in her personal life and professional life to motivate others with vision and hope.

Brenda Erickson

Reston, VA
703-467-.0272
bse715@aol.com

DR. GEORGE KASTNER has dedicated his professional life to excellence in academia, management, and entrepreneurial environments. Throughout his career he has shared this knowledge and experience with executives, managers, and business students through management consulting, executive coaching, mentoring, and teaching. As an executive coach, he has mentored numerous executives and entrepreneurs through difficult and developmental experiences. Dr. Kastner is known for his innovative approaches to business issues, development of dynamic programs for students, and active sincere involvement in advancing the level of quality of business practices. Consulting with numerous family-owned businesses, he has helped them increase the professional content in their ranks and develop governance models. He is an accomplished strategist and an interesting and engaging speaker who brings high value to every engagement.

As founding President and CEO of Reditus International, Inc., a management consulting firm that provides strategic support to firms that encounter crisis situations, Dr. Kastner has developed an approach to help CEOs build their strategic agenda and become the internal "maestro" of their teams. Until recently, as CEO and Executive President of Coldwell Banker Affiliates of Latin America, he developed the current business model and assembled (in less than two years) a powerful and effective management team developing operations in Columbia, Venezuela, Panama, Nicaragua, Honduras, Belize, Guatemala, El Salvador, Peru, and Ecuador.

For fourteen years, Dr. Kastner served as Senior Vice President of Arthur D. Little Inc. and Director of Global Key Accounts, leading strategies and consulting for global clients. Dr. Kastner started his teaching and research activities while at The University of North Carolina in Chapel Hill as a teaching fellow at the graduate program of The School of Public Health. After graduation he joined the faculty at IESA in Venezuela during which time he was a full professor holding positions as the Director and Founder of the Advanced Management Program, member of the Academic Council and member of the school's Executive Committee. In recent years he served as mentor and coach two University Deans, and was invited to work with new faculty on teaching methods.

Dr. Kastner has lead seminar programs as a visiting scholar at graduate schools around the world, including Cornell University, UVM, NYU, MIT Sloan School, Uniandes in Bogota, The Hult International Business School, The Technion in Israel, and a newly launched Management Institute in Prague. Dr. Kastner currently teaches in the graduate programs at IESA in Venezuela and Hult International Business School in Boston and Dubai. He enjoys learning and sharing his knowledge and experiences with other executives and entrepreneurs throughout the world.

Dr. George Kastner

1418 Meadows Blvd.
Weston, Fl 33327

305-218-5659
Gtkastner@reditusinc.com
Gtkastner@gmail.com